Women, Murder and Femininity

Cultural Criminology

Series editor: **Mike Presdee**, Sometime Senior Lecturer in Criminology, University of Kent, UK

Titles include:

Ruth Penfold-Mounce
CELEBRITY CULTURE AND CRIME
The Joy of Trangression

Willem Schinkel
ASPECTS OF VIOLENCE
A Critical Theory

Lizzie Seal
WOMEN, MURDER AND FEMININITY
Gender Representations of Women Who Kill

Cultural Criminology
Series Standing Order ISBN 978–0–230–53558–9
(*outside North America only*)

You can receive future titles in this series as they are published by placing a standing order. Please contact your bookseller or, in case of difficulty, write to us at the address below with your name and address, the title of the series and the ISBN quoted above.

Customer Services Department, Macmillan Distribution Ltd, Houndmills, Basingstoke, Hampshire RG21 6XS, England

Women, Murder and Femininity

Gender Representations of Women Who Kill

Lizzie Seal
Durham University, UK

© Lizzie Seal 2010
Softcover reprint of the hardcover 1st edition 2010 978-0-230-22275-5

All rights reserved. No reproduction, copy or transmission of this publication may be made without written permission.

No portion of this publication may be reproduced, copied or transmitted save with written permission or in accordance with the provisions of the Copyright, Designs and Patents Act 1988, or under the terms of any licence permitting limited copying issued by the Copyright Licensing Agency, Saffron House, 6-10 Kirby Street, London EC1N 8TS.

Any person who does any unauthorized act in relation to this publication may be liable to criminal prosecution and civil claims for damages.

The author has asserted her right to be identified
as the author of this work in accordance with the Copyright,
Designs and Patents Act 1988.

First published 2010 by
PALGRAVE MACMILLAN

Palgrave Macmillan in the UK is an imprint of Macmillan Publishers Limited, registered in England, company number 785998, of Houndmills, Basingstoke, Hampshire RG21 6XS.

Palgrave Macmillan in the US is a division of St Martin's Press LLC,
175 Fifth Avenue, New York, NY 10010.

Palgrave Macmillan is the global academic imprint of the above companies and has companies and representatives throughout the world.

Palgrave® and Macmillan® are registered trademarks in the United States, the United Kingdom, Europe and other countries.

ISBN 978-1-349-30838-5   ISBN 978-0-230-29450-9 (eBook)
DOI 10.1057/9780230294509

A catalogue record for this book is available from the British Library.

A catalog record for this book is available from the Library of Congress.

10   9   8   7   6   5   4   3   2   1
19 18 17 16 15 14 13 12 11 10

Transferred to Digital Printing in 2012

For Damien

Contents

Preface and Acknowledgements	ix
Introduction: Women, Murder and Femininity	1
Feminist research and women who kill	2
Stories of women who kill	4
Gender regulation and women who kill	5
Murder, meaning and culture	9
Developing a feminist framework	12

Part I

Five Gender Representations of Women Who Kill	23
The masculine woman	24
The muse or mastermind dichotomy	38
The damaged personality	50
The respectable woman	63
The witch	73
Conclusion to Part I	83

Part II

1 Gender, Murder and Mid-Twentieth-Century England and Wales	89
Womanhood in mid-twentieth-century Britain	91
Homicide law in England and Wales in the 1950s	96
Mid-twentieth-century prosecutions for murder	98
Sample selection	99
Analysing textual material	100
Techniques of discourse analysis	103
2 Gender Representations of Twelve Mid-Twentieth-Century Women Accused of Murder	106
The masculine woman	106
The muse/mastermind dichotomy	117
The damaged personality	129
The respectable woman	142
The witch	154

3 Conclusion to Part II	**164**
Gender regulation	164
Murder and meanings	169
Appendix – Two Further Cases from the Sample	174
Hilde Adames (DPP2/3098)	174
Alice Louisa Lyons (DPP2/3020)	174
Notes	176
Bibliography	180
Index	203

Preface and Acknowledgements

I have spent more than a decade thinking about gender representations of women who kill. I originally became interested in this topic in the summer before I spent the third year of my degree in Portland, Oregon. I saw a documentary on television that argued women found guilty of murder in the United States were more likely to be executed if they were portrayed negatively, for example, as lesbians. I was fascinated, and troubled, by the idea that the type of woman someone was depicted as could have such a profound influence over what happened to them. I believed I had settled on my undergraduate dissertation topic. During the winter semester in Portland, I read Margaret Atwood's (1997) *Alias Grace*, which fictionalises the mid-nineteenth-century case of Grace Marks, a young Canadian housemaid who was found guilty of murdering her employer. In the event, I wrote my dissertation on the trials of two mid-nineteenth-century American women found guilty of murder, examining how their womanhood was represented and how this reflected the era's assumptions about the nature of women.

Several years later, I commenced a research project on gender representations of women accused of murder in mid-twentieth-century England and Wales. This book is partly based on that research, but also reflects my wider interest in women, murder and femininity, even going back to some of the issues covered in the documentary I watched one summer evening in the late 1990s.

I'd like to thank Philip Smith for his advice on how to approach a cultural reading of cases of women who kill. Thanks to Daniel Conway for telling me about the case of Daisy de Melker; I'd never heard of her before. Thanks to Mom, Dad, Ruth, Marlene and Brian for their support in asking me how things were going book wise. Many thanks to my husband, Damien, and my best friend, Beccy, for their enthusiasm about the book and their unstinting belief in me.

Quotations from *The Times* on pages 147, 148, 149, 158 and 159 reproduced with permission from News International, ©*The Times*.

Lizzie Seal

Introduction: Women, Murder and Femininity

This book provides a feminist reading of gender representations of women who commit, or are accused of, 'unusual' murders.[1] All types of murder by women are relatively unusual, but when women do kill, the victims are most likely to be their own children or a male partner (Ballinger, 2000; Frigon, 2006). Other sorts of killing by women are rare and arguably have the potential to be even more shocking. Illustrative cases that have figured prominently in the popular imagination include those of Myra Hindley and Aileen Wuornos. Myra Hindley, along with her boyfriend, Ian Brady, participated in the murders of five young people in Manchester, Britain, in the 1960s (Birch, 1993; Storrs, 2004). Aileen Wuornos shot dead seven men she solicited as a sex worker on a Florida highway in the late 1980s and early 1990s (Shipley and Arrigo, 2004; Pearson, 2007). The 'unusualness' of these cases and their distance from more 'explainable' types of murder by women help to explain their notoriety.

Women commit far fewer murders and other types of homicide than men do (Verhoeven, 1993; Chan, 2001; Jensen, 2001),[2] but when they do, it is more disquieting. Whereas '[v]iolence is an accepted attribute of most recognised masculinities' (D'Cruze et al., 2006, p. 46), killing by women violates norms of femininity, such as nurturance, gentleness and social conformity. It disturbs culturally held notions not only of how women should behave, but also of what a woman is. In this sense, women who kill trouble the masculine/feminine gender binary by transgressing its boundaries, making gender constructions of women who kill an essential area for feminist analysis.

Women who kill abusive male partners unsettle gender norms by defending themselves through the use of fatal violence (Morrissey, 2003; Carline, 2005a). However, this is not a culturally unthinkable use of violence by women, especially if they are perceived to be psychologically impaired as a result of experiencing abuse. Women who kill their own children transgress understandings of motherhood and violate its social and cultural foundations (Meyer and Oberman, 2001; Barnett, 2006; West and Lictenstein, 2006). The mother who kills can be represented as a figure of feminine evil, echoing the myth of Medea, who murdered her sons after being abandoned by her lover, Jason (Hendin, 2004). However, there are also more sympathetic views of women who kill their children, especially if they are newborns. Women who kill abusive partners and mothers who commit filicide are likely to receive greater understanding if they are thought to be mentally unbalanced (Nicolson, 1995; Wilczynski, 1997; Barnett, 2006). Therefore, although women who kill their own children or abusive male partners are not necessarily perceived to embody norms of femininity, they are not culturally unthinkable.

The majority of murders by women where the victim is someone other than their own offspring or a male partner are not 'serial killings' in the manner of Myra Hindley or Aileen Wuornos. The definition of 'unusual' murder by women used in this book is a loose one. This is because the aim is not to explore a discrete or identifiable category of killing. Rather, there has been a fuller feminist exploration of gender constructions of women who have killed their own children or abusive male partners than of other types of murder. 'Unusual' cases are understood to include those where women have killed, or been officially accused of killing, other relatives, friends, acquaintances, strangers and other people's children. Women who committed multiple homicides, which included male partners and/or their own children amongst their victims, are also examined as multiple killing by women is rare.

Feminist research and women who kill

Feminist research into women who kill abusive male partners relates to wider scholarship on women's experiences of domestic violence and to theoretical assessments of women's subordinate position in society. In addition to highlighting the impossible situation of women in dangerous relationships, such research has examined the inequities and inadequacies of the criminal justice system in dealing with these cases (Radford, 1993; Stanko and Scully, 1996; Leonard, 2002). It has also explored how negative gender stereotypes appear to affect legal outcomes (Nicolson, 1995; Carline, 2005b; Russell and Melillo, 2006). From a feminist position, it is possible to view women who kill violent male partners as taking justifiable action. They can be seen as defending themselves from life-threatening violence, albeit in ways that the criminal justice system does not always recognise as legitimate. Women who kill abusive male partners have been the subjects of a substantial amount of feminist research and activism (Carline, 2005a), which has established the importance of this issue and contributed to legal reform.

Women who kill their own children are potentially more troubling for feminism, especially for theories which conceptualise motherhood as the foundation for a system of feminist-derived ethics based on the notion of care (see Gilligan, 1982; Noddings, 1984; Tronto, 1987). However, there is a range of feminist arguments and research that identifies the oppressive role of motherhood in relation to both women's lived experiences and to constructions of femininity (Miller, 2005). Feminists have analysed the everyday difficulties and pressures of motherhood, especially for socio-economically disadvantaged women, and have criticised the symbolic role of motherhood in shaping normative feminine identities (see Romero et al., 2003; Choi et al., 2005; Dodson, 2007). Both of these approaches to motherhood have been employed by feminist research into women who kill their children (Barnett, 2006; Oberman and Meyer, 2008). Such cases can not only be disturbing to feminist values, but can also be analysed using feminist insights and arguments.

Other types of murder by women are arguably more transgressive of feminism's boundaries than women who kill abusive male partners or their own children. This may be especially so if the woman's victims are other women, or those occupying socially and economically marginal positions (Ballinger, 2000). However, as several researchers in the area have argued, it is important that feminist scholars do turn their attention to a wider range of cases by women (Bell and Fox, 1996; Ballinger, 2000; Morrissey, 2003; Shipley and Arrigo, 2004). It is crucial that feminist research does not confine itself to 'ideologically sound' cases of women who kill and those that are easy to sympathise with. If feminists ignore women whose 'deeds fall between the cracks of the normative representation of women' (Frigon, 2006, p. 4), then the broader feminist project of challenging derogatory stereotypes and restrictive gender norms is undermined.

Further to these aims, feminist analysis must be extended to unusual cases of women who kill so that a wide variety of feminine subjectivities can be explored and deconstructed. Scholarship concerning women who kill abusive male partners or their own children has, for obvious reasons, focused on women in heterosexual relationships. This means that the constructions of femininity such research has uncovered tend to centre on women's roles as the intimate partners of men and as mothers. This is important to examine, and research into women who kill abusive male partners, or commit filicide, has highlighted the restrictive aspects of these representations (Russell and Melillo, 2006; West and Lichtenstein, 2006), as well as some of the disadvantages for women that institutionalised heterosexuality entails. However, there is less attention to women's more diverse subjectivities beyond heterosexual partnerships and motherhood. Consideration of unusual cases of murder by women enables analysis of a wider range of gender representations (Pearson, 2007) and offers new angles on women's construction as wives and mothers.

There is much important feminist research from a range of disciplines, including criminology, law, cultural studies and social history, which explores issues of gender representation in unusual cases of women who kill. However, this is the first book to take such cases as its primary topic of analysis.

Stories of women who kill

Discourse (understood as the fixation of meaning), narrative and stories are indispensable concepts for analysing gender construction. Cultural representations of women who kill tend to draw on stock stories, which may be familiar from media and fictional portrayals (Morrissey, 2003). The various elements of a woman's case and aspects of her identity are subsumed into a pre-existing narrative, which follows the conventions of storytelling. These stock stories mean that there is often a certain amount of continuity to representations of women who kill, with similar narratives appearing in different times and places (McDonagh, 2003; Morrissey, 2003). Stock stories also emerge from legal processes such as court trials (Nicolson, 1995; Threadgold, 1997). Socio-legal scholars and historians of crime have noted how the criminal justice system draws on established socio-cultural narratives in order to prosecute cases (Anderson and Twining, 1991; Ewick and Silbey, 1995) and in doing so utilises and reproduces gendered stories (Graycar, 1996; Shapiro, 1999). These criminal justice narratives are multiple and frequently offer competing versions of both the events and the identities of those concerned (Korobkin, 1998; Srebnick, 2005).

As part of their adherence to conventions of narrative, legal stories are often told through different genres. The gothic is a recurrent genre for telling stories about murder. Its features are dramatisation of collapsing boundaries and liminality, the presence of monsters, and horror and sensationalism (Halttunen, 1998; Grant, 2004). Other aspects of the gothic are the importance of corpses and the significance of unknowable, threatening spaces such as urban landscapes or large houses (D'Cruze, 2006). Melodrama is another genre that lends itself to stories of homicide. The emotionally intense narratives of melodrama are driven by crisis. They usually have a female protagonist who transgresses against social norms, but is ultimately recuperated (Landy, 1991). Through these genres, stories of women who kill create and reproduce discourses of gender.

Continuity of narratives across place and time makes it possible to identify similar constructions in cases from different periods. In her study of child murder in British culture, 1720–1900, McDonagh (2003, p. 11) argues that 'the meanings of child murder are not contained within any discrete historical moment, but rather travel across them'. However, if too much emphasis is placed on continuity, the importance of context and change may be lost (D'Cruze et al., 2006). Stock stories are modified and reiterated according to the era in which they are told. Therefore, a complete and sophisticated analysis of discourses of femininity in unusual cases of women who kill heeds to be contextualised in relation to the place and time out of which they emerge.

Naylor's (1995) typology of British news stories that appeared in the 1990s concerning violent women identifies six 'common sense' stories used in the press. These were all stereotypical and derogatory, either downplaying women's violence as humorous or excusable, or emphasising the malign threat of feminine evil and deviousness.[3] Jewkes (2004) provides a meta-typology of recurrent media narratives, identified from the feminist literature, of women who commit serious crimes. She highlights eight 'standard narratives', including women as bad wives and mothers, as monstrous or manipulative and as lacking agency.[4] The media, by its very nature, tells and retells stories in order to 'give events shape and purpose' (Morrissey, 2003, p. 14). In a legal context, such as the courtroom, stock stories aid the defence and prosecution to present their cases in ways that resonate with the jury (and the judge), drawing on 'culturally specific stock formats and stock characters in their promotion of stock theories of crime' (ibid., p. 12).

Gender regulation and women who kill

The typologies created by Naylor (1995) and Jewkes (2004) indicate how certain key stereotypical constructions of violent women's femininity have delimited the range of available representations to those which are disparaging and/or disempowering, beyond which, as Birch (1993) and Frigon (2006) argue, we do not have a language with which to articulate cases of women who kill. In particular, the themes of sexuality, madness and women as housewives and carers recur. This is unsurprising in the light of feminist criminology, which has explored how these discourses of womanhood are the ones that have governed the judgment, punishment and representation of criminal women. Frigon (2006) draws on Carlen's (1983) work on 'regimes of femininity' in order to analyse the narratives that appeared in the cases of the 28 Canadian women who were found guilty of murdering their husbands, 1866–1954. She argues that 'women are punished for having stepped outside of their social norms as women, wives and mothers' (Frigon, 2006, p. 7).

Both Nicolson (1995) and Ballinger (2000) utilise Worrall's (1990) framework of the dominant discourses of femininity, namely domesticity, sexuality and pathology (to which Ballinger adds 'respectability'), to deconstruct the criminal justice system's representation and treatment of women who kill. These discourses designate the boundaries of 'appropriate femininity', the socially and culturally approved standard against which women are judged (Worrall, 1990). Nicolson (1995) explores two major English cases of women convicted of murder for killing their abusive husbands, those of Sara Thornton and Kiranjit Ahluwalia, and argues that both were judged through these discourses of femininity, with the consequence that 'the Court of Appeal treated Sara Thornton harshly and Kiranjit Ahluwalia patronisingly' (p. 190).

Ballinger (2000) analyses the appearance of these discourses in the criminal justice system in relation to the 15 cases of women executed in twentieth-century England and Wales. She points out that 91 per cent of women sentenced to death in the twentieth century were reprieved, so asks what was different in the cases of the 15 women who were not (Ballinger, 2000, p. 328). She argues that discourses of 'dangerous womanhood' were successfully mobilised in these cases, and that where women fell short of gender norms they became vulnerable to 'judicial misogyny', making it less likely their death sentence would be commuted. In relation to the use of the death penalty against American women, Heberle (2001, p. 49) contends that decisions over guilt and sentencing involve 'contests over the terms on which individual women's feminine character will be constituted and interpreted'. The importance of conformity to appropriately gendered behaviour is highlighted by Wilczynski's (1997) study of the sentencing of female and male child-killers. Women were overall more likely than men to escape prison, but those who did not appear to be subject to the informal social control mechanisms of social work, psychiatric services or their families were more likely to be perceived as 'bad' rather than 'mad' and to receive a prison sentence.

A key aspect of these feminist arguments about gender constructions of violent women and women who kill is that the discourses of womanhood they reproduce play a role in the wider social regulation of femininity. Nicolson identifies in the cases of Sara Thornton and Kiranjit Ahluwalia 'sexist stereotypes which reinforce the oppression and control of women in general' (1995, p. 186). For Ballinger (2000), the discourses of femininity against which women are judged in the criminal justice system are the same ones that regulate women's behaviour more generally and also encourage women to police themselves. The legal system is a masculine-dominated arena, and one in which the 'desired' qualities of womanhood are defined by 'making a distinction between good, mad and bad women', with violent women usually falling into the latter two categories (Chan, 2001, p. 33).

Feminist authors have argued that the criminal justice system's ability to 'discipline gender' (Heberle, 1999) can therefore serve the interests of both state and patriarchal power by reproducing discourses that circumscribe women's roles and enacting harsh punishment when these are violated. Women's use of violence poses a threat to the gender order that subordinates them – it issues a challenge to the supremacy of masculine power and the social control of women. Women who kill 'test society's established boundaries' (Jones, 1996, p. 13), especially if they appear to have acted purposefully and/or rationally (Wilczynski, 1997; Morrissey, 2003). Crossing the boundaries of gender makes them incomprehensible and dangerous (Ballinger, 2000; Heberle, 2001), which provokes the need for legal and media discourses to 'contain and limit the threat posed by such women' (Morrissey, 2003, p. 2). Jones (1996) argues that society fears both the female murderer and the feminist as their actions challenge the social order. In her examination of women who have killed throughout American history, she notes that '[a] wave of attention to women's criminality follows thunderously on every wave of feminism' (Jones, 1996, p. 14). Public anxiety about women who kill 'reflects more general, inchoate anxieties about the potential for the feminine character to disrupt the order of things' (Heberle, 2001, p. 55). Jones (1996) and Ballinger (2000) point out that women who kill are disproportionately drawn from the socially and economically marginalised, exacerbating the need to contain their threat to the structures of existing power relations.

The discursive regulation of 'good' and 'bad' enactments of femininity is an important means through which the threat posed by women who kill is neutralised. Women who seem to be especially difficult to construct in relation to acceptable performances of femininity are, according to Morrissey (2003), open to 'monsterization' and 'mythification' as evil, placing them beyond human understanding and making them outlaws. This is particularly likely in the rare cases where women have been involved in murders that entail sexual sadism. Where women are represented as more recognisably feminine, for example, when they can be perceived as victims or their actions can be explained through mental illness, they do not cross the boundaries of gender. Morrissey (2003) argues that both representations are problematic because '[i]n either case, order is restored within the dominant, hegemonic world' (p. 171) and the threat women who kill pose to 'male-dominated institutions of heteropatriarchy' is decreased (p. 170).

Ballinger (2007) explores how what at first sight appears to be judicial leniency, namely the reprieve of women from the death penalty for killing their abusive partners in England and Wales, 1900–65, actually served as a conservative strategy. The inferior status of women as a category was underlined and 'the preservation of the gendered social order' maintained (ibid., p. 477). In part, this was because women's victimhood and helplessness were emphasised in such cases. Additionally, the wider contextual background of the unequal gender order that created the circumstances in which the domestic violence took place was left undisturbed. Bestowing mercy upon these women meant that the state could appear to be benevolent whilst potentially more radical critiques of gender and class inequalities were eclipsed.

The feminist analysis of the regulatory power of discourses of femininity and their relevance to cases of women who kill is indispensable for understanding how gender constructions are central to how these women are perceived. It also enables us to assess the wider social consequences of the reproduction of constricting discourses of womanhood in the criminal justice system and the media. Crucially, this mode of analysis highlights how the use of violence by women is an affront to established power relations, and how through deconstructing gender representations of women who kill, it is possible to lay bare the workings of inequalities of power.

The insights of this work, particularly in relation to the deployment of gendered discourses, are vital to this book's analysis of unusual cases of women who kill. However, the focus on gender power and the exertion of state or (hetero)patriarchal control can obscure some of the wider cultural meanings generated by representations of women who kill. Following Heberle's (2001, p. 55) assertion, quoted above, that anxieties about women who kill reflect general, inchoate anxieties about the disruptive power of the feminine, it is also possible to argue that these disparate concerns articulate wider anxieties *through* the symbol of the feminine. This is missed in analyses which concentrate specifically on how discourses of femininity and the workings of the criminal justice system are implicated in wider patterns of social control. What is certainly an important aspect of gender representations of women who kill becomes the only aspect to receive examination. This can have the effect of making patterns of gendered social control appear to be more static and inevitable than they are and misses the opportunity to read the cases' wider symbolic resonance. The analysis in this book of unusual cases of women who kill also draws on literature that explores the cultural meanings of murder and women's criminality.

Murder, meaning and culture

The potential for the trials and publicity surrounding crimes, especially serious crimes such as murder, to generate meanings that reveal important elements of the society in which they take place is well established by cultural historians. As Phillips and Gartner (2003, p. 2) argue in relation to their analysis of the murder of an itinerant preacher in early twentieth-century Seattle, the 'wider contexts [...] and deeper meanings' of the case provide 'a window into many aspects of life and law' during the era. Kramer and Mitchell (2002) choose the case of Mary Lane, a servant in nineteenth-century Canada who shot her mistress, in order to discover 'meanings central to the culture of late Victorian Canada' (p. 6). Dolan (1994, p. 3) finds textual representations of murders and witchcraft in early modern England valuable as 'evidence of cultural formation and transformation' rather than as records of crimes. Similarly, Srebnick (2005) argues that in American historiography, many studies of nineteenth-century murders were not originally intended as histories of crime, but of culture, with issues such as gender and sexuality, and urban life at their core.

This ability for the meanings generated in particular cases of crime to illuminate the wider culture is stressed by proponents of microhistory. This is where the close analysis of one case becomes the basis for understanding the 'wider field of politics and culture surrounding and encompassing it' (Berenson, 1993, p. 8). This can include a wealth of issues such as gender, nationality, family life and conceptualisations of morality and justice (ibid.). Microhistory is not specific to legal case studies, but violent crimes offer particularly fertile examples for analysis as they showcase struggles and conflict, making clear the clashes and disagreements over meaning (Phillips and Gartner, 2003). Culture itself can be understood as a site of struggle and conflict over meaning, which is why criminal cases are especially revealing (Dolan, 1994).

The recognition that criminal cases are rich with symbol and meaning, providing an excellent means for cultural analysis, does of course extend beyond microhistorical approaches. McDonagh (2003, p. 6), who chooses not to focus on a specific 'moment' in British history, argues that '[d]iscussions of child murder frequently seeped into debates on other issues... through which society examined its own values and standards of civilized behaviour'. Appreciation of symbolic significance and plurality of meaning is central to cultural criminology, which aims to examine the contexts in which crime and violence occur (Presdee, 2000, 2004) and 'opens up the study of crime and deviance to a broader range of subjects – the city, the media, globalisation and other discourses of late modernity' (Ferrell et al., 2004, p. 6). Chancer (2005, p. 5) explores how certain high-profile cases of serious violent crime (what she terms 'provoking assaults') in 1980s and 1990s America 'became vehicles for crystallizing, debating, and attempting to resolve contemporary social problems'. As sites of conflict, cases such as boxer Mike Tyson's conviction for rape and O J Simpson's acquittal for the murder of his wife became symbolic of contested issues of gender, ethnicity and class in Reagan/Bush era America.

Analysis of cases of murder reveals significant aspects of social change. Srebnick (2005, p. 14) contends that the murder in early twentieth-century upstate New York of a factory worker Grace Brown by her lover, Chester Gillette, 'raised issues that were emblematic of transformations in American life in the first years of the twentieth-century', including those of class, community and work. This provided fertile material for novelist Theodore Dreiser, who based his *An American Tragedy* (1925) on the case. As windows into a culture, cases of murder and violent crime illuminate anxieties about these transformations. Walkowitz (1992), in her now classic study of Victorian London, examines how the case of Jack the Ripper highlighted tensions surrounding the shifting boundaries of, for example, the acceptability of women's presence in urban space. Murder represents a rending of the social fabric when 'normally unspoken cultural dispositions – feelings about sexuality, ideals of marriage and the family, normative notions of femininity and masculinity are suddenly articulated, even shouted out in dueling [sic] narratives' (Strange, 1999, p. 693).

This articulation highlights cultural boundaries but, as Walkowitz (1992) explores, it also demonstrates their porousness. Shapiro (1996) analyses stories of female criminality in fin de siècle France as expressions of cultural tension that had disparate effects. Within debates and struggles regarding the meaning of female criminality, she identifies both resistance to change and evidence that it was occurring. The boundaries of acceptable behaviour were permeable, which induced anxiety and readjustment. In particular, Shapiro (1996, p. 4) argues that the 'special symbolic resonance' of femaleness meant that crimes by women were especially likely to be endowed with meaning and to become sites of cultural struggle. Uncertainties over gender relations became connected to concerns about the nature of burgeoning mass culture in France, with female behaviour becoming a 'key interpretive grid' through which to understand the state of society (ibid., p. 9).

Berenson (1993) turns the spotlight on the trial of Madame Caillaux from early twentieth-century France. Henriette Caillaux was a society lady who shot a newspaper editor who had printed a letter that was politically embarrassing to her husband. Her trial commenced 2 weeks before the First World War began in 1914, a time of moral and cultural crisis in France. Berenson (1993, p. 12) argues that the meanings of femininity were hugely significant to the case as the ideological and cultural conflicts of the era related to sexuality, privacy, nationality and politics 'coalesced around questions of gender'. Hendin (2004, p. 30) sees the mythification of female violence in American culture as signifying 'the fear that the violence of women violates both nature and society, and reveals terrible and frightening change'. Violent women become a focus for anxiety but it is also possible for them to symbolise the excitement of change (ibid.). The discourses that construct women who kill represent an attempt to codify the rules of appropriate feminine behaviour but this inevitably takes place in a realm of contested meaning in which social and cultural boundaries are not fixed (Shapiro, 1996).

This book adopts a two-stage model in order to analyse gender representations in unusual cases of women who kill that conjoins an examination of recurrent, regulatory discourses of womanhood to an exploration of the wider, cultural meanings that these discourses generate. The choice of 'unusual' cases not only extends the feminist scholarship on women who kill, but also provides a focus on cases particularly likely to test social and cultural boundaries. It continues the process of furthering feminist understanding of portrayals of women who kill beyond the bad wife and mother tropes, to other subjectivities. The next section discusses the theoretical tools concerning gender construction and gendered subjectivity that are employed in order to undertake the analysis.

Developing a feminist framework

The importance of gender construction

Feminist theory is hydra-headed, encompassing a variety of views and approaches, which analyse gender in relation to issues of equality, difference and experience (Braidotti, 1994; Wheedon, 1997). This book adopts a poststructuralist feminist framework in order to decode representations of gender in unusual cases of women who kill. An important element of postructuralist feminism's approach to gender identity is the rejection of the notion of essential gender differences and identities (Scott, 1986; Spelman, 1988; Mouffe, 2005). Gender identity is understood to be socially and historically contingent. Therefore, it is necessary to examine the context out of which it arises (Mouffe, 1995; Gatens, 2002). Gender identities are not unitary and subjects do not possess 'authentic', core selves (Riley, 1988; Butler, 1999). Subjectivity, the positioning of social agents in discourse, is an ongoing process of construction and constitution that produces multiple identities (within the same subject) rather than a coherent, easily identifiable 'self' (Braidotti, 1994).

Poststructuralist gender theorists reject the notion of fixed differences between masculinity and femininity, or that there are essential characteristics, biological or otherwise, that belong to 'women' and 'men' (Butler, 2004). The acceptance that gendered subjectivity is produced through discourse means that femininity is not understood to automatically relate to women and masculinity is not understood to be necessarily connected with men (Halberstam, 1998; Butler, 1999). Feminine and masculine subjectivities could be created for both men and women. The emphasis placed on the multiple and flowing nature of subjectivity means that femininity and masculinity do not need to be understood as neatly separable, or discrete (De Lauretis, 1987; Butler, 1993, 1999).

The fit between social agents and gendered subject positions is an imperfect one. Women rarely fully embody feminine gender norms and men rarely fully exemplify norms of masculinity (Butler, 1999). This leads Butler (1993) to contend that all gender is drag. In part, this is because gender norms are themselves multiple and contradictory and 'are only tenuously embodied by any particular social actor' (Butler, 2004, p. 41). The subject position of motherhood offers a salient example. Although there is arguably a broad consensus that good mothering entails providing children with care and nurturance, how this nurturing should be performed is not universally agreed upon (Doane and Hodges, 1992). There is no unitary discourse of the 'good mother' for social agents to enact.

The contingent nature of gendered subjectivity is revealed in the space that opens up between constructions of gender and actual social agents (Butler, 2004). The dominant, normative versions of femininity and masculinity are hyperbolic (Butler, 1993). Subjects perform these gender identities, but they either do not inhabit them completely or perform them in unexpected or unacceptable ways. Unexpected and unacceptable performances of gender may not be culturally intelligible or recognisable – the subject in question is not easily assigned femininity or masculinity (Butler, 1999). A 'wrong' or contradictory performance of gender by a social agent opens up a gap between their performance and normative gender. In this gap, the contingent nature of femininity and masculinity is exposed (Butler, 1993). Gender is never fully determining (ibid.), leaving the possibility for 'unexpected and enabling response[s]' (Butler, 1997, p. 2).

Performativity does not mean that subjects freely choose how to enact gender, or that they do so with conscious artifice (Butler, 1997, 1999). It does, however, implicate them in the ongoing constitution and reconstitution of femininity and masculinity. Gendering is 'a compulsory practice, a forcible production' (Butler, 1993, p. 231), which is restricted and conditioned by extant discourses. All social agents are culturally assigned gender, or are somehow constructed in relation to normative gender (Butler, 1999, 2004). They are inevitably part of this process, and can improvise on, subvert or resist, regulatory norms (Butler, 2004). Nevertheless, the terms that make up their gender identity act as a 'scene of constraint', which is external to the social agent (ibid., p. 1).

The notion of femininity as not only multiple and inessential, but also performative is particularly useful for decoding representations of women who kill. Culturally, to commit murder is contradictory to femininity and therefore women who kill open up a gap between their actions and normative gender constructions. Carline (2005b) illustrates this through considering the case of Zoora Shah, who in England in 1993 was found guilty of murdering a man with whom she was in an abusive relationship. Carline argues that to the Court of Appeal, Zoora was gender unintelligible because she did not perform the acceptable gendered scripts of femininity. Her perceived lack of physical injuries and her failure to speak to anyone about the abuse she experienced were interpreted as placing her outside the recognisable 'battered woman' subject position. The Court described her as an 'unusual woman', a designation that resulted from its inability to characterise her as 'mad' or 'bad' (ibid., p. 231). She became abject from intelligible femininity but occupied a new subject position of the 'unusual woman' (ibid.).

From this discussion of gender construction, it should have become clear that whilst representations of womanhood have regulatory power and are not easily transformed, they are not impervious to change and reconstitution. Poovey (1988) argues that regulatory discourses have 'uneven' effects – due to differences in subjects' social positioning, they have differential impact, significance and power. Therefore, it is vital to consider diverse constructions of feminine subjectivity. This can be differences between women, and also within the same woman (Braidotti, 1994).

Intersecting identities

Some types of femininity are constructed as more socially and culturally desirable than others and certain femininities are constituted as more socially and culturally powerful than others (Cornell, 1995). These differences can be analysed by utilising the type of poststructuralist feminist approach outlined above, which conceptualises gender identity as split and multiple. According to this framework, 'women' are not understood as a straightforward, identifiable category (Riley, 1988). Social agents are not homogeneous, unified entities; they are 'constructed at the point of intersection of a multiplicity of subject positions' (Mouffe, 2005, p. 12). The construction of 'women' always takes place relative to other categories, which are themselves mutable (Riley, 1988). An intersectional analysis enables the complexity of gendered subjectivity to be examined.

Intersectionality pays attention to the 'interrelationships of gender, class, race and ethnicity and other social divisions' (Yuval-Davis, 2006, p. 194). Identity is seen as comprising various interlocking strands, which are mutually constitutive (Davis, 2008). Gender is only one of these strands and is not necessarily given primacy over the others (Burgess-Proctor, 2006). An intersectional approach can be used to explore positions of subordination, but also of power and hierarchy. It is applicable to 'all people, regardless of their social location'

(Burgess-Proctor, 2006, p. 38). Intersectionality analyses subjects' multiple positioning (Mouffe, 2005), as well as the places where different aspects of identity meet and overlap (Yuval-Davis, 2006).

Stubbs and Tolmie (1995) adopt an intersectional approach to analysing Australian cases of aboriginal women who kill abusive male partners. They argue that focusing solely on gender cannot adequately explain the positioning of such women and their experiences of the criminal justice system. Both the social positioning and the cultural representation of aboriginal women are shaped by gender and 'race', meaning that the intersections between these aspects of identity must be read in order to acknowledge the complexity of these cases.

An appreciation of the intersectional nature of identity further enables feminist analysis that is sensitive to the differential cultural value ascribed to different constructions of femininity (Anthias, 2002). White, middle class, heterosexual femininity is usually granted a higher symbolic value than other forms, which can be understood as negatively related to this dominant, or normative, construction. Women who are assigned the normative form of femininity are potentially, socially and culturally more powerful than other women, and stand to benefit culturally and materially from their positive association with this construction (Anthias, 2002). The multiplicity of subjectivity means that an individual can be 'dominant in one relation while subordinated in another' (Mouffe, 1995, p. 318). Threadgold (1997) compares two 1990s Australian cases of women who killed their abusive partners; one woman was white, and one aboriginal. In the trial of the aboriginal woman, certain aspects of her case, which were very similar to the white woman's case, were attributed to her 'violent culture', an explanation absent from the white woman's trial. Through a situated narrative analysis, Threadgold explores how these women were constituted, and how their genders were inscribed differently, but also how the aboriginal woman was constructed as being from a 'deviant' culture.

As discussed above, normativity is both relational and uneven. Women who kill may bear some of the markers of appropriate femininity, whilst also bearing devalued identities. The complex and contradictory nature of their subjectivities must be thoroughly decoded. Femininities vary according to whether they are assigned to older or younger women, minority ethnic or white women, and their meanings cannot be fully understood without attention to these other elements of identity. This book utilises the lens of gender in order to carry out the analysis, but is attentive to the relevance of the women's intersecting identities and to the differences between and within them.

Symbolic femininities

This chapter has discussed how analysis of cases of murder can serve as a window into a culture at a particular point in time, and explored how constructions of femininity are particularly fruitful for this analysis due to its especially symbolic nature (Shapiro, 1996). Feminist scholars who have theorised the importance of representations of femininity to constructions of the nation have explored this symbolism. Yuval-Davis (1997, p. 45) argues, 'Women especially are often required to carry this "burden of representation", as they are constructed as the symbolic bearers of the collectivity's identity and honour, both personally and collectively'. The figure of a woman, often a mother, symbolises many cultures as women are implicated in the transmission and the reproduction of the national culture (ibid.). They are viewed as repositories of the culture and also as its metaphoric limit (McClintock, 1993; Einhorn, 1996).

Women, in being especially representative of the collectivity, mark its boundaries as 'much of ethnic culture is organized around rules relating to sexuality, marriage and the family, and a true member will perform these roles properly' (Anthias et al., 1992, p. 113). The appropriate behaviour of women highlights the boundaries between one culture and another and the division between 'us' and 'them', which means that women who do not behave 'properly' cross these boundaries (Yuval-Davis, 1997). This underlines the need for the regulation of femininity (Kandiyoti, 1991). Discourses of womanhood are battlegrounds of meaning, where the correct practices, behaviours and symbols of the collectivity are contested (Yuval-Davis, 1997).

McDonagh (1997) explores contested meanings of gender and nationality in the case of Caroline Beale. Caroline was a British woman who, in 1994, gave birth in a hotel room in New York having concealed her pregnancy. She was arrested when attempting to board a plane home, carrying the baby's body in her shoulder bag. Her case became a battleground of contested meaning when she was charged with murder and incarcerated in Rikers Island Penitentiary, as it seemed she had suffocated the baby shortly after it was born. In Britain, this was constructed as evidence of excessive American punitiveness and brutality. Press coverage highlighted the fact that in more civilised Britain, Caroline's mental health problems would have been recognised and she would have been unlikely to face time in custody. American representations of the case emphasised the greater value that their system placed on getting justice for the helpless victim, something which the British seemed content to overlook. Contested understandings of punishment, justice and civilisation as they related to the treatment of women swirled around the case, which became symbolic of what it meant to be British or American.

The wider importance of symbolic representation can be understood by considering Fraser's (1995, 2000, 2007) arguments about social justice. Justice is intertwined not only with the politics of redistribution, which is concerned with inequalities in material resources, but also the politics of recognition, which focuses on inequalities in cultural representation. Both redistribution and recognition are central to questions of social justice. The analysis in this book is largely concerned with the politics of recognition, rather than redistribution. Redistribution is clearly an essential element of social justice, but in order to understand the significance of gender representation, it is necessary to utilise a politics of recognition. Cultural and socioeconomic disadvantage are often closely connected, but there are also instances of cultural devaluation that do not relate to material deprivation, for example, homophobia (Fraser, 1995). Redistribution and recognition are often not neatly separable. Issues of redistribution arise where women's gendered experiences and social positioning shape their symbolic representation, for example, their performance of the care role or their historically unequal access to financial independence.

Individuals or groups that are assigned identities that are not recognised as legitimate are culturally devalued, and are therefore prevented from participating as peers in social life. Lack of recognition, or misrecognition, becomes institutionalised as social subordination and marks out certain subjects as 'unworthy of respect or esteem' (Fraser, 2000, p. 114). An important strand of feminist politics is to promote the acceptance of difference in terms of gender identity; that is, recognition of diverse subjectivities without cultural denigration (Braidotti, 1994; Cornell, 1995; Gatens, 2002). This is an especially thorny problem when it comes to women who kill, who may be uncomfortable subjects for feminists themselves (Bell and Fox, 1996; Ballinger, 2000; Morrissey, 2003). A poststructuralist feminist framework, which places difference at the centre of the analysis, can 'recode or rename the female feminist subject not as yet another sovereign, hierarchical, and exclusionary subject', but as 'a multiple, open-ended, interconnected entity' (Braidotti, 1994, p. 158).

The construction of femininity, its interaction with other aspects of identity and attention to its symbolic significance form the main theoretical elements of the analysis of unusual cases of women who kill. As part of this gendered analysis, it is also necessary to pay attention to concepts related to transgression.

Transgressive femininities

The notion of transgression is clearly important to understanding gender representations of women who kill. The discussion has highlighted the significance of these cases in terms of the violation of norms of femininity. The argument that examining the 'strange' or peripheral illuminates the culturally central or normative is well established (see Stallybrass and White, 1986; Cresswell, 1996; Butler, 1999). For Butler (1999, p. 140), 'it is the exception, the strange, that gives us the clue as to how the mundane and taken-for-granted world of sexual meaning is constituted'. By analysing gender representations of women who have carried out acts considered antithetical to femininity, the cultural construction of appropriate femininity becomes clearer, as do the wider cultural meanings that circulate around it. This is enhanced by the concentration on 'unusual' cases – their exceptional nature is what makes them symbolically important (Stallybrass and White, 1986; Cresswell, 1996; Butler, 1999).

'Transgression' literally means boundary crossing; one who transgresses leaves the confines of acceptability and becomes 'out of place' (Cresswell, 1996, p. 22). This condition of displacement makes the transgressive troubling and potentially dangerous. Not knowing to which category something, or someone, belongs is unsettling (Douglas, 1966; Bauman, 1991). Transgressors are often framed symbolically as polluting because they have the power to disturb order (Douglas, 1966). According to Douglas (1966, p. 139), 'The polluter becomes a doubly wicked object of reprobation, first because he [sic] crossed the line and second because he endangered others'. Their strangeness and resistance to classification means that the transgressive are not fully recognisable or intelligible (Bauman, 1991; Butler, 1999). Bauman (1991) conceptualises this in his notion of the stranger, who falls outside of the friend/enemy binary and becomes ambivalent because s/he is not known.

This condition of being unfathomable can be conceptualised as abjection, which involves the breaching of boundaries and the flow between boundaries (Grant, 2004). The abject is profoundly ambivalent; it can induce both horror and disgusted fascination. Drawing on Kristeva (1982), Grant (2004, p. 122) explains, 'The abject reveals the radical permeability of borders, and horror arises from flows, the liminal and the in-between'. Liminal beings are those that appear to be symbolically neither fully one thing nor another, they are in-between and exist at the margins (Bhabha, 1996; Butler, 2000). Those that cannot be categorised – the in-between, the stranger, the borderline, the hybrid – can also become monsters (Bauman, 1991).

The significance of boundary crossing, in terms of both gender and wider cultural norms, has already been discussed in relation to women who kill, as has the potential for such women to be constructed as dangerous (Ballinger, 2000), or to be monsterised (Morrissey, 2003). Birch (1993, p. 54) argues that the power of the famous police mug shot of Myra Hindley to disturb is in 'our recognition of the abject in that photograph, the threat it invokes of all the boundaries destroyed, the collapse of rationality, the triumph of moral anarchy'. Verhoeven (1993) and Morrissey (2003) explore the representation of Tracey Wigginton as an abject 'lesbian vampire killer'. Tracey was a young Australian woman who in 1989 killed a man unknown to her, Edward Baldock, and claimed to have drunk his blood. Vampires breach the borders 'between human and inhuman, good and evil', and life and death (Morrissey, 2003, p. 107). They live off human blood, which becomes abject waste once it has flown through the body's boundaries. The media coverage of the killing exhibited both fascination that Edward could become the victim of a much younger woman, and repulsion at Tracey's use of violence and her supposed control over three female friends, one of whom was her girlfriend, who were with her on the night of the murder (Verhoeven, 1993). Women who kill who display some of the attributes of appropriate femininity are unlikely to be figured as transgressive or abject. However, for women to exert power over life and death collapses the division between femininity and masculinity and requires some cultural repair or recuperation to avoid such depictions (Morrissey, 2003).

Part I develops a typology of five discourses of womanhood that recur in unusual cases of women who kill. These are – the masculine woman; the muse/mastermind dichotomy; the damaged personality; the respectable woman; and the witch. It outlines the components of each discourse and explores their emergence through a review of well-known cases. In doing so, Part I suggests the potential of these representations for revealing key anxieties about, and moments of, social change.

Part II, which is divided into three chapters, entails a shift to a more specific context that was the subject of the empirical research undertaken for this book. This utilises the typology of unusual cases of women who kill and applies it to an analysis of the case files of 12 women accused of murder in England and Wales, 1957–1962. Chapter 1 establishes this as a pivotal time in twentieth-century British history. It explores the main social and cultural shifts of the era and how they related to understandings of gender, and identifies hopes and fears surrounding post-war modernity as particularly significant. This chapter also discusses the methodological issues attached to archival, documentary research and outlines the techniques of discourse analysis that were used to undertake the analysis. In Chapter 2, the cases of 12 women accused of unusual murders are analysed in relation to the five discourses of womanhood. Each discourse is placed within the context of mid-twentieth-century England and Wales, and the 12 cases are analysed for what they reveal about contemporary norms of femininity and how this related to the shifting social and cultural boundaries of the era. Chapter 3 concludes by drawing together the themes that emerge from these cases, as they relate to gender regulation and the cultural meanings of murder.

Part I

Five Gender Representations of Women Who Kill

Part I develops a typology of five discourses of femininity through which women who have committed, or been accused of, unusual murders have been constructed. It does this by undertaking a review of well-known cases and cases that were high profile within the place and time in which they occurred. In each section, the constituent elements of the discourse are outlined, whether these derive from expert knowledge and/or wider cultural assumptions, and three or four illustrative cases are discussed. Part I demonstrates the recurrent nature of these representations, whilst acknowledging that they carry different meanings and symbolic significance in different places and times. These five discourses are not intended to be exhaustive, either in terms of the range of gender representations of unusual cases of women who kill or in relation to each case that is examined. Individual cases are analysed through one discourse, which was important in shaping the woman's gender representation. However, this does not mean that there were no other relevant discursive constructions of gender, merely that those selected were especially prominent.

Discourse can be understood as the partial fixation of meaning through the assemblage of signs (Laclau and Mouffe, 2001), and gender identities are represented and created through discourse (De Lauretis, 1987; Smith, 1990). Discourse analysis involves the identification of discourses in a particular area of interest and unpacking the meanings they create (Foucault, 1989), which exposes their contingency (Laclau and Mouffe, 2001). This book investigates discourses of gender that emerge from cultural and legal representations of women accused of unusual murder. For the purposes of the typology, a single discourse refers to a particular type of womanhood constructed in relation to women accused of murder.

The five discourses of femininity explored were identified as part of a two-stage process, which involved familiarity with the relevant literature on women who kill and close analysis of the empirically researched cases from mid-twentieth-century England and Wales that are discussed in Part II. Insights from feminist scholarship on gender representations of violent women, including other typologies such as Naylor (1995) and Jewkes (2004), have informed the identification of five important discourses of femininity that recur in unusual cases of women who kill.

The masculine woman

The gendering of violent crime as masculine has led to a recurrent discursive construction of women who kill as masculinised. According to this representation, violent women are not really women at all, but share more characteristics with men. The archetype of the masculine criminal woman is deeply embedded in criminological thinking and there have been numerous explanations for female offending, which suggest it is indicative of manifestations of female masculinity. These will be explored further within this section. The tendency to masculinise women who kill is exacerbated in cases of women perceived as being lesbian. In addition to criminological theories on the relationship between heightened masculinity in women and the propensity to offend, biological and psychological explanations of homosexuality in women have historically linked lesbianism to masculinity.

This section explores the appearance of the masculine woman discourse in cases of women accused of unusual murder. It first considers the notion of 'female masculinity' and how this has frequently been understood as a pathological construction. It then explores the emergence of this discourse in the high-profile cases of Rose West, Aileen Wuornos and Wanda Jean Allen.

The masculine woman of criminology

The origins of the identification of criminal women with masculinity lay in the beginnings of positivist criminology itself. Lombroso's seminal *Criminal Woman*, first published in 1885 in Italy, identified the embodied masculine traits of female offenders. According to Lombroso, women were not biologically predisposed to break the law as they were by nature unimaginative and conformist. This did not signal a greater capacity in women for morality, rather their conformity was due to their passive disposition. Lombroso argued that criminal women had a more masculine physical appearance than 'normal' women and also a greater number of physical flaws and abnormalities. His similarly biologically derived theories of male offending were discredited long before his work on women (Rafter and Gibson, 2004). This was mainly due to the paucity of research into female offending. Although mainstream criminology had rejected the notion that physical stigmata indicated criminality by the early twentieth century, *Criminal Woman*, which was translated into English as *The Female Offender* in 1903, remained the only major criminological text on female offending.

The putative relationship between masculine women and criminality was developed further by criminologists in the twentieth century. Glueck and Glueck (1934) believed that body type could determine offending behaviour, and women with masculine bodies were more likely to be criminal. Cowie et al. (1968) studied delinquent girls, and concluded that certain physical traits, such as being big, were more likely to make girls aggressive. Girls who were more masculine were more likely to be delinquent. These studies differ from Lombroso's in that they did not suggest that specific physical stigmata indicated criminality. However, they perpetuated the notion that physically manifest masculinity in women was a cause of criminality.

Biological explanations for female crime are not the only ones to have posited a link between masculinity in women and offending. Other theorists have proposed that psychological identification with masculinity, or rejection of femininity, in women is a predictor of criminality. Thomas (1923) suggested that women eager for excitement and fun sometimes reject their passive feminine role in order to seek adventure and freedom. Criminologists have also drawn on Freudian notions of gender role identification, arguing that women who do not develop normal feminine attitudes are in danger of becoming delinquent (Klein, 1973; Widom, 1979).

Finally, sociological explanations for why women might commit crime have also suggested that women who perpetrate 'active' or violent crimes hold masculine values. This argument originates with Parsons (1947), who contended that boys' rebelliousness can be understood as an attempt to distance themselves from their mothers and to establish their masculinity. Girls, on the other hand, embrace the feminine role exemplified by their mothers and are more likely to be law-abiding and conformist. Cohen (1955) adopted elements of Parsons' thesis in his exploration of delinquency in boys. For working-class boys, crime could 'verify' their masculinity, the achievement of which was in danger of being thwarted by their limited opportunities. Girls needed to avoid delinquency in order to attain femininity so were likely to be conformist. When girls did rebel, they became sexually promiscuous rather than violent or criminal. To this extent, they were still performing a feminine role in searching for a mate.

These sociological studies established a powerful connection between criminal behaviour as a means of acting out or achieving masculinity, which has remained influential in criminology (see Whitehead, 2005; Byrne and Trew, 2008). The implicit conclusion to be drawn from Parsons and Cohen is that women who are involved in masculine crimes, such as murder, are identified with the masculine gender role. Some criminological research with imprisoned women examined their value systems in order to discover whether they held masculine, rather than feminine values (Widom, 1979). Theories of gender role socialisation have led to the suggestion that women's offending is usually in keeping with femininity. Women who shoplift, for example, may do so in order to provide food or other necessities for their families. Women who receive stolen goods frequently enact a supporting role to men who carry out the active part of the crime, stealing the goods. Feminist criminologist Naffine (1985, 1987) argues that the gender role socialisation thesis is problematic as it reifies masculinity and femininity, assuming these concepts can be satisfactorily defined and measured. It also ignores important differences in the social control of men and women which may affect their offending behaviour.

These criminological theories on the links between masculinity, femininity and crime ultimately construct women who perpetrate violent crimes as deviant and pathological. Whether it is because they are biologically more like men, psychologically damaged or identify with the 'wrong' gender, the perception of masculinity in women who commit certain types of crime renders them failed women.

Feminist criminologists have challenged derogatory and stereotypical views of criminal women and, in particular, have rejected the notion that women who commit crime, or certain types of crime, are masculine (Klein, 1973; Naffine, 1987; Daly, 1997; Chesney-Lind, 2006). However, it is important to review the legacy of the masculine woman in criminology because this construction has currency in popular discourse. Recent studies on the representation of girls' violence have highlighted the appearance of masculinisation discourses in relation to girls involved in gang violence (Chesney-Lind and Eliason, 2006; Ringrose, 2006). Popular representations of crime, such as news sources, films, television programmes and true crime, articulate the 'masculine woman' discourse as an explanation for women's violence or killing. Rafter (2007) argues that it is important to take such 'popular criminology' seriously as it is the primary way most people are exposed to ideas about the nature of crime.

The masculine woman of sexology

Another intellectual discipline that has produced discourses of the masculine woman is sexology, the scientific study of sex. Sexology emerged in the late nineteenth century, when writers such as Krafft-Ebing (1894) and Ellis (1897) sought to enumerate, categorise and explain different sexual identities. Nineteenth-century sexologists turned their attention to homosexuality in women and men, conceptualising it as sexual inversion. Female homosexuals were thought to possess excessively masculine traits, and males excessively female ones. The nineteenth-century sexologists interpreted inversion as a congenital defect with biological causes. The explanation for homosexuality could be found in the body (Foucault, 1990; Vicinus; 1992; Bland, 2002).

Krafft-Ebing (1894) made the first scientific attempt to classify female homosexuality, arguing that there were four categories of lesbian, each of which was more masculine, and more degenerate, than the last. The fourth category, the invert, was the most masculine, and according to Krafft-Ebing, 'possesses of the feminine qualities only the genital organs: thought, sentiment, action, even external appearance are those of the man' (quoted in Newton, 1994, p. 566). Although constructed as a biological disorder, Krafft-Ebing included cross-dressing and rejection of conventional social roles as features of lesbianism. He also focused on characteristics and traits rather than sexual behaviour.

Other sexologists agreed that lesbianism should be understood as inversion. Ellis (1897) understood homosexuality as hereditary and irreversible. Hirschfeld (1913) described sexual inverts as people of one sex trapped in the body of the other, and contended that they constituted a third sex. The European sexologists of the late nineteenth and early twentieth centuries argued that inverts should be treated with respect and accorded rights. Their work was not intended to disparage women and men who were homosexuals, but to scientifically understand human sexuality (Magee and Miller, 1992; Bland, 2002). However, the framing of homosexual bodies as 'defective' and 'degenerate' established a template for perceiving lesbianism as abnormal and ultimately undesirable (Foucault, 1990).

Sexology's development of the concept of the female invert drew on the case of a 'masculine' woman who killed. Alice Mitchell, a 19-year old who cut the throat of her friend, 17-year-old Freda Ward in Memphis,

Tennessee, in 1892, was described by Ellis as a 'typical invert' (Duggan, 1993, p. 795) in the first American edition of *Sexual Inversion*, published in 1901. Alice had on several occasions proposed marriage to Freda, to whom she was extremely close. When it appeared that Freda's affection for her had waned, Alice cut Freda's throat rather be estranged from her. The case attracted sensational media coverage, which described it as an 'unnatural crime'. As part of an insanity defence, Alice's defence attorneys emphasised her masculine behaviour and lack of interest in feminine pursuits such as sewing and needle-work (Duggan, 1993; Lindquist, 1995). Historians of sexuality have explored the importance of her case as a high-profile construction of the late nineteenth century's new lesbian subjectivity (Duggan, 1993; Lindquist, 1995; Buring, 1997).

Later psychoanalytic understandings of sexuality focused on its importance for the mental life of individuals, rather than its biological aetiology (Waters, 1999). The Freudian notion of heterosexual femininity and masculinity as indications of the attainment of maturity influenced mid-twentieth-century perceptions of homosexuality as a form of mental illness (Weeks, 1985). In the 1950s and 1960s, scientific definitions and classifications of sexuality were largely psychiatric (Jennings, 2004). Women in lesbian relationships were variously understood to be immature, tragic and likely to exhibit masculine traits (Magee and Miller, 1992; Hart, 1994; Jennings, 2004).

Psychoanalysis associated heterosexuality with positive mental health, which meant that some psychiatrists perceived homosexuality as a symptom of mental disorder, or as a mental illness in itself (Conrad and Angell, 2004). Early and mid-twentieth-century literature on psychopaths suggested a link between sexual deviance (thought to include homosexuality) and psychopathy (see Karpman, 1951). Terms such as psychopath, psychopathy and psychopathic personality have been defined in loose and wide-ranging ways. However, a definition of the psychopath as someone with little moral sense, no conscience and an inability to form deep or lasting relationships is characteristic of the way the term was used (see McCord and McCord, 1964). In the United States, in particular, the figure of the 'sexual psychopath' loomed large in the scientific and popular imagination of the mid-twentieth-century (Freedman, 1987).

In 1940s America, psychological studies suggested a link between psychopathy and lesbianism, and proposed 'the possibly greater tendency of the [female] psychopath to engage in sex acts with other girls' (Shotwell, 1946 quoted in Freedman, 1996, p. 405). In Britain and America, female only institutions began to be viewed with suspicion as breeding grounds for homosexual activity between women. This included anxieties about prisons, boarding schools and all women colleges (Jennings, 2004).

It is important to acknowledge that not all sexology constructed lesbianism as pathological. The Kinsey reports (1948, 1953) on the sexual behaviour of American men and women argued that same sex encounters should be regarded as normal experiences. Their prevalence suggested the dominance of heterosexuality was largely down to social norms (Taylor, 1999). Other mid-twentieth-century studies found that homosexuality appeared to be biologically inherent to humans and monkeys. However, the purpose of this chapter is to trace iterations of the discourse of the masculine woman and to delineate its appearance in unusual cases of women who kill, where it has usually been articulated in terms of pathology.

Lesbian and gay, and feminist, activists challenged the notion of lesbianism as connoting abnormality, deviance and pathology from the late 1960s onwards (Cruikshank, 1992; Jennings, 2007a). Abnormality is no longer the dominant discursive construction of lesbian identity and ceased to be so during the 1970s (Weeks, 2007). The American Psychiatric Association removed homosexuality from its classification of mental disorders in 1973, but it continued to be categorised as pathological by the World Health Organisation until 1988. This was also when homosexuality was removed from the British Diagnostic and Statistical Manual of Mental Disorders (DSM) (Taylor, 1999). This demonstrates the persistence of the homosexuality as illness paradigm in expert medical classifications beyond the mid-twentieth-century. It is also important to remember that, as with the masculine woman of criminology, seemingly outmoded conceptualisations of lesbian identity, which link it to violence and criminality, remain an aspect of the popular criminology of news stories, films, television programmes and true crime. They also still make an appearance in legal constructions of lesbian subjectivity (Thomas, 2005).

Negative and derogatory portrayals of female masculinity have dominated understandings of putatively masculine criminal women (Heidensohn, 1996). This does not mean that there are no positive renderings of female masculinity. For example, the 'mannish lesbian' trope, which developed from the nineteenth-century sexologists' construction of the invert, could be a subjectivity promising greater freedom and independence for early twentieth-century women (Duggan, 1993; Newton, 1994). Queer theorist, Halberstam (1998), argues that masculine female subjectivities can be infused with pride and power. However, these positive, liberating discourses and subjectivities are not usually the ones to emerge in popular or legal representations of women who kill.

Part of the reason for the absence of more liberating discourses and subjectivities is the recurrent appearance of the masculine woman as deviant trope as a means of expressing certain cultural anxieties pertaining to morality and correct behaviour. As discussed, these anxieties circulate around femininity in particular as it symbolises cultural boundaries. The perceived assumption of masculinity by women, especially in relation to violence, is often constructed through conservative discourses as a worrying power grab, and as a symptom of cultural decline. This is frequently against a backdrop of shifting mores in terms of gender and sexual relations. The chapter now examines three late twentieth-century unusual cases of women who kill that were shaped by the masculine woman discourse.

Rose West

In 1995, in England, Rose West was found guilty of the murders of ten girls and young women, including her 16-year-old biological daughter, Heather. Their remains were discovered in the basement and garden of the house in Gloucester that she shared with her husband, Fred. Fred was also accused of the murders but committed suicide whilst awaiting trial (Cameron, 1996; Winter, 2002, 2004). Rose was 41 when she stood trial, had been married and was a mother. Due to the multiple victims, Rose was labelled a 'serial killer', more usually a masculine construction. The murders of which she was found guilty took place over a 20-year period. They involved the sexual and physical torture of the victims.

Evidence presented at Rose's trial pertaining to her supposed masculinity and sexual deviance was crucial to the prosecution's case and to gaining a conviction. There was no forensic evidence linking her to the murders, she denied involvement and, before he died, Fred claimed to have been solely responsible for their commission. The prosecution argument therefore relied on similar fact evidence, which is where evidence is admitted of involvement of the accused in activities similar to those for which they are tried (Winter, 2002, 2004). Three surviving female victims of Rose West gave testimony at her trial that she raped and sexually abused them in a manner similar to that experienced by the women who were killed. Rose was convicted of murder on the basis of this testimony.

The evidence of the surviving women included details of masculine-type sexual violence by Rose, such perpetrating sexual assault with a vibrator (Winter, 2002). She was portrayed as the aggressor in these attacks, and Fred as a passive onlooker. This was despite the fact that one of the witnesses, Fred's daughter and Rose's step-daughter, had been repeatedly raped by him during her childhood. The depiction of Rose as sexually dominant and aggressive masculinised her and underlined her sexual deviance. It also emphasised how far she departed from ideal femininity and her violation of the mother role. The masculine woman discourse was successfully mobilised by the prosecution in Rose West's trial to help secure her conviction (Winter, 2004). This demonstrates the significance of this discourse beyond the constitution of deviant subjectivities – it can also play a role in the verdict and/or punishment the woman in question receives.

The shocking nature of the West case was exacerbated by the imputed involvement of Rose in what would usually be conceptualised as highly masculinised serial killings. However, the mobilisation of the masculine woman discourse also reflected socio-cultural shifts related to family life in 1990s Britain. On the surface, the Wests were an unremarkable, heterosexual, nuclear family (Wykes, 1998). The hegemony of this family form was becoming increasingly shaky in the 1990s, when the acceptability of single parent families increased and the premium placed on marriage began to decline. These changes were by no means universally approved and were the subject not only of intense debate, but also a highly moralistic response from the Conservative Government's heavily contested 'back to basics' campaign, which emphasised 'traditional' values based on the sanctity of the nuclear family (Rodger, 1995). This campaign has since been figured as emblematic of the Conservative Government's failure to understand the changing moral landscape of 1990s Britain (Weeks, 2007; Quinn, 2008). Rose West, a married mother convicted of murders involving sexual sadism, decried conservative discourses of the superiority of the 'traditional' family. As such, she was open to demonisation as a deviant, masculine 'stranger' (Bauman, 1991), who needed to be disavowed in an attempt to recuperate the ideal of the nuclear family.

The next part of this section compares the articulation of the masculine woman discourse in two cases, those of American women Aileen Wuornos and Wanda Jean Allen. Representation as sexually deviant and masculine occurred in both of their trials and in media portrayals of their cases. Aileen and Wanda were both executed, in different states, in 2001–02. American scholars who research gender and the death penalty argue that lesbian women are disproportionately represented on death row. Defeminising female defendants in capital cases appears to be a key strategy in securing the capital conviction of a woman (Farr, 1999; Streib, 2002; Mogul, 2005).[1]

Attention is paid in particular to the significance of these women's intersecting identities. The discussion examines the cases in relation to the masculine woman discourse, but this was not the only construction of these cases. Human rights organisations and anti-death penalty groups campaigned on behalf of both women and highlighted legal problems with their convictions (Amnesty International, 2000; Miller, 2004). Feminist scholars and commentators have supported Aileen's claims that she killed her victims in self-defence (Chesler, 1993; Hart, 1994), and stress the significance of her history as someone who had experienced abuse both as a child and as an adult. However, the masculine woman discourse has been the dominant cultural representation of these two cases. Crucially, it was also dominant in both women's trials.

Aileen Wuornos

Aileen Wuornos' case is famous. She has been the subject of a major Hollywood film, *Monster* (2004); there have been two cinematically released documentaries about her, *Aileen: The Selling of a Serial Killer* (1992) and *Aileen: Life and Death of a Serial Killer* (2003), and at least two TV movies. In addition to this, her case has featured in many news reports and true crime portrayals. This fascination derives from the highly unusual murders she committed and the FBI's questionable definition of her as America's 'first female serial killer' (Kohn, 2001; Pearson, 2007). Such is the proliferation of representations of Aileen that her case has become almost hyper-real (Arrigo and Williams, 2006). Recovering the 'real' Aileen from this excess of frequently derogatory images is not possible, but a feminist decoding of these representations can help to challenge them (Naffine, 1997).

Aileen Wuornos was 46 when she was executed in Florida in 2002. She was convicted in 1991 of the murders of seven men between 1988 and 1989. She made her living as a prostitute,[2] which is how she met the men she killed. Aileen solicited clients along the interstate highway, sometimes feigning distress in order to encourage men to stop. She shot to death her victims after convincing or coercing them to remove their clothes. She also stole from them, which was interpreted as her motive for the killings. At first, Aileen claimed that she had killed the men in self-defence when they became violent and tried to rape her. She later retracted this assertion, arguing that it was made up and that she deserved to receive the death penalty (Hart, 1994; Miller, 2004;

Pearson, 2007). Despite psychiatric assessments that Aileen had serious emotional and mental health problems, she was deemed competent to be executed and received no psychiatric treatment whilst on death row (Shipley and Arrigo, 2004).

In order to analyse the construction of Aileen Wuornos as a masculine woman, it is necessary to understand the cultural, social and economic significance of the constituent parts of her identity. Aileen came from a poor background in Michigan. She was raised by her grandparents, although as a young child, Aileen and her brother had been told they were their parents. Their mother had left home when they were babies and their father was never involved in their lives. Aileen was sexually abused by her grandfather and gave birth to a child, which may have been her grandfather's, when she was 15 years old. The child was put up for adoption. During her adolescence, she sometimes slept rough in the woods and media interviews conducted with her contemporaries reveal she was severely neglected and mistreated. Aileen worked as a prostitute from her mid-teens until her arrest and imprisonment at the age of 35 in 1991 (Griggers, 1995; Arrigo and Williams, 2006). At the time of the killings and until her arrest, Aileen was in a relationship with a woman named Tyria Moore. Tyria gave evidence against her in exchange for immunity from prosecution as an accessory to the crimes (Hart, 1994; Miller, 2004).

Representations of Aileen Wuornos seized on her lesbian sexuality and she was characterised in the press as a 'Lethal Lesbian Hooker' and a 'Bull-Dyke Man-Eater' (Farr, 1999, p. 60). As a violent woman who was also involved in a sexual relationship with a woman, Aileen's aggression was attributed to her status as a 'mannish lesbian'. Her subversion of the usual enactment of violence between female prostitutes and male clients, whereby the client assaults or rapes the woman, was portrayed as further evidence of her masculinity (Hart, 1994).

Other details about the killings exacerbated the depiction of Aileen as a masculine woman. Her behaviour has been characterised as 'predatory' because she met her victims whilst soliciting on the highway (Silvio et al., 2006). Her enactment of distress or difficulty in order to persuade men to stop their cars was represented in court and in the media as a fraudulent performance of femininity designed to trick unsuspecting male motorists. Rather than being a real 'damsel in distress', Aileen was a masculinised serial killer (Pearson, 2007). She even transgressed the rules of feminine killing. Instead of killing within a domestic setting, she crossed into the masculine space of the open road and open air. This made her particularly terrifying. She not only subverted the culturally understood use of violence in paid for sexual encounters, but appropriated as her own a 'masculine' method of finding and killing victims, leading to the 'first female serial killer' label (Warf and Waddell, 2002; Pearson, 2007).

The intersection between Aileen's gender and sexuality is the most obvious example of how aspects of her identity were constructed through the masculine woman discourse. The prominence accorded to her lesbianism and implied sexual deviancy was central to portraying her as masculine and aggressive. However, the masculine woman discourse also relied on other aspects of her identity. Appropriate femininity assumes a white, middle-class standard. Aileen had led a marginal existence in terms of social class. She had always been poor and made her living through working as a prostitute, robbery and theft. Her embodied presence was perceived as uncouth and therefore masculine; she shouted and swore during her trial, violating notions of feminine decorum (Basilio, 1996).

In the United States, social class and 'race'/ethnicity are historically intertwined.[3] As a white woman from a poor, unstable, rural background who had led an itinerant, criminal existence, Aileen was at the very bottom of the white social hierarchy (Griggers, 1995). She was viewed as 'white trash', a label carrying associations of violence, incest and lack of education (Wray, 2006). Her social identity was one of shame, rather than legitimacy (Griggers, 1995). Wray (2006) argues that those designated 'white trash' evade the boundaries of whiteness. Their shameful identities make them 'not quite white'. The perception of Aileen as 'white trash' also contributed to her construction through the masculine woman discourse, as the 'trash' label is both defeminising and a construction of worthlessness. Although primarily constructed as 'different' and 'abnormal' due to crossing the boundaries of femininity and heterosexuality, Aileen Wuornos' main differences from middle-class Americans were, as Griggers (1995) contends, her poverty, lack of family and status as a prostitute.

The socio-cultural stew that formed the backdrop to Aileen's conviction in 1991 also needs to be considered. Chesney-Lind (2006) has highlighted the relevance of a 'backlash' against feminism, and against women's increased emancipation more generally, to the derogatory representation of Aileen Wuornos. The notion of 'backlash' derives from Faludi (1991), and conceptualises the rise of anti-feminist rhetoric and policymaking in 1980s America. This was 'set off not by women's achievement of full equality but by the increased possibility that they might win it' (p. 14). Also by the early 1990s, important but contested gains had been made by the lesbian and gay liberation movement in the United States (Cruikshank, 1992). Aileen was constructed as a 'man hater' (Robson, 1997) and symbol of the dangers of both feminism and lesbian liberation as part of the conservative reaction against these social changes.

Wanda Jean Allen

Wanda Jean Allen's case is less well known internationally than that of Aileen Wuornos. However, her execution in Oklahoma in 2001 was reported heavily in the American media (Shipman, 2002). In 1988, she shot her partner, Gloria Leathers, during an argument outside a police station. It was the second time Wanda had shot and killed a woman. In 1981, she killed her girlfriend, Dedra Pettus, during a dispute and served 4 years in prison for manslaughter. The case against Wanda was that she shot Gloria because she feared she was going to leave the relationship. However, Wanda's defence was that she was afraid of Gloria and believed she might be killed by her. Gloria had also killed a partner in the past, and she and Wanda met whilst in prison (Baker, 2008; Philofsky, 2008).

The prosecution alleged that Wanda was the more dominant member of the relationship, although it appears that the two women perpetrated violence against each other. On the day she shot Gloria, Wanda bore an injury on her face from being hit by Gloria with a garden rake (Shortnacy, 2001; Mogul, 2005). The defence argued that Wanda had a learning disability caused by brain damage she incurred during a car accident at the age of 12. Wanda was also stabbed in the head as a teenager. Although her IQ was assessed as 69, which is within the range defined as low functioning, she was executed by the state of Oklahoma (Baker, 2008). Evidence of her disability was not introduced during the original trial and this omission was sought, and dismissed, as grounds for appeal (Streib, 2002).

Wanda was a lesbian African-American woman. She grew up in a poor, single parent family in which she provided care for her younger brothers and sisters. As a teenager, she was arrested several times for stealing food and clothing for her siblings. Her mother was an alcoholic and also had learning disabilities. As an adult, Wanda lived by claiming welfare, as did Gloria (Baker, 2008). Their argument on the day she shot Gloria was sparked by a disagreement over a welfare cheque whilst out shopping for groceries (Mogul, 2005).

Wanda was explicitly constructed through the masculine woman discourse during her trial. The prosecution described her as 'manly' and the 'man' of her relationship with Gloria (Shortnacy, 2001; Mogul, 2005). It was also alleged that Wanda 'wore the pants' (Baker, 2008. p. 80). This representation clearly relied on a negative and homophobic construction of Wanda's sexuality, characterising her through the longstanding 'invert' discourse. Her sexuality was offered in her trial as a legally aggravating circumstance, echoing sexological arguments about the deviance and pathology of lesbian relationships.

The occurrence of the masculine woman discourse in Wanda's case also needs to be understood through an analysis of the intersections between her 'race', gender and sexuality. African-American women and lesbian women share a history of being culturally represented as masculine. African-American women who are also lesbian are therefore especially likely to be perceived as masculine (Farr, 1999). As well as exploiting stereotypes of the aggressive, mannish lesbian, the prosecution in Wanda's trial relied on the image of the 'black brute' (Alford, 2006). This construction emphasises the savagery, dangerousness and inherent criminality of African-American defendants (Seitz, 2005). The prosecution gave the jury a card Wanda had sent to Gloria which depicted a gorilla and had a humorous caption, reading 'Patience my ass, I'm going to kill something'. The attorney stated, 'That's Wanda Jean Allen in a nutshell', drawing a parallel between Wanda, an African-American woman, and a gorilla (Alford, 2006, p. 342). This strategy recalls the anthropological criminology of Lombroso, which constructed the criminal body as 'atavistic' and bearing similarities with apes. It also evokes entrenched racist stereotypes about African-Americans as being primitive and animalistic (Seitz, 2005). Wanda failed to be granted an appeal on the basis of the homophobic and racist statements made during her trial and was also unable to overturn her death sentence on these grounds (Mogul, 2005).

Wanda's socioeconomic position was also salient to her portrayal through the masculine woman discourse (Philofsky, 2008). As discussed in relation to Aileen Wuornos, in the United States (and elsewhere) social class and 'race' are constructed through one another. Wanda and Gloria lived on welfare, which demarcated them as members of the 'underclass', and Wanda's deprived family background would have added to this perception. The concept of an urban underclass gained prominence in 1980s America and was delineated by theorists such as Murray (1984). He argued that welfarist policies introduced in the 1960s undermined the nuclear family and individual responsibility, creating a dependent, pathological group that could be identified as an underclass. Murray highlighted families headed by single mothers as a particular feature of this group, along with problems such as learning disabilities and alcoholism.

Critics of the underclass concept have pointed out that in the United States its construction is racialised and frequently employed as derogatory shorthand for urban African-American communities (Simon, 1993). The perception of Wanda as not only dangerous and sexually deviant, but also from the underclass served to further defeminise her and contributed to the masculine woman portrayal. Identification with the urban poor emphasised Wanda's distance from normative femininity. Like Aileen, Wanda's putative 'abnormality' lay not only in her sexuality, but also her separation from the comforts of middle-class life. Both Aileen and Wanda can be understood as the bearers of shameful identities, which embodied the violence of marginalised existence.

During the 1980s, negative portrayals of African-American women as criminal, particularly in relation to the sale and consumption of crack cocaine, gained currency and their rates of imprisonment rose sharply (Maher, 1992; Chesney-Lind and Pasko, 2004). This occurred within the context of 'tough on crime' policies in the United States and the departure from welfare-based approaches to criminal justice (Garland, 2001; Simon, 2007). Wanda Jean's case was not linked to the issue of drug use, but she was convicted at a time when portrayals of African-American women as criminal, and as a threat to society, abounded.

The cases of Aileen Wuornos and Wanda Jean Allen demonstrate the value of an intersectional approach to understanding the construction of discourses of unusual women who kill. The masculine woman discourse, in both cases, relied to an extent on longstanding associations between lesbianism, aggression and masculinity. However, it also drew on cultural representations of 'race' and class, which separate poor women and those with devalued racial identities from appropriate femininity. The effect of this discourse was ultimately not only to defeminise Aileen and Wanda, but also to construct them as having little or no moral value, which may have made their executions more palatable (Farr, 1999). The power of this discursive construction meant that despite evidence that Aileen Wuornos had mental health problems, and Wanda Jean Allen learning disabilities, they were still executed.

It is also necessary to consider how the two women's intersecting identities structurally positioned them, and the impact this had on their cases. As poor women, both Aileen and Wanda relied on court-appointed public defenders, who have an inferior record of defending capital cases in America. Wanda's lawyer had never tried a capital case before and did not introduce evidence of her learning disabilities at her original trial (Baker, 2008). Aileen's lawyer, who went by the moniker 'Dr Legal', appeared in court under the influence of marijuana and advised her to plead 'no contest' to five of the murders for which she was convicted, a strategy that did not ameliorate her sentence (Broomfield, 2003). O'Shea (1999, p. 21) points out that public defenders, who represent over 90 per cent of those on death row in the United States, are frequently unskilled in the complexities of capital cases, and are often extremely junior or specialise in other areas, such as divorce litigation.

The masculine woman discourse developed from expert constructions of female masculinity in criminology and sexology. Although these nineteenth-century constructions no longer form part of most mainstream academic discourse, analysis of three late twentieth-century cases of unusual murders by women reveals that the aberrant masculine woman haunts cultural and legal constructions of 100 years later. Masculine women who kill not only cross the boundaries of femininity, but also seem to appropriate masculine power through their use of violence, making them troubling figures. The masculinisation of criminal women is a recurrent and well-documented representation. In particular, the cases demonstrate how the masculine woman can be iterated and deployed in conservative discourses as a reaction to shifting gender and sexual relations, especially when those with subjugated gender and sexual identities – such as womanhood and lesbianism – make gains.

The muse or mastermind dichotomy

The muse or mastermind dichotomy arises in cases where women carry out killings with male partners. Such women are open to dichotomous construction as either assistants heavily under the influence of their husbands or boyfriends, or as cunning, dominant women who are able to make men do their bidding. Frequently in these cases, the woman in question is represented through both constructions, which makes her ultimately unknowable. She is either under the spell of her male partner or she controls him, but there can be considerable uncertainty as to which representation is the 'right' one. This means that the woman's degree of involvement in the crime or crimes is difficult to know for sure, which provokes anxiety about her true nature. The anxieties expressed in relation to constructions of women involved in killings with men reflect wider social concerns from the place and time in which they occur.[4]

Both sides of the dichotomy relate to the constitution of femininity according to norms of heterosexuality. Whilst it is important to acknowledge that these norms are not fixed and change according to their cultural and temporal context, some generalisations about heteronormative understandings of femininity can be made. According to these understandings, masculinity is the more powerful gender, and men broadly have power over, and are more dominant than, women. In heterosexual relationships, women assume a supportive role to men. They may also need male guidance and protection. In certain domains, such as the home, it can be acceptable for women to appear dominant. However, this does not extend to activities which are not in keeping with femininity (Connell, 1987; Jackson, 1999; Bibbings, 2004).

This sketch of heteronormative gender roles should be understood as operating at a symbolic level, whilst also having material effects. Relationships between women and men do not necessarily adhere to heterosexual norms, and certainly not everyone would accept them as constituting an ideal, for example, feminist critics of heterosexuality (see Rich, 1980; Jackson, 1999). Nevertheless, in examining discourses of behaviour that breaches the boundaries of femininity, it is important to examine the regulatory power of constructions of ideal femininity.

The 'muse' side of the dichotomy is, to an extent, consonant with approved heterosexual femininity. Women become involved in the perpetration of homicide via their relationships with men and act at their behest. Whilst this may implicate them in behaviour which violates feminine norms, they are frequently perceived as either having been duped, brainwashed or coerced into participation (Morrissey, 2003). Therefore, their actions do not reflect their true natures. Alternatively, women's willingness to assist their male partners, particularly where they do not actively perpetrate violence themselves, can be interpreted as a comprehensible enactment of the female gender role. The previous section discussed attention that has been paid within criminology to female crime, which understands much of women's offending as in keeping with femininity if it involves supportive activities such as receiving stolen goods (Naffine, 1987). Although women's participation in violent crime is potentially more shocking, it can be constructed through similar arguments.

The muse is therefore a normal woman, rather than a deviant one. However, the representation is more complicated than it first appears. The term 'muse' characterises one half of this dichotomy in order to capture the notion that women may be perceived as having inspired their male partners to commit murderous acts. Women may be viewed as secondary to the killing itself and as acting under the influence of a man, but the sexual relationship between the two can be constructed as the crime's main impetus. Where murder is constructed as representative of masterful masculinity, the role of women is to help unleash this power.

The 'mastermind' side of the dichotomy constructs the woman as the leading actor in a killing or killings committed by a female/male partnership. According to this representation, the woman is the schemer and the plotter, and she may have tricked or persuaded the man to do her bidding. The woman does not necessarily carry out, or equally participate, in the lethal violence but her desires are believed to undergird the actions. As will be discussed in relation to specific cases, these desires can be perceived as sexual or material in nature. For women to assume a dominant role over men, particularly in an unfeminine domain such as the perpetration of homicide, is counter to the normative female role. The notion of women dominating and controlling men challenges the matrix of normative heterosexuality (Butler, 1999). It also subverts the acceptable constitution of heterosexual desire and relationships as driven by masculine sexuality and action (Jackson, 1999).

The mastermind is therefore a dangerous, unsettling figure. Masterminds may be constructed as almost mythically evil, Clytemnestra-type figures,[5] their deviant behaviour placing them beyond earthly femininity. This representation can turn into a monstrous portrayal of feminine malignance, which is most famously exhibited in the case of Myra Hindley, explored below (Birch, 1993; Storrs, 2006). The mastermind discourse can overlap with the masculine woman representation discussed in the previous chapter. Rose West, who was portrayed as having an aberrant, 'masculine' sexuality, was also argued to have been the driving force behind the murders of women and young girls in Gloucestershire.

The two sides of the muse/mastermind dichotomy are often not clearly separable. Different constructions of the same woman paint her as either the helpmeet or victim of her male partner, or as the malign progenitor of the crime(s), who uses her partner to her advantage, frequently by manipulating his sexual desire for her. This lack of separation occurs because the two sides of the dichotomy are themselves inter-related. The muse who inspires masculine action elides with the mastermind who designs it. These two representations can slide over one another, rendering women constructed through these discourses liminal figures. Their true level of involvement, or degree of influence, may not be possible to finally determine, making them inscrutable. This in turn contributes to the appearance of the muse/mastermind dichotomy in cases which in particular historical moments evoke social anxieties. The centrality of the male/female sexual partnership to the organisation of gender in modern Western societies is what makes it a focus for unease when it appears to malfunction – this is perceived as indicative of wider social breakdown.

Myra Hindley

The involvement of women in killings that entail the abduction, sexual abuse and torture of victims is extremely rare. However, when women do participate in such crimes with their male partners, their cases are usually widely reported and become notorious. Although rare in actuality, when considering gender construction it is vital to analyse the representation of women such as Myra Hindley as their cases are symbolically important. The vast majority of women convicted of homicide kill their own child or a male partner, but arguably the phrase 'women who kill' is more likely to conjure images of women involved in unusual murders such as Myra Hindley and Rose West.

In Britain, Myra Hindley achieved an almost iconic status that did not dissipate with her death in 2002. She has been portrayed on the stage, in pop songs, television programmes and art works, and was a focus for press attention from her conviction in 1966 until her death (Schone, 2000; Grant, 2004). At 23, Myra Hindley was found guilty of the murders of two children, and of harbouring and providing comfort to Ian Brady, her boyfriend, knowing he had killed a third. In 1986, she confessed to involvement in the killing of a further two young people and was successful in helping the police to find the remains of one of them (Birch, 1993; Murphy and Whitty, 2006). Myra died having spent 36 years in prison. In 1966, the trial judge recommended that she serve 25 years – in 1990, the Home Secretary changed her sentence to one of 'whole life', 24 years after her original conviction (Murphy and Whitty, 2006).

Myra Hindley and Ian Brady are known as the Moors Murderers because they buried the bodies of their victims on the moors near Manchester, England. Their first victim, 16-year-old Pauline Reade, was killed in 1963. In 1965, David Smith, Myra's brother-in-law reported her and Ian to the police after witnessing Ian hatchet and then strangle to death 17-year-old Edward Evans (Birch, 1993). During their investigation, the police discovered photographs of 10-year-old Lesley Ann Downey and a tape recording of her in a distressed state, which was played in court (Murphy and Whitty, 2006). The police also found Nazi memorabilia and photographs of Myra and Ian having sex (Birch, 1993). The murders were described in court as being linked to abnormal, perverted sexual behaviour (*The Times*, 22 April 1966).

The degree of Myra's involvement in the killings is uncertain, although she took part in selecting the victims, clearing up their blood and in their burial. Her representation has largely been as a figure of feminine evil, an unnatural 'anti-mother' who participated in the murders of children (Birch, 1993; Storrs, 2004; Murphy and Whitty, 2006). However, Myra Hindley's construction has been dualistic. The prosecution's case was that Ian was the killer and Myra was his accomplice. He had corrupted and dominated her (Whitty and Murphy, 2006). As Cameron and Frazer (1987) argue, she is seen either as Ian Brady's Pygmalion, acting on his wishes and according to his plans, or she was his Lady Macbeth, orchestrating the murders and 'much more profoundly wicked' (p. 146) than he was. According to the first portrayal, Myra Hindley becomes another of Ian Brady's victims, forced to abet his masculine violence through fear. The second is the one that puts her beyond femininity and humanity, into a realm of mythical monstrosity.

There are limited discursive resources outside of the muse/mastermind dichotomy with which to construct Myra's gender identity. It is difficult to find a language that can acknowledge the complicit involvement of a woman in the sexual murders of children, from which she may have derived pleasure, which does not slide into abjection. The dichotomous representation renders her unknowable, with the 'real' Myra Hindley impossible to uncover. Birch (1993) suggests that this inscrutability partly derives from Myra's physical appearance as a young woman, particularly the famous police photograph taken after her arrest, in which she has peroxide blonde hair and dark eyes. Myra's blonde hair and attention to her personal appearance was not unusual for a 23-year-old working-class woman in the 1960s. However, the styled hairdo, which recalled a film noir femme fatale, was figured as a grotesque performance of excessive femininity (Birch, 1993) and was interpreted as masquerade, an evil, monstrous woman's failed attempt to disguise her true nature.

Karla Homolka

Like Myra Hindley, Karla Homolka participated in murders which involved abduction, torture and sexual abuse with her male partner, Paul Bernardo. She was beaten and abused throughout their relationship, which began in 1987 when she was 17 and he was 23. Karla and Paul married in 1991 and lived together in a pink clapboard house in St Catherine's, a small town in Ontario, Canada. After a particularly severe beating in January 1993, Karla left Paul and confessed to the police her involvement in the killings of two teenage girls, Leslie

Mahaffy and Kristen French, whose dismembered bodies had been encased in concrete and thrown into Lake Ontario. She also informed the police that the death of her 16-year-old sister, Tammy, in 1990, which had been ruled accidental by the coroner, had occurred as a result of Tammy being drugged with sedatives so that the couple could rape her (Riehle, 1996; Kilty and Frigon, 2007).

The police arrested Paul in February 1993 in connection with a series of rapes that he had perpetrated in Scarborough, a suburb of Toronto. However, the state was reliant on Karla's evidence to prosecute him for the murders of three young girls. In exchange for a plea bargain in which she pled guilty to two counts of manslaughter, Karla provided details of the killings. Leslie Mahaffy and Kristen French were both abducted, and Karla assisted in the abduction of Kristen. Before Paul strangled the girls, they were held prisoners for several days and were subjected to sexual abuse. Karla was sentenced to 12 years in prison and was released in 2005. In 1995, Paul was convicted of murdering Leslie and Kristen, as well as Tammy Homolka, a charge which was added in 1994. He received a life sentence. Videotapes of the sexual assaults and rapes of the three girls were uncovered after Karla's conviction for manslaughter. They depicted her seemingly enthusiastic participation in the abuse (Riehle, 1996; Morrissey, 2003; Kilty and Frigon, 2007).

Karla Homolka remains enigmatic as she was constructed both as a victim of Paul Bernardo and as his dangerous, predatory accomplice. Her own testimony stressed her position as a 'battered wife' who had little choice over her actions (Morrissey, 2003). She emphasised that she suffered and feared violence from Paul, and that he had control over her. In response to why she did not help Leslie or Kristen to escape, Karla explained that she feared Paul would kill her (she knew he intended to kill the two girls). Karla also maintained that she did not enjoy the rape and sexual abuse of the victims as she appeared to do on camera, but had to pretend in order to avoid beatings from Paul. Medical evidence relating to her victimisation was presented at her trial to support her argument that she had little control over being involved in the killings (Kilty and Frigon, 2007). This construction of Karla as another of Paul's victims removed her responsibility for the crimes and also erased any suggestion that she was sexually gratified by her participation in the rape and sexual abuse of the victims.

According to the muse representation, Karla, an attractive young blonde woman from a middle-class background, made a suitable wife for Paul, a handsome young man trained as an accountant. She was someone he could dominate, control and enlist as an accomplice in his sadistic crimes (Morrissey, 2003). Indeed, the crimes were labelled the 'Barbie and Ken' murders because of the putatively conventional appearance of Karla and Paul as an attractive, heterosexual couple (Riehle, 1996).

This surface normality and attractiveness, and the apparent match between Karla and Paul, contributed to her dichotomous construction as a dangerous, manipulative woman, as well as a powerless, victimised one. Karla was not constructed as the mastermind of the crimes themselves, but as exhibiting her skills of deception through her manipulation of the legal system. Her assertions of Battered Woman Syndrome (BWS), and the plea bargain that allowed her to escape a murder conviction and life sentence, were understood to evince her manipulative powers. According to this side of the dichotomy, Karla escaped full punishment for crimes in which she was equally culpable (Kilty and Frigon, 2007).

To an extent, Paul had enacted the 'normal' fantasies of a heterosexual man, such as participating in sexual acts with two women simultaneously and filming sexual acts between two women (Morrissey, 2003). However, Karla's participation in the crimes was highly aberrant in terms of femininity and difficult to conceptualise as other than monstrous. There was no suggestion that Karla was a lesbian (Morrissey, 2003), rather it was assumed that her pleasure derived from dominance over the young girls and satisfying Paul.

Karla's perceived deceptive use of her femininity was also understood as evidence of her talent for manipulation (Kilty and Frigon, 2007). She was trusted by her younger sister, Tammy, which enabled her to procure Tammy for Paul. Kristen French was abducted by Paul and Karla when they asked her for directions. Paul's defence counsel described Karla as a 'Venus fly trap' (Morrissey, 2003, p. 146) who lured the girls to their fate. Her prettiness and unthreatening demeanour tricked Kristen French, making it possible to kidnap her. According to this construction, Karla was a blonde femme fatale, both sex object and sexual aggressor. Whilst Paul could be understood as enacting extreme, but recognisably masculine fantasies, Karla's participation made her both dangerous and unknowable. Her motivation and how far she was a willing partner or coerced victim remain mysterious.

The involvement of women in the sexual murders of children and young people is experienced culturally as deeply troubling and is understood to be an indication of wider social ills. As boundary markers of the national culture, the immorality or amorality of women is especially disturbing. When Myra Hindley and Ian Brady were convicted in 1966, journalists such as Pamela Hansford Johnson (1967), who covered the trial for the *Daily Telegraph*, worried that their crimes illustrated what could happen when members of the relatively uneducated working class were exposed to corrupting ideas. The revelation that the couple was interested in Nazism and the 'pornography' of De Sade seemed to highlight the dangers of introducing these ideas to unprepared minds. In particular, Johnson was concerned that wide availability of pornography and notions of sexual liberation could lead to more such crimes being committed against children. Johnson's husband, C P Snow, published a novel entitled *The Sleep of Reason* in 1968, which includes a murder trial loosely based on the Moors Murders (although both murderers are female). It draws heavily on the themes of class mobility, mass education and sexual liberation, with the murder of a young boy symbolising the dark side of this new social order.

This anxiety needs to be understood against the social background of the times (Storrs, 2004; Borowitz, 2005). Secondary education for all, the expansion of higher education, other entitlements guaranteed by the welfare state, the increased social mobility of the post-war years and new levels of affluence amongst the working class meant the social complexion of Britain had changed. Working-class people could no longer be assumed to 'know their place'. Alongside shifting class boundaries, the 1960s were an era in which sexual mores were being transformed (Marwick, 1998). The Moors Murders were read as a stark warning of where all this change might lead.

In 1990s Canada, Karla Homolka and Paul Bernardo raised different spectres. Both were perceived to have grown up in comfortable middle-class homes and it seemed that Karla was close to her parents. As an attractive couple living in a small town on the shores of Lake Ontario, they appeared to lead successful, happy lives (Riehle, 1996). By the 1990s, the perpetration of sexual violence was understood to be related to past histories of abuse and mistreatment. Women involved in criminality were conceptualised as likely to be from unstable, marginalised backgrounds (Kilty and Frigon, 2007). Karla and Paul had both led seemingly normal childhoods, untroubled by violence. Although Karla was abused by Paul, her middle-class, two-parent family background made these experiences appear inexplicable. Karla Homolka and Paul Bernardo raised the frightening possibility that violent, dangerous criminals could be indistinguishable from 'normal' people. Their crimes suggested a subterranean darkness lurking in quiet small town Canada. This was experienced as culturally troubling because Canadians often favourably contrast relatively peaceful Canada with the more violent

United States, emphasising its 'careful gun laws' and the 'stability and safety' of its cities (Gilbert, 2006, p. 297). The case of Karla Homolka and Paul Bernardo suggested that this cultural boundary between the two countries was not so secure.

Although sexuality is an essential component of the muse/mastermind dichotomy, relying as it does on the notion of a heterosexual relationship between the woman and man involved in the killings, its discursive appearance is not restricted to sexual murder. The relationship between the perpetrators is the important detail, not the type of killing. Murders committed for financial gain, revenge or fun also exhibit this construction. The discussion of Myra Hindley and Karla Homolka examined the ultimate mysteriousness of women constructed either as the victims or dupes of their male partners, or as manipulative schemers. The mastermind can recall the trope of the femme fatale, a representation of the dangerous, enigmatic woman found in film noir (Doane, 1991). The next part of this section explores the appearance of genre-based narratives in other high-profile cases.

Martha Beck

In 1949, in Queens, New York, Martha Beck, 29, and Raymond Fernandez, 34, were found guilty of the murder of Janet Fay, a 66-year-old widow to whom Raymond was engaged. Martha and Raymond were incarcerated in Sing Sing prison until their executions in 1951. Their case was a sensation (Knox, 1998). Raymond met women through newspaper 'Lonely Hearts' clubs, otherwise known as the personal ads, either marrying them or gaining their trust so that they would give him money or sign over their assets to him. He travelled around with Martha, his girlfriend, and they posed as brother and sister. The couple was arrested in Michigan on suspicion of murdering a woman named Delphine Downing and her 2–year-old daughter, Rainelle. They reportedly confessed to these crimes, with Martha admitting that she drowned Rainelle in the bath tub. However, Martha and Raymond were extradited to New York as they also confessed to the murder of Janet Fay, who lived in Nassau County. The case against them in Michigan, a state which did not have the death penalty, was eventually dropped (Knox, 1998; Shipman, 2002). Janet Fay's was the only murder Martha and Raymond were convicted of, but the newspapers speculated they were probably responsible for many more.

Martha was represented as the dominant party in the killing during the trial, in newspaper reports and in subsequent true crime and cinematic renderings of the case (Knox, 1998). Part way through the trial, Raymond changed his defence from insanity and instead attempted to reduce the charge in his case to accessory after the fact, placing him in the subordinate role in the killing. Martha was overweight and reference to her physical appearance framed newspaper reports, which described her as 'Fat Martha' (Knox, 1998, p. 87) and a '200 pound divorcee' (Shipman, 2002, p. 72). Discussion of her weight served not only to underline her strength and dominance over Raymond, but also to highlight her assumed abnormality.

Martha's defence attempted to argue insanity, which they illustrated through reference to her abnormality. Her experience of being fat was argued to partly account for her unbalanced mind. The defence also suggested that Martha was sexually abnormal. In childhood she was raped by her brother, and this was understood to have left her with sexual problems but also to have been precipitated by her abnormality. On the advice of a doctor, Martha and Raymond practiced oral sex so that she could achieve orgasm, which was represented in court as degenerate. The prosecution denied that Martha's abnormalities constituted insanity, but rather her bad character and immorality (Knox, 1998).

Although viewed as dominant over Raymond, Martha's actions were understood through the romance genre (Knox, 1998). She was a fat, psychologically damaged woman with a history of failed relationships and Raymond treated her better than she had been treated before. This helped to explain her devotion to him. Through this lens, Martha killed other women because she was jealous of them and feared Raymond would no longer want her. The romance narrative of the 'Lonely Hearts Killers' continued whilst they were awaiting execution in Sing Sing when letters sent between them were leaked to the press. Martha, an unattractive and abnormal woman, made a parodic romantic heroine with Raymond as a weak, hesitant hero. The case could also be constructed through another genre of the era, film noir. In this version, Martha was a femme fatale preying on her lover, but instead of being a seductive blonde, she was a fat, dowdy divorcee (Knox, 1998).

The case of the 'Lonely Hearts Killers' was a sensational story that could be told through familiar genres of the day. Unlike Myra Hindley or Karla Homolka, Martha Beck was represented as a comical figure who, due to her physical appearance and background, made a rather derisory romantic heroine or femme fatale. However, as well as inducing fascination in the newspaper reading public, the case also spoke to certain contemporary anxieties. In mid-twentieth-century America, it was feared that the alienating, impersonal nature of modern life had separated individuals from communities and left them adrift in a meaningless urban landscape. Sociological concepts such as anomie (Merton, 1946, 1949) sought to explain this condition. By targeting lonely women through the personal ads, Martha Beck and Raymond Fernandez appeared to have exploited the alienating nature of modern life. The 'Lonely Hearts' killings took place in a country that, following the Second World War, was increasingly powerful but also increasingly culturally conservative and fearful, living with the ever-present threat of the newly dawned atomic age (Foertsch, 2008).

Bonnie Parker

Bonnie Parker and Clyde Barrow are perhaps the most famous American case of a heterosexual couple who committed murder together, largely because of Arthur Penn's film *Bonnie and Clyde* (1967). They were part of a gang of bandits, led by Clyde, which was responsible for around 12 murders between 1932 and 1934 in south-western and mid-western America. Their victims were mainly policemen, and they robbed small town grocery stores and gas stations, usually taking relatively small amounts of money. Their most lucrative robbery earned them less than $10,000. They were killed in a police ambush in 1934 (Potter, 1998; Hendley, 2007).

Bonnie and Clyde were celebrity bandits who were highly aware of their public image. They took photographs of themselves posing with weapons, and Bonnie wrote poems about their exploits. It was the presence of Bonnie that made Clyde's gang remarkable. Without her, they were a collection of not particularly successful small time crooks, but her involvement added romance to the gang's story (Hendley, 2007). Bonnie was in her early 20s, small in stature and very slight. Unlike Martha Beck, her appearance was considered attractive and feminine. According to her mother, who wrote a biography of her, Bonnie became an outlaw because of her love for Clyde, and the relationship between the two is a key ingredient of their mythology (Potter, 1998).

Bonnie's slight appearance and apparent devotion to Clyde mean that she is usually perceived through the muse side of the muse/mastermind dichotomy, not as Clyde's victim but as his loyal follower. However, there have been different renderings of the story and the exact nature of Bonnie's involvement in the crimes has been disputed. Some representations portray her as ordering Clyde around and suggest that she laughed whilst shooting two injured policemen dead, whereas others state that she never fired a gun (Hendley, 2007).

The appeal of Bonnie and Clyde's story in the 1930s needs to be understood within the context of Depression era America. Economic decline following the First World War and the Wall Street Crash led to an increasingly precarious existence for poor and marginally middle-class Americans. During the same era, consuming news had become part of ordinary people's leisure, through media such as newsreels and radio. Stories about modern day bandits who fought the state appealed to urban and rural Americans experiencing economic hardship (Potter, 1998). Bonnie and Clyde were not politically motivated or in opposition to state power in a direct or organised sense, but their banditry on the new interstate highways demonstrated their rejection of authority. The murder of police officers, whilst deeply shocking to those who were comfortably respectable, may have been less objectionable to people who encountered the police through forced evictions and arrests for joblessness and homelessness (Potter, 1998).

The case has been constructed through use of the American 'road' genre, in which the protagonists undertake a journey involving quest, self-discovery or escape (Primeau, 1996). This particularly applies to the 1960s cinematic rendering of the Bonnie and Clyde story, in which they were represented through this genre as romantic outlaws battling the state. The social anxieties surrounding the construction of Bonnie Parker, and the type of killing she was associated with, were conducive to a favourable portrayal. Bonnie lent novelty and glamour to Clyde Barrow's gang, and also added a romance narrative to the exploits of bandits. Although her involvement in violent crimes had the potential to disturb gender norms, she was not portrayed as an unnatural woman in the manner of Martha Beck. When Faye Dunaway played her more than 30 years later in the film version of Bonnie and Clyde's story, Bonnie Parker became a cool, stylish counter-cultural icon, representative of late 1960s rejection of conformity (Hendin, 2004; Melossi, 2008).

The muse or mastermind dichotomy exemplifies unease concerning women's involvement in violence. If they are not bit players in serious violent crimes such as murder, then they must be the malign driving force. This echoes long-standing fears of both feminine inscrutability and the feminine as a source of malevolent power. The role of the male/female heterosexual partnership in structuring normative gender relations means that where this relationship has been the source of damage and destruction, it can become a symbol of contemporary fears and dissatisfactions. This frequently entails negative portrayals of women involved in unusual murders along with men, but as the example of Bonnie Parker demonstrates, becoming a symbol of contemporary dissatisfaction can also inspire romanticised representations.

The damaged personality

In relation to women who kill, feminist researchers have examined defences and explanations that rely on notions of female pathology, particularly in relation to faulty biology. For example, in England and Wales, the Infanticide Act 1938 created a special, lesser charge than murder for women who killed their babies aged below one year, if the mother was suffering from the effects of child birth or lactation at the time (Kramar and Watson, 2006; Rapaport, 2006). In the 1980s, in England and Wales and Canada, Pre-Menstrual Syndrome was successfully used to support a diminished responsibility defence in some women's murder trials (Kendall, 1991; Rose, 2000). In North America, Australia and New Zealand, expert evidence of BWS, a condition supposedly brought on by the experience of domestic abuse, can be offered to support defences of women who kill abusive partners (Schuller et al., 2004; Russell and Melillo, 2006; Sutherland, 2006). Unlike childbirth or menstruation, BWS does not originate in the female body, but is a syndrome understood to affect women only. Feminist criticisms of these psychiatric explanations for women's killing have centred on their tendency to deny women's agency and to pathologise socially lived experiences of abuse and childcare.

This chapter does not focus on constructions of madness as such, or specifically female embodied pathologies. Rather, it examines notions of the damaged personality in relation to unusual cases of women who kill. In doing so, it concentrates on cases of women understood to have personality disorders, particularly those labelled 'psychopathic', and also explores related understandings of 'dangerousness'. Personality disorders are mental disorders, rather than mental illnesses and there is disagreement over whether they are amenable to treatment. Severe personality disorders, which are conceptually related to psychopathy, are associated with characteristics such as impulsivity, lack of remorse, aggression and inability to empathise. Individuals who exhibit such traits, alongside a lack of insight into their condition, are considered particularly likely to be risky or dangerous to others. The in-between status of the psychopath or damaged personality is such that they are neither sane nor insane, neither healthy nor ill (Kozol et al., 1972). In itself, this liminality has the power to disturb, particularly as the causes of personality disorders and psychopathy are disputed (see Moran, 1999; Royal College of Psychiatrists, 2007).

The damaged personality is a neglected area in the feminist criminological scholarship on violent women, which has tended to examine constructions of characteristically feminine types of mental disorder. Severe personality disorders, psychopathy and constructions of the 'dangerous offender' are more readily associated with masculinity (Kendall, 2005). The damaged personality is not more likely to be female than male. However, this chapter analyses the articulation of this discourse in relation to unusual cases of women who kill in order to examine its gendered effects. The development of the concept of psychopathy and related personality disorders, as well as changing views on dangerousness, will be explored. The concept of the damaged personality, and its relationship with dangerousness, originates from the nineteenth century, when secular, rather than religious, explanations were advanced for human behaviour that would previously have been characterised as 'evil' (Halttunen, 1998).

The development of the psychopath

The concept of psychopathy has its roots in psychiatric writing from the late eighteenth and early nineteenth centuries. 'Madness like' (Pinel, 1806) and 'morally deranged' (Rush, 1812) individuals were thought to engage in impulsive, socially unacceptable behaviour, for which they experienced no guilt. Pritchard (1835) argued that moral insanity was a psychiatric state characterised by disordered affect in individuals whose intellectual development was normal. Such individuals were likely to have criminal inclinations that were not altered by the threat or experience of punishment. The idea of moral insanity was characterised by two features that were later identified as weaknesses in conceptualisations of psychopathy and severe personality disorders. The first was the value judgement entailed in the identification of undesirable behaviour. The second was a lack of definitional specificity, which meant that 'moral insanity' had a potentially broad application to a diverse range of behaviour and traits understood to be socially unacceptable (Herve, 2007).

The terms 'psychopathic inferior' and 'psychopathic personality' emerged from the discussion surrounding Pritchard's notion of moral insanity (Mason, 2005). The concept of psychopathy gained currency in American criminological literature in the early twentieth century, representing the ascendance of the treatment approach that dominated penology in the United States and Britain until the 1970s (Rafter, 1997). Theories on psychopathy flourished in the mid-twentieth-century especially. The concept became far more prominent in textbooks on psychiatry in the 1950s than previously (Raman, 1986), and the term 'psychopath' gained popularity in mental health and lay discourse (Arrigo and Shipley, 2001).

Several mid-twentieth-century writers refined the definition of psychopathy. One of the most important was Cleckley, whose book *The Mask of Sanity* (1941) remains influential on understandings of the psychopath. Cleckley argued that psychopaths could be intelligent and were often superficially charming. However, they were deficient in their major affective reactions and lacked the capacity for deep feeling or empathy. He contended that psychopathy was incurable. Karpman (1941, 1946, 1948) was similarly pessimistic about the psychopath's ability to reform. He suggested that psychopaths were profoundly emotionally immature, and therefore childlike in their emotional experiences. They should not be understood as devoid of emotions, but as unable to experience complex ones such as empathy, guilt and remorse. This immaturity meant that psychopaths exhibited poor self-control over their disruptive and aggressive impulses. Arieti (1963, 1967) concurred that the psychopath feels only 'short circuited' emotions such as anger, frustration or elation.

In the mid-twentieth-century, psychopathy, which was characterised by anti-social personality traits, was thought to be closely linked to criminality. During this era of belief in the potential for reform through treatment, psychopaths were those who were beyond rehabilitation due to their faulty personalities (Johnstone, 1996). Psychopathy therefore helped to provide an explanation for the limits of treatment. In Britain, Henderson (1939) devised a schema of three types of psychopathic personality, which influenced the development of British conceptions of the condition. The types were aggressive, socially inadequate and creative. As well as displaying anti-social traits, the socially inadequate psychopathic personality failed to lead a normal life based on marriage and employment, without welfare intervention. This designation was linked to understandings of 'feeble-mindedness', which was perceived as entailing low social functioning. The notion of inadequacy was related to earlier eugenics inspired perceptions of inherent inferiority (Wootton, 1959).

McCord and McCord (1964) drew on the previous literature to stress the psychopath's maladaptive personality and lack of social emotions. They also emphasised the notion of psychopaths as immature and childlike individuals who seek out instant gratification. The McCords suggested that some people were biologically predisposed to psychopathy, which could be triggered by parental rejection. Children who did not have the opportunity to become attached to their parents failed to learn how to develop significant emotional ties to others.

In England and Wales, moral defectiveness was a category of mental defectiveness under the Mental Deficiency Act 1927 (which replaced the 1913 designation of 'moral imbecile'). The Mental Health Act 1959 changed the legislation regarding mental disorders, and made 'psychopathic personality' a legal status for the first time. Although classified as a mental disorder, it was not a mental illness (Williams et al., 1960). Two kinds of psychopathic personality were recognised: the aggressive and the seriously irresponsible (Walker and McCabe, 1973). The Mental Health Act 1983 retains psychopathic disorder as one for which patients can be compulsorily admitted to hospital, under the proviso that medical treatment will be able to alleviate their condition (Johnstone, 1996).

Mid-twentieth-century critics of terms such as 'psychopath' and 'psychopathic personality' suggested that these were 'wastebasket' designations for difficult, incorrigible people. They lacked clinical specificity and could too easily become catch-alls for a wide range of socially disapproved behaviours. If psychopathic personality could be such an elastic term, it cast doubt on its validity (Biggs, 1955; Wallinga, 1959; Wootton, 1959). Other terms began to receive preference over psychopathy in the 1950s and 1960s. In 1952, the DSM I, produced by the American Psychiatric Association, included a definition of sociopathy, rather than psychopathy. Sociopaths were 'chronically anti-social individuals' who were 'frequently callous and hedonistic, showing marked emotional immaturity, with lack of responsibility' (quoted in Herve, 2007, p. 46). The American Model Sentencing Act 1963 contained reference to offenders suffering from a 'severe personality disorder indicating a propensity toward criminal activity' (quoted in Guttmacher, 1963, p. 381).

Notions of severe personality disorder largely replaced discussion of 'psychopathic personality' in psychology and psychiatry during the latter half of the twentieth century. These were defined by the DSM III (1980) as distinct from clinical syndromes, but as enduring conditions discernible from behavioural traits. Anti-Social Personality Disorder (ASPD) built on, and replaced, the sociopathy definitions given in DSM I. ASPD has similar traits to psychopathy, such as aggressiveness, impulsivity and disordered affect. There is disagreement over whether the terms can, or should, be used synonymously but it is often suggested that most psychopaths can also be diagnosed with ASPD, although not all individuals with ASPD are necessarily psychopaths (Hare, 1993; Herve, 2007). DSM IV (1994) defines ten personality disorders, which are gathered into three clusters: odd-eccentric, impulsive-erratic and anxious-avoidant. ASPD is part of Cluster B, 'impulsive-erratic', and this type of personality disorder is the one most readily associated with violent or criminal behaviour and, as will be discussed below, dangerousness (Lenzenweger and Clarkin, 2004).

Personality disorders are now diagnosed through the use of psychological testing instruments, which provide behavioural criteria. This is argued to have improved the specificity and validity of these conditions (Lenzenweger and Clarkin, 2004). However, debate remains over the utility of diagnosing personality disorders, and whether these diagnoses highlight socially unacceptable behaviour rather than a somatic disorder (Moran, 1999). The term ASPD is now much more likely to be used than psychopathy. However, Hare's (1980, 1993) Psychopathy Checklist (PCL) and its revised version (PCL-R) revived interest in psychopathy as a condition that could be scientifically tested. Inspired by Cleckley's (1941) analysis of the psychopath, the PCL-R contains 20 characteristics in a clinical rating scale. These include glibness, shallow emotions, impulsivity, lack of responsibility and lack of empathy. Use of the checklist allows psychologists to make a diagnosis of psychopathy.

Damaged personalities are constructed legally and culturally, as well as medically. Different medical terms may be used interchangeably in legal and popular representations. Therefore, a defence made in court on the basis of psychopathy or ASPD does not necessarily adhere strictly to psychological or psychiatric definitions. The psychopath is a potent symbol of danger and evil, portrayed in novels, films and television programmes. These depictions contribute to wider cultural understandings of psychopathy and severe personality disorders.

Psychopathy, evil and dangerousness

Conditions such as psychopathy and ASPD create individuals who are perceived as ungovernable and unable to change. Their violent behaviour is seen as lacking rational or explicable motivation and can be difficult to predict. Although suffering from a recognised disorder, such individuals are often perceived as impossible to treat or reform. These characteristics are close to notions of evil, which is usually understood to describe behaviour that is beyond the rules of human conduct, or to express actions that are other than human (Mason et al., 2002).

Psychopathy and severe personality disorders can operate as synonyms for evil in forensic and legal settings. Mason et al. (2002) found that mental health professionals working in a high-security psychiatric hospital in England considered certain mentally disordered offenders, who had committed violent crime, evil. Ruffles (2004) examines the equation made between psychopathy and ASPD, and evil, in Australian courts. She argues that diagnoses of conditions that share the characteristics of evil allow the courts to make moral judgements about violent offenders under the cover of rational, scientific terminology. These offenders are considered particularly dangerous and receive harsher sentences.

Dangerousness is closely associated with psychopathy and ASPD (Kozol et al., 1972). Measures to control the dangerous have a long history. English law constructed the poor as likely to be dangerous from Elizabethan times onwards, imposing penalties on beggars and vagabonds (Prins, 2002). Alongside the perception of the criminal poor as dangerous, a psychiatric notion of dangerousness developed. This was applied to individuals who appeared sane, but committed terrible homicides apparently without motivation. Psychiatrists drew on the notions of moral insanity outlined in the previous section to explain such crimes (Foucault, 1978). This led to a growing acceptance that insanity could attack the emotions whilst leaving thought and consciousness intact.

The criminal anthropologists of the late nineteenth-century argued that instead of legal responsibility, the crucial question was the amount of danger an individual posed to society. Distinctions needed to be drawn between those who could become less dangerous through treatment, and those who were impervious to intervention (for whom they recommended long-term incarceration or death). The notion that the state should be responsible for reducing and managing risks to the general population developed during the second half of the nineteenth-century (Foucault, 1978; Pratt, 2000). This included risks from certain individuals. The International Union of Penal Law adopted the term 'dangerous being' in 1905, around the time resistance to psychological and sociological approaches to criminality diminished (Van Hamel, 1911; Foucault, 1978). The English and Welsh Prevention of Crime Act 1908 introduced preventive detention for repeat offenders (not all of whom would be 'dangerous'), codifying the importance of public protection (Pratt, 2000; Prins, 2002).

By the mid-twentieth-century, concerns about the need to protect the public from dangerous offenders through the use of indeterminate detention focused on psychopaths and people with personality disorders. Certain jurisdictions in the United States had instituted sexual psychopath laws by the 1950s. Legislation in Europe and North America often focused on the importance of detention for the purposes of treatment. In Denmark, courts could recommend individuals for 'psychopathic detention' (which was indeterminate) in specially staffed institutions (Guttmacher, 1963). As discussed earlier, the introduction of 'psychopathic personality disorder' under the Mental Health Act 1959 in England and Wales sanctioned compulsory admission to hospital. The Criminal Justice Act 1961 introduced the Extended Sentence for those deemed a potential threat to society (Prins, 2002).

Mid-twentieth-century measures that aimed to control individuals with psychopathy or personality disorders tended to exhibit optimism that a combination of treatment and training could help to rehabilitate people with these conditions. The United States Model Sentencing Act 1963 specified dangerous offenders as those 'suffering from a severe personality disorder indicating a propensity towards criminal activity' (quoted in Guttmacher, 1963, p. 381). The Act decreed that dangerous offenders should receive sentences that were long enough to effect rehabilitation, but if this failed, would have them prolonged to a period of 30 years. The focus was on the nature of the offender and their potential threat to the public, rather than the crime committed (Flood, 1963). The Model Sentencing Act's approach was typical of the era's penal welfarism, which placed faith in the powers of treatment and training to work for most offenders (Garland, 2001).

Attitudes and legislation towards dangerous offenders hardened in America, Britain, Australia and New Zealand in the late twentieth century. There was a trend towards longer sentences for a variety of criminals, with measures such as California's 'three strikes' laws leading to life sentences for individuals who would not necessarily be considered psychiatrically dangerous (Pratt, 2000). The management of risk began to play an increasingly prominent role in the operation of the criminal justice system and public protection became even more of a priority (Kemshall, 2004). In England and Wales, there were controversial proposals for the indeterminate detention of the 'dangerous severely personality disordered', which could be authorised on the basis of specialist assessment alone, without the individual having committed a crime (Mullen, 1999). This was not introduced, but use of indeterminate sentences for sexual and violent offenders increased in Britain and elsewhere in the late 1990s and early twenty-first century (Kemshall and Maguire, 2001; Hudson, 2005).

Debates over dangerousness are important to bear in mind in relation to the damaged personality discourse of women who kill. The issues surrounding homicide are slightly different from the ones discussed in relation to the use of indeterminate sentences, as both murder and manslaughter can result in long periods of incarceration without special measures. However, the use of imprisonment for public protection shows the development of the dangerous offender as a symbol of risk. Comparing the sentences different women received is difficult as practices vary across jurisdictions and time periods. Laws on homicide also differ, meaning that direct comparison of verdicts is also problematic. However, it is possible to analyse the discursive construction of different cases and whether an association is made between a condition such as psychopathy or a severe personality disorder and being a threat to the public.

The rest of this section examines three well-known cases of women and girls who killed young children and were viewed as having psychopathic or severe personality disorders. It discusses their liminal status as 'neither sane nor insane' and the unease their seemingly motiveless crimes provoked. As a secular strategy to make sense of 'evil' (Halttunen, 1998), the damaged personality inevitably becomes a focus for discussions of social failure. These can either centre on the forces that created a damaged, dangerous individual or the lack of protection accorded to their victims that made it possible for the harm to take place.

Mary Bell

Mary Bell's case is one of the most notorious of a child below the age of 14 being found guilty of killing other children.[6] In Newcastle, north-east England, in 1968, she was convicted of the manslaughters of 4-year-old Martin Brown and 3-year-old Brian Howe, both of whom lived in her local area. Martin's body was found in a derelict house in May 1968. It was assumed that he had died accidentally, but 2 months later Brian's body was found on some waste ground. He had been strangled and cut with scissors and a razor (*The Times*, 6 December 1968). The pathologist determined that it was likely that Brian had been strangled by a child as the marks on his neck suggested less force than an adult would use (Sereny, 1995). This led the police to connect Martin's death to Brian's, although no marks had been found on his neck. They collected statements from around 1200 children in Scotswood, the area of Newcastle in which the deaths had occurred (ibid.).

Two children, Mary Bell, 11, and Norma Bell, 13, gave inconsistent statements. They lived next door to each other, but despite sharing the same surname, were not related. Mary told the police she had seen a local 8-year-old boy hit Brian Howe and had also seen this boy playing with scissors. That Brian had been injured with scissors was not a publicly known detail. The police questioned the boy Mary had referred to, but ruled him out. They took further statements from Mary and Norma, and the two girls accused each other of having strangled Brian. They were charged with his murder, and also with the murder of Martin Brown (Sereny, 1995).

At trial, Mary's defence called two psychiatrists as expert witnesses, who testified that she was a psychopathic personality. The first doctor explained that this was characterised by aggression, lack of shame or remorse and lack of feeling for other humans. He recounted that Mary had discussed the boys' deaths in an unemotional way, which indicated this condition. The second psychiatrist stated that Mary had a serious disorder of personality and was 'very dangerous' (Sereny, 1995, p. 164). Norma's defence argued that she was an immature child who fell under Mary's influence. They stressed Mary's intelligence and powers of manipulation, as well as describing her as 'wicked' and 'evil'. The prosecution likened Mary to a 'Svengali' and stated, 'In Mary you have a most abnormal child, aggressive, vicious, cruel, incapable of remorse, a girl, moreover, possessed of a dominating personality, with a somewhat unusual intelligence and a degree of cunning that is almost terrifying' (*The Times*, 14 December 1968).

Norma was acquitted of both murders, whilst Mary was found guilty of manslaughter due to diminished responsibility. In his sentencing remarks, the judge commented that Mary was 'dangerous' (Sereny, 1995, p. 187) and 'a very grave risk to other children' (*The Times*, 18 December 1968). Although diagnosed as having a psychopathic disorder and therefore eligible for a hospital place, nowhere could be found with suitable facilities. The judge sentenced Mary to detention for life, explaining that she would be released when it was deemed safe to do so. She was sent to the Special Unit of Red Bank Approved School in Lancashire, which until she arrived had been for boys only (Sereny, 1995).

The discursive representation of Mary Bell was shaped not only by her gender, but also the fact that she was a child who had killed other children. This provoked feelings of horror. In addition to being diagnosed as a psychopathic personality, and therefore as somewhere between sanity and insanity, Mary was also viewed as an abject child. Terms such as 'psychopathic' and 'dangerous' mixed with 'wicked' and 'cunning' during her trial, demonstrating the overlap between them. The press reporting of the case described Mary as a 'bad seed' and an 'evil birth' (Sereny, 1995, p. 164), which recalled fictional horror stories of murderous children.[7] At the time, Mary's crimes appeared incomprehensible. Although diagnosed by psychiatrists as a psychopathic personality, they knew little of her background and did not know that as a small child she had been prostituted by her mother and subjected to serious sexual abuse (Sereny, 1998).

The case of Mary Bell was also troubling because, from a conservative perspective, it appeared to symbolise the moral decline of late 1960s Britain. As discussed in relation to Myra Hindley, the changing cultural landscape of this time brought with it fears that society would breakdown if 'traditional' standards of decency and duty were contravened. As a child, Mary represented the future (Jackson and Scott, 1999), and the future of Britain's 'permissive' society seemed bleak. From the vantage point of the close of the 1960s, the 'horror story' of the case took its place beside iconic events such as the Altamont Festival and the Manson Family murders, both of which occurred in America in 1969,[8] and which symbolised the 'fallout' from the 1960s (Hunt, 2002, p. 95). The following two cases involved women who worked as nurses, and exemplify late-twentieth-century notions of risk anxiety (Beck, 1992).

Genene Jones

Genene Jones began working as a nurse in Texas in the 1970s. She was employed at the Pediatric Intensive Care Unit of Bexar County Medical Center between 1978 and 1982, during which time it was noticed that an unusually high number of the babies she cared for experienced multiple cardiac or respiratory arrests when she was present. There were also a disproportionately high number of deaths occurring on the Unit. The unusual patterns of arrests and deaths, which were linked to Genene's shifts, were noticed by her colleagues and the hospital convened a panel of outside medical experts to examine the records. The panel did not find sufficient evidence of homicide to warrant reporting Genene to the police. The hospital restricted employment on the Unit to registered nurses, which disqualified her from working there (Furbee, 2006).

Genene found a new job in a paediatric clinic 60 miles away from the Bexar County Medical Center in September 1982. Her patients again experienced unusually high levels of respiratory arrest. After working at the new clinic for 9 months, a 15-month-old girl died after receiving an injection from Genene. A missing vial of succinylcholine chloride, a muscle relaxant, aroused suspicion concerning the respiratory arrests of her patients. In 1984, she was convicted of the murder of the 15-month-old girl and later in the same year was found guilty of injuring another child by injecting them with muscle relaxant (Thunder, 2002; Furbee, 2006). At Genene's murder trial, the court admitted evidence from earlier suspicious incidents and she was sentenced to 99 years in prison (Lucy and Aitken, 2002).

Hare (1993) refers to Genene's case in order to illustrate an aspect of psychopathy; capacity for deceitfulness and manipulation. Drawing on journalist Elkind's (1990) book on Genene, *The Death Shift*, Hare suggests that she was an accomplished liar who was easily able to alter details about her past when giving an account of her life. Genene is frequently interpreted as having injured and killed children in her care in order to cast herself as the hero of the situation and because she derived a morbid pleasure from the process of trying to revive them (Elkind, 1990; Kocsis and Irwin, 1998). Her defence at trial was that she had not injected the children with fatal amounts of succinylcholine and that there was no direct evidence against her. Therefore, psychiatrised explanations did not form part of the legal discourse surrounding the case. However, in academic and true crime literature, Genene is often portrayed as either psychopathic or suffering from a severe personality disorder and it is also suggested that her harming of young children can be understood as Munchausen's Syndrome by Proxy (MSbP) (Elkind, 1990), which is discussed further below.

Beverley Allitt

Beverley Allitt began work as an enrolled paediatric nurse on a short-term contract at Grantham and Kesteven General Hospital in Lincolnshire, England, in February 1991. In the few months following her employment, there was a suspicious increase in child deaths on her ward, and a rise in the number of cardiac and pulmonary arrests. A post-mortem examination of one child revealed that they had been injected with a large amount of insulin before pulmonary arrest. No reasons could be found for the rise in such incidents and the hospital determined that a member of staff was harming children on the ward. After a police investigation, Beverley was arrested in May 1991. In May 1993, she was convicted of murdering four children who were in her care at the hospital by injecting them with insulin and potassium chloride and by smothering. She was also found guilty of attempting to murder a further three children and the grievous bodily harm of six others (Brown, 2000; Lucy and Aitken, 2002).

Discussion of Beverley's damaged personality was a significant aspect of the sentencing stage at her trial. She denied the charges against her and did not attempt a diminished responsibility defence (D'Cruze et al., 2006). However, the defence submitted information relating to her mental state for the judge's consideration when sentencing. Newspaper reports state that Beverley had a 'rare personality disorder known as Munchausen's Syndrome by Proxy' (*The Guardian*, 18 May 1993). MSbP is not a type of personality disorder, but refers to a specific kind of child abuse defined by Meadow (1977). In such cases, a carer, usually a mother, induces symptoms or illnesses in a child in order to gain medical attention. Beverley had also displayed signs of Munchausen's Syndrome, which is where an individual fakes symptoms or harms themselves in order to attract attention (see Bools et al., 1994; Rosenberg, 2003). She had a poor sick leave record whilst training as a nurse, and regularly visited hospital with minor injuries that staff who examined her suspected she had self-inflicted (*The Guardian*, 18 May 1993).

The confusion between MSbP and personality disorder could have resulted from inaccurate media reporting, or it may be that this is how it was represented in court. Research into MSbP suggests that perpetrators of this type of abuse often have personality disorders, and this may be why MSbP was represented as if it constituted a personality disorder. Confusion over the precise medical details of Beverley's diagnosis does not prevent analysis of her discursive construction as a woman with a damaged personality. In addition to MSbP, Beverley was anorexic at the time of her trial, a visual marker of her troubled mental state. In sentencing, the judge described her as 'severely disturbed', 'cunning' and 'manipulative'. He gave her 13 life sentences and informed her that it was unlikely she would ever be released (*The Herald*, 29 May 1993). He stated that there was 'no real prospect' she would cease to be a danger to others, and that public protection required her 'permanent containment' (*Press Association*, 28 May 1993). Beverley was legally and discursively constructed as inherently dangerous. In 2007, the high court ruled that she must serve a minimum of 30 years in prison (*The Guardian*, 6 December 2007). She is incarcerated in Rampton Hospital, a secure psychiatric facility in England for high-risk individuals sectioned under the Mental Health Act 1983.

The construction of Genene Jones and Beverley Allitt exhibits some of the long-standing features of the damaged personality discourse. Both women were perceived to lack any motive for harming children in their care, beyond serving the needs of their own twisted psyches. Although elements of the behaviour of both women had been considered unusual, they masqueraded as 'normal' until the discovery of their crimes, in that they did not appear to be deranged or deluded. Descriptions of the women as being without conscience, liars, cunning and manipulative are in keeping with iterations of psychopathy and severe personality disorders that recall a moral language of evil. In these cases, the gendered effects of a discourse that hinted at evil were compounded by the women's roles as nurses. The nurse is a figure of feminine nurturance, protection and duty. Violation of this role, especially through perpetrating harm against children, evokes 'Angel of Death' representations (D'Cruze et al., 2006) whereby the nurse becomes a symbol of horror.

As late-twentieth-century cases, the prosecutions of Genene Jones and Beverley Allitt demonstrate increased preoccupation with managing risk. The 'risk society' is conceptualised as one in which anxieties about risk, and the limited capacity of experts to deal with them, became a pervasive concern (Beck, 1992). In particular, fears around the risk of harm to children intensified, as the world of childhood came to be seen as unpredictable and unsafe (Jackson and Scott, 1999). Both women were nurses who killed child patients and their cases raised questions about how their harmful behaviour could go unnoticed. They also raised the terrifying possibility that women with medical expertise and a professional role caring for children could be the ones to pose a threat to them. An Inquiry was established after Beverley Allitt was found guilty, which considered the circumstances that led to the deaths and injuries of children at Grantham and Kesteven General Hospital. The Allitt Inquiry Report (1994) suggested that she was able to remain undetected because she was not noticeably abnormal and did not behave in an obviously unusual fashion. Although Beverley had been known to enjoy the attention she received from the various minor injuries that she had at school and college, and her sickness record at college was poor, the Report argued this was not sufficiently unusual to be able to foresee harmful behaviour on her part. It seemed that distressingly, the risk that she posed was not apprehended.

Beverley Allitt's ability to 'pass' as normal was a troubling aspect of the case and a constituent part of her construction as dangerous. Although she was someone with apparent quirks, she wore the 'mask of sanity' described by Cleckley: she could not be instantly identified as possessing a damaged personality and therefore as dangerous. The judge's remarks that Beverley was a danger to the public and her incarceration in Rampton Hospital demonstrate that once recognised as such, she was regarded as unlikely to change.

The damaged personalities discourse can supersede other explanations for behaviour. Although certain constructions of psychopathy and severe personality disorders have argued that such conditions result from a combination of innate and environmental factors, the appearance of these conditions in unusual cases of women who kill can serve to restrict explanations to the unfathomable actions of a damaged individual. This reliance on notions of inherent 'dangerousness' shows the role of the damaged personalities discourse as providing a secularised version of 'evil', which appears to presage social breakdown or disintegration.

The respectable woman

The respectable woman discourse arises in cases where a woman is portrayed as embodying some of the traits of appropriate femininity. 'Respectable' women who kill are not perceived as deviant or transgressive in terms of social expectations. Explanations for their actions which suggest mental or physical health problems may be advanced, but unlike the masculine woman or damaged personality discourses, respectable women are not understood to have breached the boundaries of femininity. They are not threatening or dangerous. Representation as respectable can appear to contribute to securing conviction of a lesser charge, a lighter punishment or an acquittal by constructing the woman as someone who does not deserve to be found guilty.

Respectability is a relational concept which varies across place and time and is deeply imbricated in constructions of class, gender, 'race'/ethnicity and sexuality. Historically, respectability for women is associated with white, middle-class, heterosexual womanhood. This does not mean that women who depart from this characterisation cannot be respectable, but that they are likely to need to work harder to attain and maintain this status (Skeggs, 1997; Wolcott, 2001). White, middle-class, heterosexual women are assumed to possess this privileged identity. Respectability is theirs to lose. Women with normative or highly valued social identities can surrender their respectability and some of the advantages it entails, but they do so after violating its standards. Working-class women, women of colour and lesbian women, on the other hand, need to continually prove their respectability through dress, speech and behaviour, the markers against which they are judged (Skeggs, 1997).

The notion of respectability is closely tied to perceptions of moral worth (Skeggs, 2005). In order to attain a moral identity, it is necessary to be seen as respectable, and therefore conforming to socially approved codes of gendered behaviour. A recurrent feature of feminine respectability is sexual propriety (see Stoler, 1989; Giles, 1992). What constitutes acceptable sexual activity alters according to the cultural and historical context (Mosse, 1985). Historically, women have been judged more harshly than men if they do not meet expectations of appropriate sexual behaviour in terms of chasteness and monogamy, and these norms have played a more important role in the regulation of femininity than masculinity.[9]

Attaining a moral subjectivity is not solely based on judgments of sexuality. Class is also a key indicator of moral value (Sayer, 2005a, 2005b). In Western countries such as Britain, the United States and France, a constellation of indicators including education, cleanliness and 'taste' shape class identities (Bourdieu, 1984; Peiss, 1987). Stupidity, squalor and bad taste are associated with certain working-class cultures. These working-class identities are constructed as not only disreputable, but also lacking moral worth. In Britain, this has been figured as the division between the 'rough' and 'respectable' working class (Roberts, 1984; Tebbut, 1995; McKibbin, 1998). The rough do not work, do not keep tidy homes, use coarse speech, drink and eat too much and have families that are too large. They lack restraint, an important symbol of working-class and middle-class British respectability. The classed nature of respectability is highlighted by the fact that this demonstration of restraint is not required of the British upper class.

The relational nature of respectability is also demonstrated through its connection with racial identities. Colonial European constructions of whiteness emphasised its inherent moral value and superiority over non-white subjectivities (Stoler, 1989; McClintock, 1995; Fitzgerald and Muszynski, 2007). The association between value and whiteness later had implications for the constitution of whiteness in relation to non-white immigrant populations. In twentieth-century Britain, working-class respectability became explicitly coded as white (Bonnett, 1998). Urban areas where immigrants from the Caribbean and South Asia settled in the mid-twentieth-century were regarded as sites of disorder, and the respectability of white families who remained in such areas was called into question (Waters, 1997). In the United States, notions of class, 'race'/ethnicity and respectability are intertwined. African Americans have historically been constructed as over-sexed, lazy and as living in dysfunctional families and communities (Scott, 1997). White people perceived to have similar failings have been labelled 'white trash', a derogatory term that highlights their lack of respectability and tenuous relationship with whiteness (Wray and Newitz, 1997; Wray, 2006).

Respectability is constituted across different axes of identity and areas of social life. Like other aspects of identity, it is not a fixed quality, although women's social positioning profoundly affects whether they can successfully be represented as respectable (Skeggs, 1997). Being accused of murder, a crime both unfeminine and shocking would seem to automatically contravene respectability. However, middle-class white women can maintain their respectability, even when suspected of murder (Hartman, 1995). Notions of respectability also circulate in other women's cases. If they can be persuasively identified with aspects of feminine normativity, they can be portrayed as having attained respectability. This is particularly the case if the woman can be positively contrasted with her victim.

The successful identification of women who kill with recognisable features of respectability or femininity is an act of discursive recuperation, whereby deviant subjects are recovered back into a dominant discourse (Foucault, 1990). Analyses of recuperation frequently emphasise its troubling nature, as the transformative potential of acts of subversion and resistance are undermined by slotting them back into existing power relations (Alcoff and Gray, 1993; Epstein et al., 2000). In the unusual cases of women accused of murder, discursive recuperation can be a means of securing an acquittal or lighter penalty and holds obvious advantages for the woman in question. It also ensures the erasure of the deeply troubling challenge to conventional gendered behaviour that such women pose.

The respectable woman discourse exemplifies the tendency for women to be constructed as boundary markers of the national culture; in the case of the respectable woman, the qualities of normative femininity are delineated, but so too are desirable national attributes. In turn, these are filtered through constructions of class and ethnicity (Stoler, 1989; Fitzgerald and Muszynski, 2007). Notions of 'respectable' womanhood are often culturally conservative and, as such, are mobilised in order to shore up the status quo in terms of gender and other relations. However, competing interpretations of what constitutes 'respectability' are also indicative of social change, and the concept can be appropriated by those with subjugated identities – for example, feminists can emphasise the link between femininity and respectability as a means of arguing for the increased social status of women (see Burton, 1994). The discussion of Rose West explored how recuperation of the culturally conservative ideal of the nuclear family entailed her vilification and disavowal. Recuperation of the violent woman herself into respectability can be a way not only to smooth over the gender troubling aspects of her behaviour, but also as an attempt to protect the boundaries of the nation's morality.

Some of the most well-known cases of women who kill to be constructed through discourses of respectability are from the nineteenth century, and epitomise the symbolic power of the gendered status embodied by an American or European 'lady' (see Roberts, 2002). However, respectable femininity should not be understood as an antiquated concept. Feminist criminologists have highlighted the importance of judgments about the respectability of female defendants in court and the criminal justice system in more recent contexts (Kruttschnitt, 1982; Worrall, 1990; Renzetti, 1999).

Lizzie Borden

Lizzie Borden is chronologically the later of the two nineteenth-century examples that will be explored but she is discussed first because of her almost iconic status as a respectable woman who supposedly 'got away with' murder. Her case is perceived to be emblematic of sentimental notions of white, middle-class womanhood and her story has been retold in novels and stories, poetry, films, television programmes, plays, opera and dance (Nickerson, 1999). The enduring fame of the case means that it has been assigned a variety of cultural meanings, not only in late-nineteenth-century America but also in other eras (Robertson, 1996; Filetti, 2001).

Lizzie, 32, was acquitted of the axe murders of her father and stepmother, Andrew and Abby Borden, in New Bedford, Massachusetts in June 1893. On the morning of 4 August, 1892, Abby was killed with blows from an axe while she changed sheets in the guest bedroom of the Borden family's house in Fall River. Her skull was shattered. Andrew had left the house at 9.15 a.m. in order to go to town. He returned at 10.45, by which time, unbeknownst to him, Abby was dead. After changing out of his outdoor coat, Andrew took a nap downstairs on the sofa. At 11.05 a.m., Lizzie discovered his dead body and alerted Bridget Sullivan, the maid and the only other person who had been in the house during that morning. Lizzie sent Bridget out to get help. In the meantime, Lizzie spoke to a neighbour and the police were called at 11.15 a.m. by someone in the street who owned a telephone. Bridget and a neighbour later discovered Abby's body after a doctor had arrived and examined Andrew. The coagulation of the blood from her wounds indicated she had been killed over an hour before he had (Robertson, 1996; Nickerson, 1999).

The only likely suspects for the murder were Lizzie and Bridget. Most of the doors in the Borden house were kept locked, making it difficult for an intruder to get in. An outsider would also need to have managed to hide from both women for the time between the murders, in a house that was not particularly large. Bridget had no motive to kill the two people for whom she worked, and with whom she lived. She had also, Lizzie concurred, been in the attic bedroom and outside cleaning windows when the killings would have happened. Lizzie, on the other hand, stood to inherit a substantial amount of money as the result of Andrew and Abby's demise. She also gave the police an inconsistent account of her movements during the murders (she claimed to have been in the barn). Two weeks prior to the killings, Lizzie had attempted to buy prussic acid, a poison, and had been refused, although this evidence was excluded from her trial (Robertson, 1996; Nickerson, 1999).

Lizzie's social position explains the contentious nature of her trial and why it became a press sensation. The Bordens were an old and established family in Fall River. Most of the family lived in the exclusive part of town, but due to Andrew Borden's parsimony, Lizzie lived in a less salubrious setting amongst Irish immigrants, in a house that did not have the comforts expected by the upper middle class of the day. This was through choice on Andrew's part, as his wealth was equivalent to that of a present-day millionaire (Robertson, 1996; Nickerson, 1999).

Consequently, Lizzie occupied a liminal position. In terms of ethnicity and social class, she belonged to the town's elite, but was geographically displaced from it. Her living circumstances also meant that she could not entertain, or dress, as a lady would perhaps anticipate (Robertson, 1996; Nickerson, 1999). Nevertheless, as a white, middle-class woman from New England who carried out charity work and taught Sunday school, Lizzie symbolised late-nineteenth-century American understandings of what it meant to be civilised (Shaw, 1997). This partly accounted for the prosecution's difficulty in convincing a jury that she was guilty, and for the support she received from the national press. At the time, the 'true woman' was the guardian of civilised morality and behaviour. For her to have violated this with such acts of savagery was close to being unthinkable (Nickerson, 1999; Roggenkamp, 2005).

However, Lizzie's status as an ideal woman was not completely assured. As an unmarried woman of 32, she was a spinster, rather than a fulfilled wife and mother (Roggenkamp, 2005). This necessitated her dependence on her father and to an extent made her an unenviable and pitiable figure. Her defence, in its recuperation of Lizzie from the violent axe murderer, stressed this dependence to the all male jury by emphasising her helplessness and referring to her as a 'little girl' (Shaw, 1997; Nickerson, 1999; Filetti, 2001). The prosecution, however, played on a different representation of the unmarried woman. American attitudes to spinsters were changing, towards finding them distrustful and objects of suspicion, rather than merely pitiable (Roggenkamp, 2005). The prosecution highlighted Lizzie's lack of emotion and seeming masculinity. Her motive was greed, a profoundly unfeminine failing which implied a desire for independence (Robertson, 1996; Nickerson, 1999; Roggenkamp, 2005).

These competing representations of Lizzie exemplified a number of anxieties and tensions surrounding late-nineteenth-century American womanhood. The need to believe in the version of Lizzie as a domestic, pious and dutiful daughter upheld conservative notions of true womanhood. However, Lizzie's support from temperance and women's organisations, including leading feminists, signalled the emergent New Woman, who demanded equality and rejected the need for masculine protection (Nickerson, 1999; Filetti, 2001; Roggenkamp, 2005). These supporters believed that her femininity and respectability had been unfairly traduced (Shaw, 1997). Respectability was an essential component of the New Woman, who was educated and autonomous, with active contributions to make to the well-being of society and civilisation (Smith-Rosenberg, 1986).

The contested nature of womanhood, respectability and civilisation in late-nineteenth-century America, coupled with an expanding national press, helped to establish the case of Lizzie Borden as one of the most famous murder trials in that nation's history (Roggenkamp, 2005). Although her acquittal has been read as the triumph of a discourse of respectable womanhood, the case against Lizzie was circumstantial. There was no physical evidence tying her to the deaths of her father and step-mother, and she would need to have cleaned herself up very quickly, in a house with no running water, between murdering Andrew at around 10.45 a.m. and alerting Bridget to his death at 11.05 a.m. (Uelman, 1998). However, as a story which is permanently unfinished, Lizzie Borden's case remains a site for multiple interpretations of femininity and respectability.

Celestine Doudet

In Paris in 1855 Celestine Doudet, a governess, was tried for the involuntary manslaughter of one of her pupils, Mary Ann Marsden, and on charges of physically abusing four of Mary Ann's sisters. Celestine was acquitted of the manslaughter of Mary Ann but received a fine and a sentence of 5 years in prison for the mistreatment of the other girls (Borowitz, 2002). Her case reveals the complex and contested ways in which mid-nineteenth-century respectability was established via norms of sexuality and child-rearing, and the role unmarried women played in upholding these norms.

Celestine was of Anglo-French parentage and grew up in Rouen in north-west France. Her father, a captain in the French navy, lost his money and determined that his daughters should be educated and become governesses, as he could not afford marriage dowries for them. Celestine's parents retired to England, but after her father died in 1839, her mother returned to France to live in Paris. Celestine joined her there and worked as a tutor, although shortly afterwards left for England to work as a wardrobe mistress for Queen Victoria. Celestine left her royal appointment with a personal recommendation from the Queen and worked as a governess for a variety of aristocratic English families. In 1852, she was employed by Dr James Marsden, a widower, as governess to his five daughters in Malvern, in the English midlands (Hartman, 1995).

Governesses were the focus of considerable cultural interest in mid-nineteenth-century England, which was out of proportion to the number of families who would have employed them. Novels such as Charlotte Bronte's *Jane Eyre* (1847) depicted the governess' travails and relative powerlessness. Their social position was ambiguous as they were respectable, middle-class, educated women whose families could not support them. Therefore, they were engaged to work for wealthy families in a capacity which mirrored that of a servant (Hughes, 2001).

Shortly after Celestine commenced working for James Marsden, her mother died. She proposed that she could move back to her mother's apartment in Paris and establish a small school, at which the Marsden girls would be live-in pupils. James agreed, and gave Celestine some money with which to educate and care for his female children (Hartman, 1995). Part of the Victorian governess' role was to ensure the moral education of her charges and to enforce sexual discipline (Hughes, 2001). James suspected his daughters of masturbation and, according to Celestine, asked her to cure them of it (Wolff, 1995). In the mid- and late nineteenth-century, masturbation was considered physically and psychologically damaging, a cause of infertility and madness (Hunt, 1998; Whorton, 2001). It was feared girls who masturbated would become nymphomaniacs and prostitutes (Hartman, 1995). In the 1850s and

1860s, doctors began to recommend cures based on punishment and surgery (Wolff, 1995; Whorton, 2001).

Celestine's sister, Zephyrine, worked at the school but left, disgusted at Celestine's cruel treatment of the Marsden girls. She informed neighbours that they were not fed properly, were often kept locked or tied up, and were also beaten. Neighbours attempted to intervene by writing to James about his daughters' predicament and also by contacting the police. A police officer visited, but found nothing out of order and James was reluctant to take action on the basis of the letters he received. He had visited the girls twice in Paris whilst in Europe on a trip with his new wife. He did not return until July 1853, after Mary Ann's death (Hartman, 1995; Borowitz, 2002).

James was disinclined to complain to the police, or to support the police investigation that Celestine's neighbours initiated. He feared the scandal that would result if his instructions to Celestine to cure his daughters of masturbation were made public. He had employed her out of concern for the girls' future health and increasingly despaired of them when Celestine reported she found it difficult to prevent them from masturbating. They had also been examined by doctors who attributed their ill health and frailty to masturbation (Hartman, 1995). Eventually, James pressed charges in 1855 and Celestine was tried in two different courts for the manslaughter of Mary Ann, and the physical abuse of the other girls (Borowitz, 2002).

The case demonstrates the role the governess could play in the sexual regulation of children. As a respectable, unmarried woman, Celestine was viewed by James as a suitable guardian of his daughters' moral welfare. Her defence was that her treatment of the girls merely fulfilled James' wishes and instructions (Hartman, 1995). Although many observers in England and France excoriated Celestine's behaviour, she also had supporters who campaigned for her release from prison. She was freed in 1858 after serving 3 years of her sentence and received employment offers for governess posts with English families (Borowitz, 2002). The French correspondent for *The Times* described how the Bishop of Nancy had made a request for mercy on her behalf, and that despite the 'prejudice' that had been expressed against her, Emperor Napoleon III, by releasing Celestine, had 'done the most graceful act a monarch can perform for the suffering and the innocent' (*The Times*, 10 July 1858). As an Anglo-French woman, Celestine crossed the boundaries of national identity during an era when they were becoming increasingly consolidated (see Powell, 2002), which may have stirred negative feelings towards her. Conversely, as a respectable governess, she had attempted to regulate the boundaries of feminine sexuality, which upheld moral order and stability. These nineteenth-century cases demonstrate the appearance of the respectable woman discourse as a means of mitigating the circumstances surrounding violent killings. Lizzie Borden and Celestine Doudet were from middle-class to upper middle-class backgrounds, which meant that their respectability was assumed, rather than something which needed to be proven. This does not mean that there were no negative representations of them. Lizzie Borden was perceived as masculine and heartless and Celestine Doudet as wicked and cruel.

As the discussion of these cases has also revealed, despite being respectable, women could still occupy socially ambiguous positions such as the governess and/or spinster. Construction as respectable did not guarantee positive representation, or indeed acquittal, but it enabled supporters to identify or sympathise with these women. It also allowed the defence to present the accusations against Lizzie as manifestly ridiculous, a strategy not open to women perceived as disreputable. In Celestine's case, concerns on the part of James Marsden over the preservation of his family's respectability delayed her prosecution. These women's cases also demonstrate the emergence of cultural anxieties in terms of nineteenth-century middle-class women's acceptable public and private roles, and their symbolic status as bastions of morality. Another important facet of the respectable woman discourse is the process of recuperation, through which a woman accused of murder is incorporated back into intelligible femininity. This can take place even where the woman does not originate from a respectable background, as in the late-twentieth-century American case of Karla Faye Tucker.

Karla Faye Tucker

Karla Faye Tucker was executed in Texas in 1998 for the murders of Jerry Dean and Deborah Thornton. In 1983, along with her boyfriend, Daniel Garrett, she broke into their apartment and violently killed them. Karla repeatedly struck both Jerry Dean and Deborah Thornton with a pickaxe. In a confession that was played for the jury during her trial in 1984, Karla claimed to have experienced orgasm each time she struck with the weapon. At this time, she was very far from being respectable. She was a drug addict and worked as a prostitute. The murders were committed under the influence of illegal drugs. Her assertion that she was sexually gratified by the murders did nothing to ameliorate their shocking and deeply unfeminine nature (Knox, 2001; Howarth, 2002).

72 *Women, Murder and Femininity*

During her time on death row, Karla became a born again Christian and married her prison chaplain. By 1998, she was a religious 38-year old of attractive and conventionally feminine appearance (Farr, 1999; Rapaport, 2000; Knox, 2001). She appealed for clemency from the Governor of Texas, George W. Bush, on the grounds that she had been rehabilitated and was no longer the same person as the one who had wielded the pickaxe (Kobil, 2003). Karla was supported, politically and financially, by prominent members of the evangelical Christian right, such as Pat Robertson and Jerry Falwell, who were not against the death penalty in principle but opposed her execution (Farr, 1999; Rapaport, 2000). Robertson described Karla as 'a beautiful person' and asserted 'Her speech and demeanour reflected sublime virtue' (Robertson, 2000, p. 580). He argued that she had become a different person, which rendered her execution barbaric.

Bush denied clemency, partly on political grounds but also due to Texas state procedure (Howarth, 2002; Kobil, 2003). In order to commute the death sentence, the state's Board of Pardons and Parolees, whose membership had been selected by Bush, needed to make a recommendation to this effect, but as is the convention in Texas, no such recommendation was made (Robertson, 2000). Karla Faye Tucker became the first woman to be executed in the state since the Civil War era, and the second woman in the United States following the reinstatement of the death penalty in 1976 (*New York Times*, 3 February 1998).

Karla's feted transformation from drug-crazed, pickaxe-wielding murderess to sweet and gentle Christian lady represents her discursive recuperation into appropriate femininity. This was successful to the extent that to some, she could not be identified with the deviant, over-sexed woman she had been. Her case generated intense media interest, which was mainly supportive in nature (Halmari and Ostman, 2001). The recuperation of Karla into femininity and the assignation of respectability can be contrasted with the cases of Aileen Wuornos and Wanda Jean Allen. Acceptance of Karla's metamorphosis was aided by her whiteness and heterosexuality. This made her execution culturally traumatic in a way that the state killings of Aileen and Wanda were not (Farr, 1999; Howarth, 2002). Although Karla's transformation did not ultimately save her from the death penalty, her execution provoked discussion of capital punishment's legitimacy and renewed the vigour of abolitionist campaigns (Howarth, 2002). Her case gained international attention, with letters requesting clemency being sent to Bush from the European Parliament and the Pope (*New York Times*, 3 February 1998).

Her recuperation inserted her into the respectable woman discourse, although unlike the other cases examined so far, she was not respectable at the time of the killings.

The support Karla Faye Tucker received from the religious right illustrated the American 'culture wars' during the second term of Bill Clinton's presidency. Once recuperated as a virtuous Christian 'lady', Karla was appropriated by evangelical Christians such as Robertson and Falwell as a symbol of moral American womanhood. At the same time as her execution was debated, Clinton's sexual involvement with Monica Lewinsky, a young White House intern, dominated both the news media and talk shows (see Lipkin, 2000; Jones, 2001). Karla Faye Tucker served as a cultural juxtaposition to the promiscuous, 'liberal' and Jewish Monica Lewinsky. Although Karla was a symbol of virtuous American femininity for sections of the religious right, there was a tension with the 'tough on crime' direction of criminal justice policies in the 1990s, which had seen execution rates climb (Simon, 2007). Ultimately, it was unlikely that a pro-death penalty Republican governor with presidential ambitions such as George W. Bush would take a role in reprieving her. Karla Faye Tucker's discursive recuperation as a respectable woman, who could represent imperilled American womanhood, demonstrates the symbolic potency of this representation, and its relationship with contests over the 'proper' meanings of national culture.

The witch

This section is concerned with the appearance of the witch discourse in cases of middle-aged and older women who were accused of multiple killings. Women who killed male partners and their own children will therefore be discussed, although only in cases where the woman was thought to have more than one victim. Images of witches are extremely diverse. However, a durable stereotype of the witch as an older woman can be identified in American and European cultures between the eighteenth and twentieth centuries (Davies, 1999, 2001). This is not to argue that this is the only witch representation to emerge in 'Western' cultures, but this particular stereotype, which is a familiar image of the witch, is the one that will be analysed.

Before outlining this iteration of the witch discourse, it is necessary to explain the aspects of witches and witchcraft that will not be explored. Firstly, none of the cases included are of women who were actually accused of witchcraft. Cases are drawn from the twentieth century, when belief in witches and witchcraft was in decline (Davies, 1999,

2001). The cases are not necessarily ones in which the occult or magic were understood to play a role. Rather, this section will examine the witch discourse as shaping a particular representation of femininity that bore resemblance to the familiar cultural stereotype of the witch. This is a negative stereotype that portrays older women as threatening and malignant (Demos, 1983; Codd, 1998; Davies, 1999). There are positive representations of witches, not least certain feminist reclamations of the image of the witch and the practice of witchcraft (Purkiss, 1996; Gibson, 2007). However, echoes of the witch as a symbol of feminine deviance haunted certain twentieth-century constructions of women who kill. In this sense, the witch is a shadow discourse in these gender representations. It is not fully there, but it conditions the portrayals of femininity in certain women's cases.

This focus on the trace of the witch in discourses of femininity, rather than on women believed to be witches, means that the persecution of those accused of witchcraft in Early Modern Europe and seventeenth-century America will not be discussed. Feminist interpretations of 'witch hunts' as a holocaust perpetrated against women have been challenged to the point of being discredited by most historians working in this area (Purkiss, 1996; Gaskill, 2008). Women were often the accusers in cases of suspected witchcraft, and the majority of female accused were not healers or midwives (Harley, 1990; Holmes, 1993). Comparisons will not be made between twentieth-century criminal justice processes and the punishment of women believed to be witches three centuries earlier.

The figure of the witch is a subterranean presence in the cases selected for analysis. There are a number of folkloric characteristics associated with witchcraft. In addition to being old, the witch was frequently a widow. She could be sexually ravenous, with the power to weaken and contaminate men (Roper, 1991; Rowlands, 2001). She was likely to be poor. The beggar witch was a poor woman who used her powers to take revenge on those who refused to give her money or alms (Davies, 1999; Dillinger, 2004).

Witches were completely evil and utterly malicious. They had made a pact with the devil, and met at secret gatherings to perform harmful magic (Dillinger, 2004). The witch was also a shape-shifter, who could disguise herself by taking the form of an animal (Davies, 1999). Her ability to deceive and disguise, as well as her intention to cause others harm, manifested itself in murderous behaviour, particularly through the use of poison (Roper, 1991). The witch would harm and kill randomly (Dillinger, 2004). Although, on the one hand, witches could be identified through physical signs such as being old and ugly (Demos,

1983; Davies, 1999), on the other, their status as ordinary women made them indistinguishable from those around them. The witch was dangerous because her evil nature was hidden and potentially unknowable (Dillinger, 2004). She was both mysterious and unremarkable. Once a witch had been discovered, she was known to be such by her bad reputation (Rowlands, 2001).

Witches were often marginal and therefore liminal figures. They were women who existed in problematic relation to established social networks and interactions, and took the blame for social misfortunes (Roper, 1991; Purkiss, 1996). This responsibility for social misfortune is an enduring aspect of the witch discourse, meaning that it represents social shifts and anxieties. European and American representations of witches also had a racialised aspect, with colonial 'others' viewed as practitioners of witchcraft (Purkiss, 1996). The women discussed in this section were all white so the image of the witch as racial other did not appear in their cases. However, issues of racial or ethnic identity will be explored where relevant.

In her analysis of representations of older female offenders in the British media, Codd (1998) argues that depiction of women as powerful or controlling echoes folk legends of the witch. This portrayal is especially likely to arise in cases of women perceived to be bad carers. The cases under discussion pertain to women of 45 or over, who committed, or were suspected of committing, multiple killings. This was in violation of their roles as wives, mothers or other types of carer. As bad carers, women represented through the 'witch' discourse symbolise other social failures. Caring is so intimately tied to women's normative roles, especially culturally acceptable roles for older women (such as the kindly grandmother figure), that its profound breach in the form of multiple killing suggests wider social malaise. The witch discourse is examined in relation to three cases and its relationship with broader social concerns is explored.

Belle Gunness

The story of Belle Gunness retains an enduring mystery. On 28 April 1908, her farm in La Porte, Indiana, USA, burnt down. Belle lived there with her three children and ran the farm. Police searched the remains of the buildings and found the bodies of three children and a headless woman in the basement of the house. They assumed that these were the bodies of Belle and her children, although they could not find her head. On 30 April, they arrested Ray Lamphere, a handyman who had worked for Belle. He had been arrested earlier in the year for 'annoying' her and she had brought trespass charges against him 2 weeks before the fire. Ray was charged with arson and murder. Organs from the four bodies from the basement were tested and were found to contain poison. The police surmised that Ray poisoned Belle and her children, before setting light to the farm (Hinton, 1999; Flowers and Flowers, 2004; Scott, 2007).

The case changed dramatically with the arrival of Asle Hegelian in La Porte. Asle came in search of his brother, Andrew, with whom he had worked as a farmer in South Dakota. Like Belle, the Hegelians were Norwegian immigrants. Andrew had responded to Belle's advert in a Norwegian language newspaper, in which she described herself as a wealthy widow looking for a husband. He had left South Dakota in early January and Asle had not heard from him since, which was unusual as the two brothers were very close. Asle wrote to Belle, who claimed that Andrew had gone to Chicago. By tracing his brother's money transfers, Asle determined that Andrew had sent money to a bank in La Porte (Langlois, 1983; Hinton, 1999; Scott, 2007).

When he saw a news clipping about the fire, Asle travelled to Indiana, worried that his brother may have been hurt. Once in La Porte, he found two of Belle's neighbours digging amongst the rubble of her property and asked them to help him investigate any holes or 'soft spots' that had been filled in around the farm. In digging up one such hole, Asle discovered a sack containing the dismembered body of Andrew. The police dug up other soft spots and discovered ten more bodies. In all, there were nine male bodies and two female. One of the female bodies was Belle's adoptive daughter, Jennie, who had supposedly left for a Californian finishing school in 1906 (Hinton, 1999; Scott, 2007).

It emerged that the male bodies were all Norwegian immigrants who had answered Belle's adverts for husbands. Once they had deposited money in her account, it appeared Belle killed them and buried them on her property (Hinton, 1999). The police still suspected Ray Lamphere of being involved, although further details that emerged about Belle cast doubt on this. The murder charges against him were dropped and he was sentenced to 20 years for arson. Ray gave conflicting accounts of how much he knew of Belle's deeds. He claimed that she poisoned a woman in order to make it seem like she had died in the fire (Flowers and Flowers, 2004).

Belle was born in 1859 in Norway, the daughter of a poor agricultural worker. In the early 1880s, she emigrated to America and joined her sister in Chicago. In 1883, she married her first husband, Mads Sorenson, with whom she had four children. Two of her children died and, although they showed symptoms consistent with poisoning, Belle's explanation that they died from an illness was accepted. She received insurance money from their deaths, and later from some properties that burnt down. When Mads died, police and local people in the Illinois town where they lived suspected that Belle had poisoned him, but this was not proven. In 1902, she married Peter Gunness, who died shortly afterwards from a head injury that Belle claimed was caused by a meat grinder. She used the insurance money from his death to buy the farm in La Porte (Hinton, 1999; Scott, 2007).

The discovery of Belle's past made it seem likely that she was primarily, if not solely, responsible for the bodies unearthed at the farm. It was assumed that she had killed her two husbands and the children, and also that she was still alive and had escaped (Scott, 2007). After the bodies were discovered, newspapers invented a variety of monstrous epithets for Belle, such as 'woman Bluebeard', 'Gunness Monster' and 'Hell's Belle' (Hinton, 1999, p. 337). The Bluebeard analogy was the most enduring and 'Lady Bluebeard' remained a nickname for Belle Gunness (Langlois, 1983).[10] Such names explicitly linked her with monsters and represented her as witch-like. A variety of explanations emerged as to why Belle had committed her crimes. Some of these were expert discourses of insanity or inherent criminality. Popular explanations drew on the supernatural, arguing that she was possessed by the devil, or that her house was inhabited by evil spirits. It was also suggested that she had special powers which enabled her to hypnotise her victims (Hinton, 1999). In this sense, Belle Gunness became an early-twentieth-century witch.

Other elements of her story contributed to the witch representation. Belle was a stout woman, strong from her work on the farm and not considered to be attractive. She maintained a degree of distance from La Porte's social networks, made possible by possessing her own land (Scott, 2007). Her alleged killings allowed her to achieve and maintain financial independence. She requested that the men who came to her farm sign their money over to her, which inverted normative matrimonial arrangements, whereby women became dependent on men (Langlois, 1983). Her method of attracting victims was in keeping with the sexually voracious widow, who lures men in order to prey on them.

One of the most significant aspects of the witch discourse in relation to Belle Gunness is the notion of the shape-shifter. As an immigrant woman who had married, and therefore changed names, more than once, Belle had adopted and cast off different identities. However, it was her disappearance after the fire that made her a legendary figure.

Numerous sightings were reported shortly afterwards and in the months that followed, one as far afield as Mexico (*New York Times*, 14 June 1908).[11] Possible sightings continued over the years. In 1914, she was thought to be in a cabin in Saskatchewan, Canada (*New York Times*, 27 March 1914). In 1931, a woman named Esther Carlson was tried for murdering an old man, and was suspected of being Belle Gunness (Scott, 2007). However, Belle, if she lived on after the fire, was never discovered and her disappearance and transmogrification into someone else attested to her shape-shifting powers.

As Protestant Northern Europeans, Norwegian immigrants to the United States such as Belle and her victims were generally regarded by the dominant culture as 'safe' and easily assimilable (Schultz, 1994). By the early twentieth century, when the bodies were discovered at Belle's farm, Norwegian-Americans were perceived as contrasting positively with 'new' immigrants from Southern and Eastern Europe, who were largely Catholic or Jewish and were represented as a threat to the quality of the nation. However, assimilation was a contested topic within Norwegian-American settler communities, many of which in the period before the First World War sought to establish Norwegian churches and to preserve the use of the Norwegian language in the United States. The debate around tensions between the preservation of Norwegian culture and assimilation into American culture centred on language in particular, and Norwegian language newspapers were established as a means of shoring up ethnic identity (Schultz, 1994). By attracting male victims through adverts in Norwegian language newspapers, thus making them an instrument of danger, Belle Gunness decried these efforts at cultural preservation and disturbed notions of Norwegian-American identity.

Daisy de Melker

Daisy de Melker is one of South Africa's most famous 'spectacular' cases of murder (Comaroff and Comaroff, 2004). She was executed in Johannesburg in December 1932 for poisoning her 20-year-old son, Rhodes Cowle, with arsenic. She was also tried for the murders of her husbands, William Cowle and Robert Sproat, but was acquitted due to lack of evidence tying her to their poisonings. She was the third white, or 'European', woman to be executed since the Union of South Africa in 1910 (Kahn, 1960).[12] This, combined with the sensational nature of the crimes of which she was accused, has cemented her place in South African history.

Daisy was born in 1886 near Grahamstown, in what was then the Cape Colony, but spent most of her childhood in Bulawayo, Rhodesia. In her late teens, she returned to South Africa to train as a nurse in Durban. She married William Cowle, a plumber, in 1905 and they had five children, two of whom died during childhood (Beukes, 2004). William died in 1923 after terrible convulsions and stomach pains. The doctor who examined him identified the symptoms of strychnine poisoning but did not suspect 'foul play' (*The Times*, 19 October 1932), as he accepted William had taken Epsom salts contaminated with the poison. Daisy inherited William's money and his pension. She married Robert Sproat, another plumber, in 1926. He died, apparently of lead poisoning, in 1927 and Daisy also inherited money from him (Beukes, 2004).

By 1932, Daisy was married again, this time to Sidney de Melker, who had been a famous rugby player in South Africa (*The Times*, 18 October 1932). Her son, Rhodes, was approaching 21 and she found his behaviour increasingly difficult. He demanded that Daisy spend money on him, for example, she had bought him a car. He would also verbally and physically abuse her when angry. When he died in March 1932, the doctor certified the death as caused by cerebral malaria, which Rhodes had contracted during time spent in Swaziland (Beukes, 2004).

William Sproat, Robert's brother, had remained suspicious of Daisy and the circumstances of his brother's death. When he learned of Rhodes' death, he contacted the police, and the bodies of Rhodes, Robert Sproat and William Cowle were exhumed (Beukes, 2004). It emerged that Rhodes had died from arsenic poisoning, and traces of strychnine were found in the bodies of both husbands (*The Times*, 21 October 1932). The pharmacist who had sold Daisy arsenic shortly before Rhodes died appeared as a witness at her trial. Daisy's defence was that she had purchased it to kill a cat. The judge found her guilty of murdering her son and sentenced her to death (*The Times*, 24 October 1932). She is also suspected of having killed her other two children who died, and a fiancé from Bulawayo.

Elements of Daisy's story that are similar to the Belle Gunness case made her seem witch-like. She used poison, a covert means of killing, and appeared to have financial motives. (The murder of her son enabled her to collect from life insurance policies, although his behaviour has also been seen as a contributory factor.) She was rumoured to be sexually insatiable and her defence barrister described her in his memoirs as 'over-sexed' (Beukes, 2004). South African novelist, Sarah Millin, attended Daisy's trial and based her book *Three Men Die* (1934) on the case. In her autobiography, *The Night is Long* (1941), Millin emphasised Daisy's ugliness and stated that she had a cleft palate, recalling the witch stereotype of an ugly, deformed older woman. She also noted that Daisy did not bother to wear make-up during her trial and wore the same dress throughout.[13]

The era preceding Daisy de Melker's execution was a turbulent one for South Africa. The post-1910 Union governments debated whether to remain a dominion of the United Kingdom, or whether to attempt to establish a republic. Afrikaner nationalists supported independence from the British. South Africa became more autonomous after the 1926 Balfour Declaration and gained its own flag in 1928 (Beck, 2000). Some of the divisions within the dominant white communities between the British and the Afrikaners began to heal as a white South African identity emerged. The black African population became increasingly marginalised and disenfranchised during the late 1920s, and the vote was extended to all white men and women in 1930 (Beinart, 2001). In a period of increased empowerment for white women, Daisy (who was ethnically British rather than Afrikaans) had reversed the cultural assumptions of the South African elite that white women were in need of the law's protection, and that they automatically embodied the virtues of the nascent South African nation. She was therefore an aberration who had violated national standards of white femininity and outraged, rather than upheld, the moral superiority of her race (Comaroff and Comaroff, 2004). In this sense, Daisy became a liminal figure, troubling the boundaries of South African racial and national identity and, like Belle Gunness, she disrupted the social order.

Dorothea Puente

Dorothea Puente ran a board and care home in Sacramento, California, for indigent middle-aged and older people, many of whom had mental health problems. The social workers who placed residents in her house thought highly of her and were impressed by the standard of care she provided. However, in November 1988, two female social workers became troubled by the disappearance of one of their clients, Alvaro Montoya, from Dorothea's house. Dorothea claimed that he had gone to Mexico and then Salt Lake City, which made the social workers suspicious. They visited the house and attempted to speak to other residents about Alvaro, and were informed that it was not unusual for people to go missing from there (Pearson, 1998; Gibson, 2006).

The social workers contacted the police, who discovered a body wrapped in plastic and buried in Dorothea's yard. After being questioned, Dorothea took a Greyhound bus to Los Angeles, where she rented a motel room. Six more bodies, believed to be other tenants who had gone missing, were unearthed from the yard (Pearson, 1998; Gibson, 2006). Dorothea had the authority to cash Social Security cheques for some of her residents with mental health and chronic alcohol problems, which she had continued to do after they disappeared (*New York Times*, 18 November 1988). The police mounted a search for Dorothea, whose whereabouts were discovered after a man she spoke to in a bar recognised her from television reports. She admitted stealing the Social Security money, but denied having killed anyone. She was charged with murdering the seven people whose remains were dug up from her backyard (Pearson, 1998; Gibson, 2006).

Dorothea was born in 1929 in San Bernardino County and was named Dorothy Helen Gray. She was one of six children and both of her parents died during her childhood. She claimed to have married four times, although records indicate that she was married twice. Dorothea told people that she was born in Mexico, but she did not in fact have a Latina heritage (Gibson, 2006). In the late 1970s, she was convicted of stealing from tenants who boarded with her and made the front page of a local magazine in Sacramento (Pearson, 1998). In 1982, she was found guilty of charges related to drugging and stealing from people in her care (*New York Times*, 18 November 1988). She served half of a 5-year sentence and a condition of her parole was that she should not take on boarders. Dorothea's previous convictions excluded her from working in a state run home but she was part of California's informal welfare system, and received referrals from local mental health and community services (ibid.).

In 1989, Dorothea was charged with two more murders. One of these was of Everson Gillmouth, a former fiancé of hers, whose body was found on a riverbank in 1986. The other was Ruth Munro, a woman with whom Dorothea had opened a restaurant in 1982. Ruth put money into the business and died of a drug overdose shortly after moving into Dorothea's house. At the time, it was recorded as suicide (Howard and Smith, 2004). Dorothea was eventually tried for nine murders in 1993. The prosecution argued that she killed her tenants with an overdose of prescription drugs and carried on collecting their Social Security money. Her defence was that all, apart from Ruth Munro, had died from natural causes. Dorothea maintained that she did not inform the authorities of her tenants' deaths because she knew she should not have been caring for them. She admitted to claiming their money (Fox and Levin, 2005).

The jury at Dorothea's trial deliberated for more than 3 weeks (*New York Times*, 27 August 1993). Due to the length of time the bodies had been buried, there was little physical evidence and it was difficult to determine the cause of death (Fox and Levin, 2005). The jury found her guilty of three murders and could not reach a decision on the other six. The judge declared a mistrial for these (*New York Times*, 27 August 1993). The prosecution asked for the death penalty and, again, the jury could not reach a decision so she was sentenced to life in prison without the possibility of parole (*New York Times*, 14 October 1993; 11 December 1993).

Along with details familiar from the other cases discussed so far, such as Dorothea's status as an older woman and her use of hidden methods to kill her victims and suspected victims, the elements of the witch discourse related to women's care work are also relevant. As a woman who used her position as a carer to harm vulnerable people, Dorothea was a troubling figure. Her case exposed gaps and shortcomings in California's welfare system (Greener, 1991), making her represent not only her own crimes, but also wider social disaggregation.

Dorothea's most culturally disturbing and witch-like propensity was her talent for shape-shifting. She was able to hide her previous convictions, for crimes that bore similarities to her murders, from social workers and her local community. She was well regarded and social workers noted that their clients' overall health tended to improve once they were placed in her house. Tenants experienced her differently, stating that she drank heavily and could become bad tempered and violent. Some of them expressed dissatisfaction about living with Dorothea, but social workers ignored them, believing board and care represented their best option from a limited range, and that she offered them a good service (*New York Times*, 8 August 1993; Pearson, 1998).

The dissonance created by the images of Dorothea as a reliable caregiver and as a violent woman who killed and stole from vulnerable people was troubling and indicated that she could take on and cast off identities as necessary. The two versions of her character were difficult to reconcile. The *New York Times* noted that, '[a] white-haired woman who wears large glasses and floral-print dresses, does not fit the stereotype of a serial killer' (8 August 1993). Other details, such as uncertainty about how many times she had been married and her ethnic identity, contributed to perceptions of her ability to deceive, disguise and change.

Dorothea's crimes came to criminal justice and public attention in November 1988, the month that Republican candidate and Vice President, George Bush, won the American election following two terms of the Reagan administration. Before assuming the Presidency, Ronald Reagan had been Governor of California, which was Dorothea's home state and symbolically America's 'Shangri-la' (Starr, 2005). California, the Golden State, stood for sunshine, stardom, opportunity and innovation. Reagan, a right-wing, populist Republican, capitalised on his movie star past and folksy charm, emphasising national optimism and arguing that under his Presidency it was 'Morning in America' (Jenkins, 1994). In particular, he pursued economic policies based on reduced public spending and fewer taxes. A case like Dorothea's highlighted the social fissures and breakdown that could ensue following Reagan-style welfare cuts, and existed in stark contradiction to both the image of the Californian promised land and of its avuncular adopted son.

The witch discourse arises in cases where a middle-aged or older woman appears to be responsible for multiple killings. When revealed as 'malign', rather than as harmless or caring, these women unsettle norms of older women's femininity and appear almost supernaturally evil. As discussed, the 'witch' discourse is a subterranean representation as it does not imply that the women in question are actually believed to be witches (although some of Belle Gunness' nicknames connoted a supernatural being). The three cases explored demonstrate the role of the witch in symbolising social misfortune or cultural anxiety, where the shocking discovery or suspicion of multiple killings by older women appears to indicate deeper social problems or challenges. In this sense, the witch discourse exemplifies this book's dual approach to analysing cases of women accused of unusual murder, where the crossing of gender boundaries is considered alongside the cultural meanings generated by the cases.

Conclusion to Part I

Part I has examined regulatory discourses of gender as they appeared in unusual cases of women who kill, and has suggested their relationship with wider cultural anxieties. The variety of cases demonstrates how the different constructions of womanhood (or of lack of womanhood) recur in different places and times (McDonagh, 2003; Morrissey, 2003), frequently carrying the traces of older constructions. However, this review of well-known unusual cases also shows that these tropes of gender become symbolic of issues that arise out of specific contexts, such as the perceived social changes to 1960s Britain in the cases of Myra Hindley and Mary Bell, or the forging of the white South African nation in the 1930s in the case of Daisy de Melker.

The five identified discourses play a role in gender regulation as they highlight the boundaries of appropriate femininity. The significance of these discourses in outlining the metaphoric limits to womanhood can be seen in the recurrence of boundary crossing as a major theme, be it the boundary between masculinity and femininity, or between sanity and insanity, or, as in the case of the witch, the margins of the social order. Liminality is also key, with discourses such as the muse/mastermind dichotomy and the damaged personality constructing subjects who cause category confusion, making them seem dangerous. The respectable woman representation demonstrates that women who kill are not necessarily figured as transgressive, but that escaping or transcending condemnation or abjection involves discursive recuperation (Morrissey, 2003), which is likely to be partial and to exist alongside more derogatory portrayals.

The continuing discomfort caused by women who kill and the recourse to discourses of gender denigration through which to represent them highlight the threat they pose to established power relations (Ballinger, 2000; Heberle, 2001), and the need to contain their potentially disruptive power (Jones, 1996; Morrissey, 2003). This 'disciplines' femininity (Heberle, 1999) as it constrains what constitutes an acceptable gender performance (Butler, 2004). Whilst the unacceptability of murder in ethical terms is beyond dispute, the potential for women who kill to become culturally unintelligible or abject in terms of gender demonstrates the ongoing maintenance of femininity as weaker than, and subordinate to, masculinity.

The five discourses that constitute the typology are not solely relevant to women who kill, but construct women in relation to other situations. The masculine woman and damaged personality representations derive from expert, medicalised knowledge (which can be translated into popular knowledge), but the other three are not expert attempts to explain criminality or female deviance, they emerge from wider cultural norms of womanhood. Previous feminist research has shown that gender constructions of women who kill have relevance beyond each particular case – they relate to the social positioning and representation of women more generally (Nicolson, 1995; Jones, 1996; Ballinger, 2000).

It is useful here to make recourse to the poststructuralist feminist framework that shapes the analysis of the cases in this book. Feminists need to be wary of how far they generalise the category of 'women' as it is multiple and can attach to diverse constructions of femininity (Riley, 1988), meaning that 'women' do not constitute one easily identifiable group. This complicates our understanding of the regulatory power of discourses of women who kill – the instances of cultural subordination they encode may not exert control over all women, as there are important power differences between women (Anthias, 2002).

An intersectional approach, which accounts for the complexity of multiple identities, helps to make this clear. The portrayal of Aileen Wuornos as a masculine woman relied not just on stereotypes of the lesbian woman as aggressive, but also the derogatory 'white trash' representation, an intersection of 'race' and class. Wanda Jean Allen was constructed as masculine through negative portrayals of her sexuality, the 'black brute' stereotype and constructions of the 'underclass'. Poovey's (1988) conceptualisation of discourses' regulatory effects as 'uneven' is useful here. In the context of the late 1980s and early 1990s United States, 'white trash' and 'underclass' representations as they intersected with constructions of womanhood were potent elements in the increased criminalisation and punishment of women (Maher, 1992; Chesney-Lind and Pasko, 2004). However, this did not impact equally on all women, but differentially affected poor minority ethnic and white women.

The respectable woman discourse, which can enable women who kill to be represented positively, is more likely to be available to middle-class white women than to other women, and is a discourse with uneven benefits. Although this representation tends to re-encode certain constraining elements of femininity, such as sexual propriety and the performance of duty, it accrues *potential* advantages to women who can be constructed through this discourse. This exemplifies Mouffe's (1995) point that subjects can be dominant in some representations and simultaneously subordinate in others, and Cornell's (1995) argument that feminists should acknowledge the relative social power that attaches to the subjectivities of middle-class white women.

The review of well-known cases demonstrates how the five discourses of femininity can become wider symbols of social shifts and anxieties specific to particular times and places. The case of Karla Homolka became a symbol for anxieties about Canadian identity and the maintenance of distinctiveness from the United States in the 1990s; the case of Martha Beck represented fears of the effects of urban disconnectedness in mid-twentieth-century America. Due to the especially symbolic nature of femininity, unsettling female behaviour becomes an 'interpretive grid' through which to understand society's ills (Shapiro, 1996,

p. 9). Discourses of womanhood in unusual cases of women who kill do more than regulate the boundaries of gender – they are vehicles for the expression of cultural anxieties and struggles over meaning (Berenson, 1993; Phillips and Gartner, 2003).

The struggle for meaning is particularly acute in the case of Karla Faye Tucker, who by the time of her execution in the United States in 1998 had been adopted by sections of the Christian right as a symbol of virtuous American womanhood. For some, she became a repository for the national culture (see Einhorn, 1996). This was a highly contested meaning, which did not accord with the aims of punitive criminal justice policies, or, conversely, designations of American womanhood that did not rely on whiteness and Christianity. The construction of Karla through the respectable woman discourse also demonstrates the contingency of the meanings attached to discourses of femininity (Laclau and Mouffe, 2001). It would be difficult to predict that the case of a formerly drug-addicted female axe murderer would become a cause celebre for figures of the Christian right such as Jerry Falwell and Pat Buchanan. Attention to contingency enables an appreciation that discourses are not fixed and neither are the social circumstances out of which they arise.

Combining analysis of regulatory discourses of gender with attention to social and cultural transformation enables us to see gender relations and the wider social order as shifting and dynamic. This is not to see representations of femininity as unconstrained, but to acknowledge that they are part of a changing landscape, in which cultural boundaries are porous (Walkowitz, 1992; Shapiro, 1996). Discussion of the case of Rose West explored how the demonisation of her as a sexually deviant masculine woman must be understood against the background of changes to family life in 1990s Britain and shifts in terms of acceptable morality. Our examination of unusual cases of women who kill needs to be attentive to the 'burden of representation' carried by women (Yuval-Davis, 1997, p. 45), but it also needs to explore the construction of certain subjects as 'unworthy of respect or esteem' relative to others (Fraser, 2000, p. 114). In doing so, it can analyse the drawing of cultural boundaries around the normative and the worthless; the included and the excluded. This can best be done through a close examination of cases from a particular time and place.

Part II will address one specific context, that of mid-twentieth-century England and Wales. Through empirical analysis of case files, it explores the discursive construction of femininity in 12 cases of women accused of unusual murders, 1957–62, and analyses how this intersected with some of the major social and cultural changes of the era.

Part II

1
Gender, Murder and Mid-Twentieth-Century England and Wales

The period 1957–62 is a pivotal one in twentieth-century British history. This transitional era marks the growth of the 'affluent' society in which consumer goods became widely available and affordable with the advent of near full employment and a rise in average earnings. Sandbrook (2005, p. xx) explains that, '[i]t was in the mid-fifties, after all, that rationing and austerity came to an end, consumer activity began rapidly escalating, the first commercial television channel was established, and the retreat from empire began in earnest'. Social changes that would transform British society were underway. Hennessy (2007) characterises the early 1950s as a continuation of the 'long 1930s', when the culture of day-to-day life remained consistent with the interwar period. Between the early and late 1950s, Britain changed from 'a right, tight, screwed-down society walled in every way' (Hennessey, 2007, p. 5, quoting a senior civil servant in the Home Office) to one in which the ice started to break (ibid., 2007, p. xvii). He describes the major changes that took place in the late 1950s and early 1960s as social 'dam bursts', which preceded the liberalising trends of the later 1960s.

Harold Macmillan's Conservative governments of 1957–1963 benefited from identification with Britain's affluent society in which life had improved for ordinary people. Prime Minister Macmillan believed that the Conservatives needed to be enthusiastic about social change and modernisation, especially in order to win re-election in 1959 (Jarvis, 2005). They adopted a modernising social agenda, which included legalisation of betting shops in 1960, extended opening hours for pubs and bars in 1961 and the loosening of restrictions on 'obscene' publications, which led to the famous trial of D H Lawrence's 'Lady Chatterley's Lover' in 1960 (Hennessy, 2007).[1] The Homicide Act 1957, discussed further below, limited the application of the death penalty and the Wolfenden

Report of the same year recommended the decriminalisation of sex between consenting adult males (although the corresponding legislation was not passed until 1967).[2]

The Tories' willingness to embrace certain aspects of social modernisation indicates that they perceived important changes were underway, which they needed to reflect and encourage in order to appeal to the electorate. This was necessarily a contested process, as not all Conservative politicians, and certainly not all of the Party membership, approved of measures of social liberalisation (Jarvis, 2005). Even for Macmillan, the changes wrought in Britain's affluent society were a cause for anxiety. One source of such was how long affluence would endure – this was the theme of his famous 'having it so good' speech (Hennessy, 2007).[3] Another was how the British people would respond to their greater freedom to take responsibility for their own moral existence (Jarvis, 2005). There was a concern, held by those on the right and left of the political spectrum, that the affluent society of consumer goods and easier living was morally damaging and had the potential to undermine social bonds. It is important to bear in mind these worries about modernity and social change that cast a shadow over mid-twentieth-century optimism.

Coupled with anxiety about the possible coarsening effects of the affluent society, with its superficial, flashy seductions, there were fears that Britain as a nation and as a society was in decline (Black and Pemberton, 2004). 'Declinism', as Black and Pemberton (2004) term it, could encompass dissatisfactions related to Britain's post-war transition from a colonial to post-colonial nation and its perceived loss of power. However, declinism was also articulated in concerns that something was wrong with British society, as exemplified by Penguin's early 1960s series entitled 'What's Wrong with Britain?' (see Earle, 1961; Hill and Whichelow, 1964). This could be dismay at the ascendance of working-class Britons at the expense of its traditional ruling class, or conversely frustration that the working class could be bought off with cheap, mass produced goods, whilst sacrificing solidarity and the chance to make radical changes to British society.

The changes taking place in Britain in the late 1950s and early 1960s are the context against which the cases of 12 mid-twentieth-century women accused of murder will be analysed. The hopes and fears generated by modernity is a key theme that shaped the representation of femininity. Modernity can be broadly defined as transformations in governance, new formations of subjectivity, the expansion of technology and the enhanced status of expertise coupled with the professionalisation of knowledge (Conekin et al., 1999). Modernising changes to British society can be identified from the late nineteenth century onwards, but the contested meanings of modernity in the particular context of the late 1950s and early 1960s are the ones that will be considered in decoding 'unusual' cases of women accused of murder.

In order to examine the meanings of femininity constructed in mid-twentieth-century cases of murder, it is necessary to appreciate the shifting nature of British identities during the period. Post war, citizenship became wedded to national identity, and working-class British people were accorded status as citizens in ways they had not previously enjoyed, both through the benefits of the post-1945 welfare settlement, and their symbolic transformation from subjects to active citizens (Brooke, 2001). In the 1950s, the British Empire was in retreat and immigration from the Caribbean and Indian sub-continent was increasing. At the same time that citizenship and national identity became synonymous, the meanings of Britishness were changing, which led to 'a veritable crisis of national self-representation' (Waters, 1997, p. 208). If women are especially symbolic and representative of the nation, then these contemporary shifts in national identity form an important part of the backdrop to mid-twentieth-century constructions of British womanhood.

Womanhood in mid-twentieth-century Britain

The 1950s and early 1960s are popularly regarded as an era that was especially restrictive for women, when gains made during the Second World War were lost and women's domestic roles as wives and mothers were re-inscribed (see, for example, Millard, 2008). Although domesticity and motherhood were symbolically central to appropriate femininity in mid-twentieth-century Britain, it is important to delineate a subtler picture of both constructions of femininity and the experiences of women at this time. It is also necessary to understand that gender relations and identities were undergoing significant changes in the areas of employment, consumerism, the family and sexuality.

Post war, greater numbers of married women and women with children entered paid work as part-time shift patterns introduced during the war were retained (Summerfield, 1998; Wilson, 2006). This led to debates concerning whether mothers undertaking paid work would damage their children and exacerbate social problems such as juvenile delinquency (Wilson, 2006). However, paid work could be regarded as not only acceptable, but also desirable, for married women with children as it enabled them to contribute to the household income and achieve a higher standard of living. This interpretation was often advanced by married women workers themselves (ibid.). Contemporary feminist sociology constructed paid employment as a duty for educated married women, as long as they did not have small children, arguing that their skills and labour should not be withheld from the economy (see Myrdal and Klein, 1956; Hubback, 1957).

The burgeoning consumer culture of the 1950s that followed the post-war austerity years meant that women, who bore responsibility for the upkeep of the home, became consumers of domestic products and appliances. New science and technology entered the home through women, making them drivers of modernisation (Geraghty, 2000). Post war, the role of housewife became professionalised as women were expected to incorporate new technologies and new knowledge into their management of the household (Geraghty, 2000; Giles, 2005). The availability of domestic service for middle-class women had been in decline since the interwar period and working-class families, by the 1950s, were more likely to be able to buy or rent a whole house. Domestic labour in one's own home gained greater status and 'bestowed dignity and purpose' on many women (Giles, 2005, p. 72). Through maintaining a tidy, well-ordered home working-class women in particular could demonstrate their self-worth and respectability, and their commitment to a better future. However, those who did not adequately perform the role of industrious housewife signalled their lack of respectability and a failure to keep up with modern society (ibid.).

Sexual norms were shifting and being reconstituted in the mid-twentieth-century, albeit within limits. Heterosexual monogamy was the only widely accepted venue for sexual behaviour and desire, and certainly the only respectable formation of sexuality (Weeks, 1989). Perceived sexual pathologies, such as homosexuality, gained greater attention (mainly in relation to men, rather than women). Although this constituted non-heterosexual subjectivities as being outside of British citizenship, it paradoxically expanded the range of possible sexual identities and practices (Weeks, 1989, 2007; Swanson, 2007). Modern urban life as the facilitator of a diverse range of non-normative sexual encounters was a source of anxiety, which signalled a threat to the containment of sexuality within the marriage partnership (Swanson, 2007).

The boundaries of heterosexual interaction shifted in the interwar period, when it became socially acceptable for men to take unaccompanied women out to restaurants, theatres and clubs. This led to the blurring of the boundaries between respectable women and those in the role of prostitute or mistress (Cook, 2004). By the 1950s, a wife was perceived as a sexualised woman, who would ideally be willing and able to sexually pleasure her husband and, in turn, to be sexually gratified by this (ibid.). 'Expert' views on female sexuality were dominated by Freudian interpretations, according to which sexual desire and experience of vaginal orgasm were considered to be elements of 'mature' sexuality (Hall, 2000; Cook, 2004). Pleasurable sexual activity was important for emotional depth in marriages and families. Cook (2004) argues that in the 1940s and 1950s, engagement in, and enjoyment of, sexual activity with her husband became defined as part of a wife's marital duty. Increasingly, the failure of women to achieve orgasm was regarded as their own failing, rather than a shortcoming of their husband's sexual performance. This was part of a libertine shift in terms of understandings of heterosexual male sexuality, in which emphasis on masculine restraint was lifted and women's sexual role was seen as primarily to satisfy men.

Sex outside of marriage was largely considered to be unacceptable for women in the late 1950s and early 1960s. As a continuation of interwar trends, the notion existed that it was advantageous for women to experience some sexual activity prior to marriage, for example, mutual masturbation. This could be understood as acceptable for couples who intended to marry (Cook, 2004). An advice manual published in the 1950s suggested that sex might be beneficial between heterosexual couples who were committed to one another, but not yet married (Lewis, 1992). The manual was withdrawn, but its advice indicates that attitudes towards sex were beginning to shift as part of a heavily contested process. Women and girls who were viewed as 'promiscuous' were anathema to appropriate femininity in the mid-twentieth-century and 'promiscuity' was sometimes regarded as evidence of psychiatric disturbance (Cox, 2003). Motherhood outside of marriage was viewed as deviant and usually entailed social censure from the respectable (Fink and Holden, 1999). It was also constructed through expert discourses as indicative of psychological problems (see Young, 1954).

The marriage partnership was understood to be ideally a 'companionate' one, with women and men performing their allotted roles of homemaker and main breadwinner, whilst providing each other with support and comity (Finch and Summerfield, 1991). This had been a middle-class construction of ideal marriage from the 1930s onwards, and by the 1950s was arguably the ideal template for working-class marriages as well (Finch and Summerfield, 1991; Light, 1991). Companionate marriage was the modern form of heterosexual partnership, replacing the old-fashioned model of male domination and female submission, and understood as beneficial to the nation's citizens and their children (Collins, 2003; Holden, 2007). The emphasis was on 'equality, intimacy, sharing and communication' (Collins, 2003, p. 90). This does not mean that marriages were necessarily companionate in actuality and contemporary sociological studies, such as *Coal is our Life* (1956), suggest a more patriarchal model retained currency in certain working-class communities. Equality was conceived as a shift in status towards the valuing of the different roles women and men performed. The companionate marriage implied that husbands and fathers would be 'domestic' in the sense that they would enjoy spending time in the home with their families and would provide some assistance with the chores (Collins, 2003). It did not entail men sharing the full burden of domestic work and childcare. These remained women's work, both symbolically and in practice.

In mid-twentieth-century Britain, motherhood was constructed as the apotheosis of femininity (Riley, 1983; Fink, 2000). Women who did not bear children were frequently perceived to be unfulfilled and lacking, as motherhood was a ' "natural" driving force to all women' (Holden, 2007, p. 15). Psychoanalytic inspired expert opinion, popularised through magazines and radio broadcasts, emphasised the vital importance of the mother child bond and argued that without constant maternal attention, small children suffered irreparable psychological damage (see Winnicott, 1944; Bowlby, 1953). Although opinion such as this could be construed as designed to sequester women firmly in domestic space, post-war social policy did not involve a co-ordinated attempt to do so (Riley, 1983). The welfare settlement assumed nuclear families based on a male breadwinner/female carer model, but as discussed above, there were also inducements for married women to undertake paid work (Lewis, 1999). However, the perceived importance of motherhood to women's fulfilment and to children's well-being (and ultimately that of the nation) underlined women's position in the gender order as carers, and promoted an idealised vision of mothering, which was difficult to attain.

In the 1950s and early 1960s, respectability, 'having good social standing and [...] socially or conventionally acceptable morals and standards' was not solely a middle-class preserve and working-class women could be regarded as respectable (Tinkler, 2006, p. 133). However, this was experienced as a more contingent identity than for middle-class women (ibid.). For working-class women, respectability needed to be worked at and maintained. Sexual probity, financial restraint and domestic neatness and cleanliness were key markers of working-class respectability

(Roberts, 1995; Tebbutt, 1995). Women's appearance and the state of their homes were visual cues from which to read their level of respectability (Tinkler, 2006). Working-class men were also subject to standards of respectability, which included performing paid work sufficient to support their family, not drinking too much and refraining from brawls and street fights (Mort, 1999; Francis, 2002).

The Second World War helped to alter notions of citizenship and, more fundamentally, what it meant to be British. During and following the war, the symbolic status of working-class people increased (Rose, 2003). They came to symbolise the British 'people', a designation they were not accorded in the interwar period, when the 'people' were conceptualised as middle class (Light, 1991). Post war, the working class was attributed a higher level of humanity, a change aided by the 1945 Labour government and the institution of the welfare settlement, which included universal entitlement to secondary education and health care (Bonnett, 1998). Working-class people who were not respectable, those regarded as lazy, shiftless and dirty, were not understood to be part of the people, or, arguably, to attain the same level of humanity (Waters, 1997; Rose, 2003).

This change in the nature of citizenship and of 'Britishness' itself was not fully inclusive. The working class was conceptualised as 'white' and minority ethnic people were not included in the symbolic rendering of Britishness (Bonnett, 1998; Rose, 2003; Webster, 2007). White women were especially representative of the nation, specifically a homely, domesticated version of Britishness (Webster, 2001, 2007). They were the guardians of home and 'became a common image of a nation under siege by immigrants' (Webster, 2007, p. 10). Immigration from the Commonwealth increased sharply during the 1950s and the Immigration Act 1962 imposed restrictions on this for the first time (Saggar, 1999), making Britishness synonymous with whiteness both symbolically and legislatively. This had implications for minority ethnic people living in Britain, who were for the most part locked out of respectability and full citizenship, both in terms of formal legal equality and of figurative belonging (Waters, 1997; Rose, 2003; Webster, 2007).

Appreciation of the shifting and contested nature of aspects of femininity and women's experiences in mid-twentieth-century Britain is essential in order to effectively read the constructions of gender that arise from the analysis of the empirically researched cases. These cases occurred at a time of pivotal social and cultural change. They have also been chosen because they took place after the law regarding murder was overhauled by the Homicide Act 1957.

Homicide law in England and Wales in the 1950s

The law regarding homicide in England and Wales changed in 1957, largely as a result of contemporary debates about the use and application of the death penalty, which was a contentious issue (Christoph, 1962; Bailey, 2000). A Royal Commission on Capital Punishment was established in 1949 and delivered its report in 1953. The Commission's terms were narrowly defined to explore ways to limit, rather than abolish, the death penalty. After gathering evidence from a variety of experts, it recommended extension of the provocation defence and that the jury should decide on questions of insanity and criminal responsibility (this had previously been decided by the trial judge). It also suggested that death should not be the only punishment for murder available to the judge, but that life imprisonment should also be an option.[4] The Commission rejected the idea of introducing diminished responsibility as a partial defence to murder, and also eschewed suggestions for American-style degrees or types of murder (Cmnd. 8932, 1953).

In the 1950s, the notorious cases of Timothy Evans, Derek Bentley and Ruth Ellis intensified the debate surrounding the death penalty. Timothy Evans was executed in 1950 for the murder of his wife and baby. After initially confessing, he claimed his neighbour, John Christie, was responsible for the murders. Three years later, the remains of six women's bodies were discovered in and outside John's flat (Paget et al., 1953; Block and Hostettler, 1997). In 1953, Derek Bentley was present when his 16-year-old friend, Christopher Craig, shot a policeman. Derek was 19 and said to be of 'low intelligence'. Although according to the police he uttered 'Let him have it' before Christopher pulled the trigger, controversy surrounded whether Derek had in fact said this and, if so, what it meant. As a minor, Christopher was not eligible for execution and it was felt this may have influenced the decision not to reprieve Derek (Block and Hostettler, 1997).

Ruth Ellis' case caused particular unease and re-ignited discussion over whether women should be hanged. Unlike the cases of Timothy Evans and Derek Bentley, there was no doubt that Ruth was responsible for causing the death of her lover David Blakely, whom she shot five times outside a pub in London (Ballinger, 2000; Minkes and Vanstone, 2005). In 1955, she became the last English woman to be hanged. Analyses of Ruth's failure to win a reprieve have concentrated on her portrayal as a woman who violated 1950s gender norms. She had sexual relationships, and a child, outside of marriage and her job as a night club hostess was widely understood at the time to connote prostitution. It is suggested that Ruth's physical appearance of peroxide blonde hair and heavy make-up elicited disapproval and contributed to a perception of her as a 'promiscuous' and disreputable woman (Rose, 1988; Ballinger, 2000).

David's perceived caddish behaviour towards Ruth meant that she attracted sympathy from some members of the public and the execution of an attractive 28-year-old mother of two caused outrage and dismay (Block and Hostettler, 1997). A large crowd gathered outside the prison to protest on the night it was carried out (Block and Hostettler, 1997). Other mid-twentieth-century executions of women such as Margaret Allen and Styllou Christofi did not attract the same level of public support or interest and have not left the same imprint on the collective memory. Margaret Allen was executed in 1948 for the murder of an old woman whom she beat to death. Margaret appeared in court dressed in men's clothes and was perceived as homosexual (Ballinger, 2000; Oram, 2007). In 1954, Styllou Christofi strangled her daughter-in-law and set fire to her body. She was a 53-year-old Cypriot woman and could speak no English (Ballinger, 2000; Minkes and Vanstone, 2005). Ruth Ellis, who was white, British, relatively young, physically attractive and heterosexual, could more easily be assimilated into femininity than either Margaret Allen or Styllou Christofi. This may account for the public sympathy she received (see Pierrepoint, 1998).

The Homicide Act 1957 was passed in response to the recommendations of the Royal Commission on Capital Punishment and the controversy surrounding the executions of Evans, Bentley and Ellis. The Act legislated for some of the Commission's recommendations, such as widening the provocation defence to include 'things said' as well as 'things done'. Murder ceased to be a capital offence in all cases and a mandatory life sentence was introduced for non-capital cases. Against the Commission's recommendations, diminished responsibility was established as a partial defence, which would reduce murder to manslaughter in cases where the accused suffered from an 'abnormality of mind' at the time of the killing. The Act established a distinction between capital and non-capital murders, which was reminiscent of a system of degrees of murder. Certain types of murder were subject to the death penalty, such as those committed in the course of a robbery or if caused by a gun or explosion. Murder was also a capital offence if committed on two or more separate occasions (Edwards, 1957; Prevezer, 1957; Hughes, 1959).

The selected cases enable a close examination of the period after the Homicide Act, and of the significance of wider social and cultural shifts as British identities were being reshaped. In addition to contemporary gender norms and the law surrounding homicide, it is necessary to give an overview of the prosecution process in England and Wales in order to further contextualise the circumstances of the women's cases.

Mid-twentieth-century prosecutions for murder

Until the Magistrate's Court Act 1967, there was a committal hearing before the main trial in cases of murder, which was held in the Magistrate's Court. This was to establish whether there was a prima facie (sufficient evidence) case to proceed with (Wootton, 1978). The prosecution called its evidence and depositions (evidence taken under oath that can be used in court) were taken from the witnesses, and the defence had the opportunity to cross-examine them (Devlin, 1960). Anyone charged with murder was entitled to free legal representation (ibid.). In theory, a magistrate could find that there was no prima facie case, but in practice this was extremely rare, and the committal hearing was a precursor to a criminal trial held in the Assize or Central Criminal Court (Wootton, 1978).

The exceptions to this were if the defendant was found unfit to plead, or if they pled guilty to murder or a lesser charge, such as involuntary manslaughter (Devlin, 1960). Once committed, the murder charge was dismissed and the trial proceeded on the indictment, which stated the nature of the charge(s) with legal accuracy. The accused was arraigned upon the indictment, which was the formal reading of the criminal complaint in court, and pleaded to it. Before coming to trial, the case for the prosecution was prepared by solicitors in the office of the Director of Public Prosecutions (ibid.).

Before the trial, the accused was remanded in prison and kept in the prison hospital on the observation ward. This involved round the clock observation and regular written reports by nursing staff. The prisoner was interviewed by the prison medical officer, and he produced a report for the prosecution (HO/301, Evidence to the Royal Commission on Capital Punishment, Sir Frank Newsam, 4 August 1949). This contained the doctor's recommendation as to whether the accused was fit to stand trial and whether he thought she was suffering from diminished responsibility at the time of the killing. Frequently, the accused was also interviewed by a psychiatrist.

Once the case reached trial, the judge could withdraw it, if, in his opinion, there was not enough evidence. Judges also had the power to reject or exclude evidence. If the judge allowed a case to be heard, he could still direct the jury to find the defendant not guilty if he felt the case had not been sufficiently proved (Devlin, 1960). In court, the prosecution opened the trial with its argument against the accused, and called its evidence. The defence could cross-examine the witnesses. After the closing speech by the prosecution, the defence called its evidence, and the prosecution could cross-examine the defence's witnesses. The defendant could choose whether or not to give testimony in their own defence (their statement to the police was usually read out as evidence by the prosecution). The prosecution could call evidence in rebuttal, for example, an expert medical witness to refute a defence of diminished responsibility (see Rock, 1993 on the conventions of the criminal trial).

After the closing argument of the defence, the judge made his summing up. This summarised the evidence of the case that had been put to the court and directed the jury as to which options were open to them – for example, whether they could find the defendant guilty of manslaughter due to provocation or diminished responsibility, rather than murder. The judge's summing up did not have to allot equal time to both sides, and he could give his own opinion and suggest (although not direct) which way the jury should make their decision (Allen, 2004). However, this did not necessarily mean the jury would choose the verdict indicated by the summing up. Until the 1960s, the jury was selected from adults who owned property or paid a certain amount of rent per month. Therefore, poor or itinerant members of society were not eligible for jury service (Blom-Cooper and Morris, 2004). Until the 1970s, women could be prevented from sitting on juries, either by a peremptory challenge from the defendant or by the judge's discretion. Judges tended to exercise this power in cases perceived to be shocking. For example, no women sat on the jury for the trial of Myra Hindley and Ian Brady in 1966 (Logan, 2008).

As mentioned above, murder was subject to mandatory sentencing, but manslaughter, or any other charge of which the defendant may have been found guilty, was subject to discretionary sentencing. Those women who were found guilty could apply for leave to appeal against their conviction (convictions could be overturned, but the Court of Criminal Appeal could not order retrials until 1964 (Samuels, 1964)) and the women found guilty of manslaughter could apply for leave to appeal against the length of their sentence (Thomas, 1964).

Sample selection

The empirically researched cases explored in this book all occurred after the Homicide Act became law in March 1957. The death penalty had been restricted, and the new defence of diminished responsibility could be used. Only one woman, Mary Wilson in 1958, was sentenced to death after the Homicide Act (the last executions to be carried out in England and Wales were in 1964, before the death penalty's effective abolition in 1965). Her case is analysed in the section on the witch discourse.

The mid-twentieth-century examples have been selected from cases of women accused of unusual murders between March 1957 and the end of 1962. They were identified from Morris and Blom-Cooper's (1964) *A Calendar of Murder*. This contains a thumb nail sketch of all the 764 murder indictments in England and Wales during this period. As such, it is an invaluable source for identifying unusual cases involving women from this time, as unlike official statistics, details of each killing are provided. Another advantage is that it includes women indicted for murder, rather than simply those convicted of it, meaning that cases where women were acquitted or found guilty of a lesser charge are discussed.

During the period Morris and Blom-Cooper (1964) cover, 98 women were indicted for murder. Of these, 18 fit the definition of being unusual outlined in the introduction. Twelve of these cases are analysed in relation to discourses of femininity. Of the remaining six cases, four have case files still closed to the public, preventing close analysis. Two exhibited only fragmentary discursive constructions of femininity. This is partly due to having more limited documentation than in some of the other cases, but also because a particular interpretation (or particular competing interpretations) of their womanhood does not emerge from the available documents. Shards of meaning in relation to how their femininity was constructed and understood can be discerned, but there is not enough evidence to reconstruct their cases in way that I have for the other 12. I have written about one of these women, Alice Lyons, elsewhere and explored how she was seen as pitiable (Seal, 2009b). The other, Hilde Adames, was found unfit to plead for reasons of insanity. This accorded her a marginal status in the criminal justice system and it could be that the absence of a clear discursive representation of her womanhood highlights the marginalisation and silencing of defendants in this category. However, the methodological limitations attached to analysing her case make drawing firm conclusions impossible. The details of both cases are included as an appendix.

Analysing textual material

Part II applies the model of five discourses of femininity that recur in cases of women accused of unusual murder to empirically researched cases from mid-twentieth-century England and Wales. This involved analysing documents from case files that are held in The National Archives, London. These files contain witness statements, depositions, police reports and medical reports, and provide a wide range of material that emerged from different stages of the criminal justice process. In cases where an appeal was attempted, there is also the judgment of the appeal court and extracts from the trial transcript. Newspaper reports have also been accessed as a means of gaining further information about the women's trials.

Analysis of files from mid-twentieth-century English and Welsh cases of women accused of unusual murder allows a close reading of criminal justice documents and the use of direct quotes from this material in order to explore discourses of femininity. The constructions of womanhood that appear in these cases can be firmly placed within the context of their particular place and time, with reference to the cultural and social forces that shaped them. They can also be read for how the particularly symbolic nature of femininity means that representations of womanhood also relate to contemporary hopes, fears and anxieties.

Some of the empirically researched cases were high profile at the time but others were not, and received scant attention from the newspapers. The purpose of the analysis of these mid-twentieth-century women's cases is to explore how representations of femininity arose in the criminal justice system (Robertson, 2005) and to examine the role of these discourses in mundane, as well as notorious, examples. In their analysis of newspaper representations of women who kill men in California, Bakken and Farrington (2009, p. 8) state that 'questions of gender and image extended beyond the coverage of high profile cases' and D'Cruze et al. (2006) similarly argue that issues of gender, 'race' and class emerge from cases that exemplify the banal, as well as the spectacular. The value of paying attention to cases that either did not become or remain well known is that they demonstrate both how the negotiation and reproduction of norms of gender, class and 'race'/ethnicity were part of the everyday workings of the prosecution process and how the workings of the criminal justice system exhibited contemporary concerns about the state of society. The discussion of each discourse of femininity is undertaken in relation to contested meanings of modernity in the late 1950s and early 1960s, and connects the representations of the women to the historical literature on, for example, sexuality, motherhood and respectability in mid-twentieth-century Britain. As Canning (2006) argues, the historical analysis of discourses of femininity must link texts to context.

Another important contextual detail to consider is the institutional nature of the case file documents. For the most part, documents such as police reports and medical reports reflect the institutional and expert discourses of the criminal justice system, not the views of the female defendants or the victims' families. These voices are difficult to uncover, as statements and interviews were recorded by criminal justice personnel and cannot be unproblematically regarded as the views and opinions of the people from whom they were taken (D'Cruze, 2001; Robertson, 2005). Sources such as the defendant's statement to the police or the psychiatrist's report result from exchanges that were asymmetrical in terms of power relations and social position (Thornborrow, 2002). This must be acknowledged when undertaking the analysis. However, discourse analysis regards all texts as complex and multi-layered, arising from intricate matrices of power and is therefore the best method for approaching texts of this nature.

Case file documents are hugely significant, as they played an active role in the lives of the women to whom they relate (Prior, 2003). The narrative of the case constructed by the police report frequently shaped the narrative created by the prosecution. The assessments of prison doctors and psychiatrists influenced the type of defence the women could use, and the disposals they received. The focus on the discourses of femininity the files produce does, however, mean that the women's own voices remain largely submerged, as they do in criminal justice settings. The power to define 'truth' in the cases lies mainly with criminal justice personnel such as police officers, psychiatrists and judges rather than with defendants and ordinary witnesses (Valverde, 2003).

The fact that the documents represent institutional and expert discourses is not detrimental to the analysis, as Part II is concerned with decoding mid-twentieth-century representations of femininity that appeared in the criminal justice system and relating these to significant socio-cultural shifts. The focus of this book is on uncovering how analysis of the symbolic representation of femininity in unusual cases of women accused of murder also uncovers contested cultural meanings. Documents held in prosecution files, which are stored in the National Archives, are products of the bureaucratic functioning of the state and construct official meanings. A cultural analysis reveals how these official meanings are redolent with the wider hopes, fears and anxieties of their place and time, which helps to demonstrate the limits of their fixity in the face of impending social and cultural change.

Although emblematic of state power, the criminal justice system should not be construed as monolithic or as automatically oppressive in every instance (Valverde, 2003). Prosecuting murder in the 1950s and early 1960s involved police officers, doctors, clerks, solicitors, barristers and the judge. These various actors did not necessarily tell the same story about a case. For instance, a police report can be far more sympathetic towards the defendant than the argument made by the prosecution barrister in court. The judge's summing up could lean towards the defence's argument, rather than the prosecution's. The jury did not always reach the verdict the judge's summing up favoured. The focus on the production of discourses of femininity against a backdrop of shifting norms and identities requires us to interpret the creation of meaning as a dynamic process, rather than a static, unidirectional one.

Techniques of discourse analysis

Discourse analysis and techniques drawn from deconstruction were used to perform close textual analysis of sources such as witness statements, police reports, medical reports, trial transcripts and newspaper stories. Although it is possible to follow a particular model or scheme of discourse analysis, a 'multiperspectival' approach was adopted instead, which employs a variety of concepts as and when they are deemed useful (Phillips and Jorgensen, 2002). These concepts were chosen after engaging with the case files, and have been judged appropriate to the analysis of gender construction in unusual cases of women accused of murder. These concepts guided the analysis of the documents and, along with awareness of the historical context, were important for identifying constructions of gender. They have been used with a light touch in the discussion of the cases, in that the concepts shape the analysis but are not referred to explicitly.

One such concept is the nodal point (Laclau and Mouffe, 2001). This is a privileged discursive point that allows for the contingent fixation of meaning within a discourse. Female subject positions are constituted in relation to the privileged position of appropriate femininity, with deviant and 'failed' femininities negatively constructed in relation to it. Feminine identities radiate out from the nodal point of appropriate femininity. The closer they are to it, the greater social and cultural value they have (Laclau and Mouffe, 2001). In mid-twentieth-century Britain, married motherhood operated as a nodal point, with the value of other feminine identities being assigned relationally.

Concepts related to the dynamic, interactive nature of texts help to further illuminate the analysis. These include polyvalence, the potential for the same text to generate multiple meanings (Foucault, 1979), and multivocality, the possibility for identifying multiple voices within the text (Bakhtin, 1986). These enable understanding of the emergence of inconsistencies and contradictions. The case file material is understood as dialogic, that is, it inevitably speaks against the existing background of what has previously been spoken (Bakhtin, 1986). This background includes the criminal law, relevant statute and the institutional functioning of the criminal justice system, but it also includes the wider social and cultural field of gender representation and social change in mid-twentieth-century Britain.

Another useful concept is that of the shadow discourse. This is a discourse that conditions meaning without being explicitly present (Castle, 1993). The witch representation is an example of this as there is no explicit labelling of women as witches in mid-twentieth-century criminal justice documents. Rather, elements of the witch discourse, such as an emphasis on women's bad character or their marginal position within their community, shape their representation.

Iterability is a notion drawn from deconstructionist theories. It refers to the process by which words and phrases gain meaning through being repeatable, but in their repetition, change or modify their meanings slightly (Binder and Weisberg, 2000). For example, 'prostitute' is a symbol of feminine deviance that has long-held negative meanings, which are repeatable in different contexts. However, it is modified by the particular social and historical context in which it is constructed. In mid-twentieth-century Britain, understandings of 'prostitute' were shaped by changes in legislation such as the Street Offences Act 1959 and cultural shifts regarding the greater acceptability of unaccompanied women in public space. Iteration is key to understanding why gender constructions in unusual cases of women who kill (and of womanhood more generally) may have certain commonalities and continuities across different times and places. However, representations across time and place also have differences and specificities, which is why a study of a particular context such as mid-twentieth-century Britain is illuminating.

Finally, for a multiperspectival discourse analysis of cases of women accused of murder, the Derridean concept of haunting is useful. Texts often carry the traces and echoes of older discourses and they are haunted by these past constructions (Derrida, 1994). This helps to understand why documents such as police reports, medical reports and trial transcripts from the mid-twentieth century can contain traces of older constructions of deviant feminine identities such as 'lesbian' or 'prostitute' that echo late-nineteenth-century conceptualisations. The rest of Part II is devoted to the analysis of 12 mid-twentieth-century cases of women accused of murder. It employs the same typology of discourses of femininity used in Part I, but, as it concentrates on a tightly defined time period, gives greater attention to the cultural meanings the discourses reflected and generated.

2
Gender Representations of Twelve Mid-Twentieth-Century Women Accused of Murder

The masculine woman

By the 1950s in Britain, perceived 'masculinity' in women was associated with lesbianism or 'female homosexuality'. Jennings (2007b) argues that post-war discourses of lesbian identity were variously constructed in medical texts, popular psychology, magazines and newspapers and by lesbian women themselves. For the cases explored in this section, medical and psychological representations of female homosexuality are particularly relevant, as these understandings shaped the portrayal of the women in question as 'masculine' in the criminal justice system. According to many psychiatric and popular psychological explanations for 'female homosexuality', lesbians were immature, emotionally stunted women, who were 'unable to develop equal relationships and prone to angry outbursts and alcoholism' (ibid., p. 3). They were destined for unhappy, tragic relationships with other women, which, it was believed, could not be properly fulfilling (see Bergler, 1958). Female homosexuality was also understood to be related to heightened aggression and masculine traits (Magee and Miller, 1992).

After emerging during the interwar period, lesbian identities in Britain were consolidated in the 1950s and 1960s as a recognisable lesbian subculture and nightlife developed in London and other urban areas. At this time, women developed their own social networks and their own understandings of lesbianism as a sexual identity. Nevertheless, 'same sex desire between women in post-war Britain was shaped and defined by silence' (Jennings, 2007b, p. 6). Lesbianism was severely at odds with the contemporary normative ideal of marriage and motherhood for women. The three mid-twentieth-century cases discussed below need to be understood within this context of female homosexuality as taboo in 'mainstream' culture, and as a subjectivity frequently constructed through expert medical discourses as pathologically abnormal.

Yvonne Jennion

Yvonne Jennion, a 23-year old, was found guilty of murder and sentenced to life in prison in 1958. She lived in St Helens, north-west England, with her mother and 4-year-old daughter. She had never been married and did not have a job. Yvonne visited her aunt, Ivy, one morning in October in order to borrow some money. Ivy lectured her about being unemployed and living off her relatives. When Yvonne responded angrily, Ivy slapped her face and the two women began fighting. When Ivy's back was turned, Yvonne hit her across the head with a heavy ashtray, leapt on top of her and manually strangled her. She then took the cord out of a pair of pyjamas that were in the room and finished strangling Ivy with this.

Yvonne was known to the local police, but their suspicions were also aroused by the fact that she was the last person to see Ivy alive. In a witness statement, she maintained that as she left the house, she noticed that Ivy's gate was unlocked and that 'any man could get in and get her' (DPP2/2834, Police report, 14 October 1958). The police took another statement from Yvonne, this time a suspect, in which she admitted to having killed Ivy.

Yvonne appears to have led a troubled adolescence, during which she ran away from home several times. As a result of running away, she twice spent time in approved school.[1] She was interviewed by a child psychiatrist at the age of 15, who diagnosed a severe neurotic conduct disorder, which was manifested in being out of her mother's control (her father died when she was 14) and in her 'promiscuous' sexual behaviour. The latter referred to lorry drivers Yvonne claimed to have had sex with when she ran away. The psychiatrist suggested that she experienced severe anxiety about her basic sexual identity and that she feared she might be homosexual.

The trial proceedings were shaped by the fact Yvonne had admitted causing Ivy's death. The question was not whether she had killed her aunt, but whether she was fully responsible for her actions and therefore a murderer. Her defence was diminished responsibility due to psychopathic personality disorder and simple schizophrenia. The prosecution countered that she was 'bad tempered' and 'immoral' rather than ill. Expert psychiatric witnesses appeared for both sides. The judge's summing up was sympathetic to the defence's argument of diminished responsibility, but the jury found Yvonne guilty of murder.

The masculine woman discourse in Yvonne's case was structured by the child psychiatrist's report from when she was 15, a copy of which is included in her case file. The report states that she 'showed more of the adventurous virile spirit of a boy than the gentler feminine instincts natural to her sex' and had 'so much of the masculine in her make-up that she may develop into a homo-sexual, as so many of them [masculine girls] do' (DPP2/2834, Child psychiatrist's report, 12 May 1950). The police report and prison medical officer's report both summarise the child psychiatrist's opinion that, aged 15, Yvonne was considered to be in danger of becoming homosexual. Under cross-examination at the committal hearing, a detective chief inspector opined, 'I would describe her as being mannish, and to a point, irresponsible. I agree that she is abnormal' (DPP2/2834, Detective Chief Inspector Dowson's deposition, 29 October 1958). The description of Yvonne as 'mannish' was repeated in the psychiatrist's report carried out whilst she was in prison and by the judge in his summing up.

The appearance of the masculine woman discourse in Yvonne's case appears a little confusing as her sexual relationships in adulthood seem to have been with men, for instance, her relationship with the father of her child. The perception of Yvonne as a lesbian or 'female homosexual', a medicalised term frequently employed in the 1950s (see Caprio, 1957), appears to have been largely based on the child psychiatrist's report and her supposedly 'mannish' demeanour and behaviour. She also claimed in an interview with a psychiatrist that she had sexual experiences with other girls whilst at approved school.

Psychoanalytic constructions of homosexuality argued that it could be latent and was not necessarily manifested in actual same sex relationships with women (Magee and Miller, 1992). The child psychiatrist's report on Yvonne mentioned her 'disregard for her appearance, and tomboyish behaviour' as indications that she was homosexual, and that 'she remained more of a boy than a girl until the age of puberty' (DPP2/2834, Child psychiatrist's report, 12 May 1950). His comment that Yvonne was 'more of a boy than a girl' recalls the inversion construction of early-twentieth-century sexology explored in Part I.

The defence utilised the portrayal of Yvonne as masculine to support their case of diminished responsibility. The defence cross-examination of Eva Jennion, Yvonne's mother, sought to bolster the argument that Yvonne had always been mannish and therefore strange. She revealed that as a child Yvonne preferred 'boyish games' and 'the company of boys'. When asked if Yvonne liked to wear boys' clothes, her mother replied, 'Yes, if she could get them' (J82/160, Defence cross-examination of Eva Jennion, 8 December 1958).

The construction of the invert emerged most clearly in Yvonne's case in the judge's summing up of her trial. He advised the jury:

> If I were sitting as one of your number I would be inclined to think of the case along these lines – I suppose it is not nearly subtle enough for the mental doctors, psychiatrists, or the like – but I cannot help thinking that if she is partly a young man with the body of a woman she must be emotionally queer. (J82/160, Judge's summing up, 9 December 1958)

The judge acknowledged that his interpretation was balder and more simplified than that of the expert evidence heard during the trial. His characterisation of the 'young man with the body of a woman', whether he realised it or not, echoed Hirschfeld's (1913) formulation of homosexuality as a 'third sex', where it was possible for a man to exist in the body of a woman.

The prison medical officer questioned Yvonne about her sexuality when he interviewed her. This is likely to have been because of the influence of the contemporary psychoanalytic notion that sexuality was central to human behaviour, and the criminological interpretation of women's offending as being related to sexuality. He would also have had the opportunity to read the child psychiatrist's report that diagnosed Yvonne as homosexual. He stated:

> She maintains she is essentially homosexual, and indulged in certain homosexual practices during the period she was at the approved school... It would, therefore, appear that she is abnormally sexed and comes into the category of bisexual having an interest in both forms of sexual activity. (DPP2/2834, Prison medical officer's report, 31 October 1958)

Like the prison medical officer, the psychiatrists who assessed Yvonne focused on her sexuality. The report of one asserts, 'She said she had lesbian experiences with another girl while in an approved school on a fifty fifty basis' (DPP2/2834, 30 November 1958). These statements about Yvonne's sexuality need to be understood within the context of exchanges that were profoundly unequal in terms of power relations. It cannot be known exactly how Yvonne characterised her sexuality, or how much significance she attached to her answers. What survives in the archival record was shaped by expert medical interpretations, as it was the doctors who wrote the reports. However, Yvonne's agreement that she was homosexual formed an important part of her diminished responsibility defence.

The defence employed the masculine woman discourse to provide a psychological explanation for the aggression Yvonne displayed in killing Ivy. They drew on contemporary associations between lesbianism, masculinity, psychopathy and violence. During the cross-examination of the pathologist at Yvonne's trial, the defence counsel stressed the 'frenzied' nature of the attack upon Ivy, and asked

> would you be prepared to say or not as to whether the particular injuries and damage you found indicated that it was rather out of character with a woman having caused it – a normal, sane, self-controlled woman? (J82/160, Defence cross-examination of pathologist, 8 December 1958)

The defence argued that Yvonne was abnormal and therefore not fully responsible for her actions. It called two expert medical witnesses who testified that she had mental disorders; one that she had psychopathic personality disorder, and the other that she had psychopathic personality disorder and simple schizophrenia. The judge's summing up suggested that the link between lesbianism and pathological violence argued by the defence was a plausible one:

> It could be the position, perhaps, here, having regard to her trouble – she maintained that she derived no sexual satisfaction, although she tried it with men, except with people of her own sex – that something happened, may be [sic] one of the very things described which, in this case, caused her to behave in a manner which was as the Prison Doctor said, impulsive and explosive, but also without her intent. (J82/160, Judge's summing up, 9 December 1958)

The masculine woman discourse was used strategically by the defence in attempt to gain a lesser verdict in a case where the perpetration of the crime was not in doubt. This tactic did not work for Yvonne, who was found guilty of murder, despite the judge's summing up. This indicates the difficulty of using a devalued subjectivity, such as the masculine woman, as a defence.

The prosecution countered the defence of diminished responsibility by calling rebutting medical evidence, which argued Yvonne could be regarded as legally responsible for her actions. The prosecution counsel did not explicitly contradict the masculine woman representation, as his description of Yvonne as a 'bad tempered', 'immoral' woman who had committed a 'brutal' murder was to an extent in keeping with this discourse (J82/160, Prosecution closing argument, 8 December 1958). It was not in the prosecution's interest to re-feminise Yvonne, but simply to dispute that her undesirable qualities were grounds for a verdict of manslaughter.

Norma Everson

Norma's case is also one in which the masculine woman discourse was prominent and closely tied to perceptions of her sexuality. In 1961, she was found guilty of the murder of Winifred Lord, a neighbour. On the June night of the killing, Norma returned to the flat she shared with her friend Gladys, having already been to Winifred's house to see if Gladys was there. She discovered that the door to the bedroom she shared with Gladys was locked, so she banged on it. When Gladys opened the door, Norma saw that Winifred was in bed and realised that Gladys and Winifred had been in bed together. She was 'furious' and told Gladys to leave the room (CRIM1/3700, Norma's statement, 8 June 1961). While Gladys was making a cup of tea, Norma stabbed Winifred four times, killing her. She then left the flat and went to a friend's house.

Norma and Gladys resided in north London. They had lived together at different addresses for approximately 4 years and they shared a bedroom. Not long before Norma stabbed Winifred, Gladys had left the flat and sent a letter claiming she had gone to a holiday camp. She was in fact a few streets away at Winifred's house. Norma had asked Gladys not to invite Winifred to their flat again, which accounted for her anger on the night of the killing.

Norma was 33 and worked as a van driver. As a younger woman, she had been in the army. A week before stabbing Winifred, she had tried to gas herself. On the day of the killing, Norma had not eaten for 2 days, had drunk heavily and taken prescription medication containing barbiturates. A psychiatrist who examined her recommended that there were sufficient grounds for a diminished responsibility defence, but her defence at trial was one of provocation. Norma claimed that Winifred tried to attack her and ran onto the knife herself. She also maintained that when she left the flat, she did not realise Winifred was dead. The prosecution stressed that Winifred had been stabbed four times and that when the police arrived to take Norma in for questioning, she nodded her head. She was found guilty of murder.

The mannish lesbian trope figured prominently in the medical professionals' reports on Norma. Her perceived masculinity was identified from her appearance and behaviour, rather than any description from Norma of sexual experiences with women:

> Upon examination she was dressed in trousers and pullover, and her changes of attire have followed this pattern whilst she has been custody. She was a tanned, strong featured woman whose general health was good. (CRIM1/3700, Prison medical officer's report, 12 July 1961)

> It could be said from the prisoner's mode of dress which is masculine and from the kind of occupations she has engaged in that she has shown some evidence of a more masculine orientation than the average woman. (CRIM1/3700, Psychiatrist's report, 17 July 1961)

The comments about the masculine nature of Norma's attire need to understood within their mid-twentieth-century context. Respectable women rarely wore trousers and conventional dress entailed skirts, high heels and use of make-up (Tinkler, 2006). Norma's trousers and pullover may have been interpreted as the clothing of a 'butch' lesbian, who was the 'masculine' party in a lesbian relationship (see Jennings, 2006). The medical reports echo Krafft-Ebing (1894) in their stress upon Norma's masculinity as demonstrated by her choice of clothes and her 'occupations' as a van driver and time spent in the army.

The doctors involved in Norma's case assumed that she and Gladys were in a sexual relationship, although Norma insisted that they were not. The psychiatrist stated:

> having read the statements of certain witnesses and the police history, I was naturally concerned in examining the prisoner to enquire into to her attitude to sexual matters. The prisoner said that sex was a subject which she had always found embarrassing to discuss and which she had not even discussed with Miss Power [Gladys]. She said that she had at no time in her life experienced any sexual attraction towards anyone. (CRIM1/3700, Psychiatrist's report, 17 July 1961)

Unlike Yvonne's case, the doctors who assessed Norma did not suggest that lesbian orientation connoted mental illness. The psychiatrist concluded that Norma's denial of homosexuality meant that sexual jealousy should be excluded as a motive for killing Winifred. He claimed that Norma felt provoked by Winifred and recommended:

Since it would appear that a plea of diminished responsibility will be made in this case on the grounds that the prisoner was seriously provoked at a time when she was under the influence of drugs and alcohol, further investigation of the latter possibility would seem to be preferable to the expression of opinions [about sexual jealousy] which must be speculative. (Ibid.)

Despite this, Norma's defence was provocation rather than diminished responsibility, probably because her own narrative of the killing argued that she felt threatened by Winifred. The psychiatrist's report suggests that the pathological aspects of female homosexuality would have been worth exploring if Norma had been willing to overtly adopt a lesbian subjectivity.

Norma's rejection of a lesbian identity did not prevent her relationship with Gladys from coming under scrutiny during her trial. The judge's summing up described Norma and Gladys as 'friendly, you may think in an abnormal and perhaps perverted friendly way' and noted 'they lived together, at any rate part of the time, with quarrels and reconciliations' (J82/150, Judge's summing up, 25 July 1961). He also reminded the jury that Norma 'gave a large part of her earnings to Miss Power' (ibid.). This last detail underlined Norma's putative masculinity as it appeared she had appropriated the 'masculine' role in the relationship, subverting a key heterosexual norm of the mid–twentieth century; that of providing economically for a dependent or semi-dependent woman.

The portrayal of Yvonne and Norma as masculine women was closely tied to their perceived lesbian sexuality. Their unconventional lifestyles and use of violent behaviour also contributed to this discourse, as constructing them as masculine women provided an explanation for their aberrant actions. However, it is also worth considering the significance of the two women's social class backgrounds.

Although working class, neither woman was desperately poor or marginalised. Yvonne's delinquent past and time in approved school marked her as disreputable, as did her status as an unmarried mother (see section 'The witch' on mid-twentieth-century perceptions of unmarried motherhood). Being a lone mother accounted for her lack of employment, as she had been dismissed from positions because of this. Respectable working-class women of her age would be married if mothers and in paid work if single. Yvonne was outside of these categories. The ideal feminine performance for a young working-class woman in the 1950s entailed a visible effort to appear well groomed and attractive, without being too glamorous and therefore 'common' (Tinkler, 2006). Yvonne's rejection of this performance contributed to her discursive construction as 'mannish'. She was an unmarried mother who lived in a female headed household and as such was outside of heterosexual norms. This, combined with her propensity for running away as an adolescent, also pushed her further from appropriate femininity and contributed to the masculine woman representation.

The case file material on Norma suggests that she was perceived as a 'butch' lesbian which was associated with working-class lesbian women. Feminine working-class women engaged in occupations such as cleaning, hair-dressing, low-level clerical positions or worked on factory production lines. Norma's job as a van driver was unconventional and 'masculine'. Mid-twentieth-century working-class women were already one step removed from ideal femininity, which connoted an upper middle-class standard of avoiding work, paid or unpaid, which was dirty and unpleasant (Giles, 2005). Women such as Norma and Yvonne, who did not participate in an ongoing performance of femininity in terms of their appearance and lifestyle, were open to construction as masculine.

Marilyn Bain

Early one morning in September 1962, either Marilyn, 25, or her flatmate, Jan, 33, phoned for an ambulance to collect Jan from the flat they shared in London. She had a knife wound. Both women had stayed up all night, drinking and playing Ludo. At some point, they had started quarrelling and physically fighting. Marilyn had injured Jan in the ribs with a knife, although she could not remember doing so. At the request of the police, she later searched the flat and found a blood stained knife in the kitchen, which she gave to them. Jan began to recover in hospital, but her wound became infected, and 3 days after being stabbed, she died from peritonitis. At the committal hearing, the pathologist stated that from the position of the wound, it could have been caused by Jan 'falling' or 'pitching' against the knife and it was in a part of her body that required little pressure to cause the injury (CRIM1/4013, Pathologist's deposition, 16 October 1962). Although indicted for murder, the court accepted Marilyn's plea of guilty to involuntary manslaughter and there was no trial. She was sentenced to 3 years in prison.

Marilyn was working as an army nurse in 1959, when she met Jan at the Gateways, a lesbian club. Later that year she was demobbed, and went to live with her. Marilyn was barred from the club in 1960 for being drunk, but Jan continued to go there. They had a sexual relationship until Marilyn started seeing a man, and 'homo-sexual relations' (CRIM1/4013, Marilyn Bain's statement, 17 September 1962) between the two women stopped. Jan engaged in sexual intercourse with men for payment and Marilyn earned money from performing 'nude exhibitions' (CRIM1/4013, Prison medical officer's report, 2 October 1962) for some of Jan's clients. She also received money from her family, whom she told she was working as a nurse. In 1960, Marilyn was placed on probation for 18 months for stealing two wing mirrors off a car whilst drunk. Her probation officer arranged for her to attend a clinic for alcoholism, and she went three or four times.

Unlike Yvonne and Norma, Marilyn was not constructed as sexually abnormal, but as someone who lived a dissolute life. This could partly be due to her own statement, in which she described her relationship with Jan as 'homo-sexual at first'. However, she began to have arguments with Jan after their 'homosexual relations' stopped when Marilyn started seeing a man. She explained that, 'The rows between us were caused because Jan wished she could be normal like me' (CRIM1/4013, Marilyn Bain's statement). Marilyn explicitly defined her sexuality as 'normal' and this may have influenced how she was perceived by the psychiatrist and prison medical officer who examined her.

The prison medical officer's report did not pay close attention to the issue of homosexuality, but made reference to Marilyn 'engaging in homosexual intimacies with the deceased' during an account of her life in which he stated 'she allowed herself to drift aimlessly doing odd jobs, indulging excessively in alcoholic intoxicants' (CRIM1/4013, Prison medical officer's report). He continued, 'According to her story the deceased and herself often fought with each other and inflicted injuries on each other during their frequent drunken orgies' (ibid.). The psychiatrist's report described Marilyn as having an 'apathetic and fatalistic attitude to her way of life' and as a 'drifter' (CRIM1/4013, Psychiatrist's report, 15 October 1962). 'Drifting' was understood to be a characteristic of the mid-twentieth-century 'good time girl' (Swanson, 2007). Marilyn appeared to live a life that directly contravened 'respectable' working-class or lower middle-class womanhood, which for a single woman would entail commitment to a steady job. Echoing the prison medical officer, the psychiatrist's report stated:

> At the time of the assault on the victim she and the prisoner appear to have been some hours in a drunken orgy during the evening and

night... These orgies appear not to have been uncommon in their lives. (CRIM1/4013, Psychiatrist's report)

Use of the term 'orgies' by both doctors constructs Marilyn and Jan as disreputable, drunken women and as sexually deviant, drawing on interpretations of lesbian women as alcoholic and prone to outbursts of temper (see Jennings, 2007b). This was despite the fact that according to Marilyn, she and Jan did not have a sexual relationship by the time of the killing. Her account of the evening and night that she injured Jan describes how they drank and played Ludo together, but appears to provide little scope for conceptualising it as an 'orgy'. However, the doctors seemed to regard Marilyn as leading a dissolute life of the underworld and this informed their perception.

The prison medical officer recorded that:

During her period in the hospital her behaviour has given concern to the nursing staff, who consider she exerted a bad influence on the other hospital inmates, and suspected her of engaging or attempting to engage in homosexual activities. (CRIM1/4013, Prison medical officer's report)

Although offered as an indication of Marilyn's disruptiveness, there was no suggestion from the doctor that she should be regarded as mentally abnormal. He described her as having no disease of mind, mental disorder or abnormality of mind, and the psychiatrist suggested that she was in a 'diminished state of awareness... due to fatigue and alcohol, but I do not think there is evidence of any other relevant psychiatric disturbance' (CRIM1/4013, Psychiatrist's report).

The representation of Yvonne, Norma and Marilyn as masculine demonstrates the importance of perceived incorrect or deviant performances of gender. Marilyn was not constructed as pathological, but the doctors' judgemental descriptions of her unsavoury lifestyle located her in a seedy, disreputable milieu, which they portrayed as essential to understanding her subjectivity. This incorporated contemporary interpretations of lesbianism (and male homosexuality) as an aspect of a licentious, sordid urban underworld.

The centrality of the heterosexual partnership as the normative ideal in1950s Britain has led this period to be described as a 'heterosexual dictatorship' (Weeks, 2007). In the context of mid-twentieth-century anxieties about male homosexuality, Weeks (2007, p. 21) argues that, '[a] new preoccupation with, and campaigns against, sexual perversity only underlined the terrors beneath the patina of normality'. Denunciations of lesbianism as pathological or dissolute indicated unease about the stability of womanhood as synonymous with marriage and motherhood. In different ways, the three women led lives that represented alternatives to this model, even if their lifestyles were open to derision and social censure. Yvonne was perceived as a promiscuous lone mother, Norma as a lesbian and Marilyn as perhaps not essentially lesbian, but a member of London's underworld, which existed in contravention to respectable society. In particular, Norma and Marilyn appear to have been members of the social networks of lesbian women that developed in London the 1950s and 1960s (see Jennings, 2007b). In keeping with derogatory, medicalised contemporary understandings of lesbianism, these unconventional lifestyles figured in the cases as key to understanding the women's transgressive, violent behaviour.

If we interpret the end of the 1950s and beginning of the 1960s in Britain as a time when gender and sexual relations were in flux, albeit with the heterosexual partnership as the recognised norm, the gender constructions of Yvonne, Norma and Marilyn in the criminal justice system can be understood as anxious institutional reactions to the possibility of diversity, rather than as effects of a monolithic social order. However, it is necessary to understand this within the context of an era when sexualities apart from heterosexuality completely lacked citizenship status (Weeks, 2007) and lesbian identities were largely invisible. Jennings (2007b) and Oram (2007) have analysed how 1950s newspaper reports of mid-twentieth-century murder trials involving lesbian perpetrators contributed to contemporary discourses of lesbian identity. A similar analysis cannot be undertaken of the three cases discussed in this section. Whilst Norma and Marilyn's cases barely made it into print, Yvonne's trial was reported in the national and local press. Although the local press carried detailed stories, they expunged any mention of her supposed homosexuality.

The muse/mastermind dichotomy

In exploring constructions of lesbianism, the previous section highlighted the centrality of heterosexuality to acceptable mid-twentieth-century British subjectivities. For women, this entailed marriage and motherhood, particularly as white women represented the private, domesticated spaces of idealised 'Britishness' (Webster, 2007). At the same time, norms of sexuality were shifting in the post-war era and there was a plurality of heterosexual identities (Swanson, 2007). Although in the late 1950s and early 1960s, sex was preferably to be confined to marriage, there were indications that views were beginning to shift. Sexual desire for the opposite sex during adolescence was considered normal and healthy (Jackson, 2008), although girls who acted on this desire could be viewed as psychologically abnormal (Cox, 2003).

Marilyn Bain, whose case was analysed in the previous section, was identified as a member of a seedy, metropolitan underworld, which permitted sordid behaviour such as lesbianism. Both of the mid-twentieth-century cases constructed through the muse/mastermind discourse located the women in question in a perceived urban underworld, although the city in question was Birmingham. Post-war hopes and anxieties about modernity centred on the city. British urban life represented opportunity and new experiences but it could also symbolise commotion, disorderliness and 'unmooring' (Swanson, 2007, p. 3). Cities were locales where gender and sexual identities were played out in public and their modern environments were influential on the formation of national character (ibid.).

Particularly representative of both the urban underworld and women's presence in, and negotiation of, public space was the figure of the prostitute. The Wolfenden Report of 1957 conceptualised the problem of vice mainly as one of visibility and threat to public decency (Smart, 1995; Swanson, 2007), and following its recommendations, the Street Offences Act 1959 made it easier for women to be prosecuted for solicitation (Self, 2003). The Wolfenden Report (1957, p. 79) argued that, in the context of affluent 1950s Britain, 'economic factors cannot account for it [prostitution] to any large or decisive extent' and that prostitution was chosen by women 'because they find in it a style of living which is to them easier, freer and more profitable than would be provided by any other occupation'. Although conceptualised largely as the result of personal choice or psychological flaws, the Report suggested that it was possible to rehabilitate young women who worked as prostitutes (Williams, 1960).

The prostitute was a focus for anxieties in 1950s Britain because she was a liminal figure who represented the collapse of boundaries. Firstly, she was becoming increasingly difficult to visually distinguish from the 'normal' urban woman (Swanson, 2007). Secondly, prostitution overlapped with other deviant identities and spaces. The late night cafes, espresso bars and jazz clubs of urban centres were the landscape of Britain's youth, perceived as 'exotic', multi-racial environments frequented by prostitutes, immigrants, Teddy Boys and drug dealers (Fyvel, 1961; Bailey, 1999; Jackson, 2008). These were sites of danger, where young girls could be drawn into prostitution (Jackson, 2008). Prostitution was also associated with immigration and fears of 'miscegenation' which could pollute British identity (which was conceptualised as white). In Birmingham, the red light district of Balsall Heath was also an area of non-white immigration (Hubbard, 1998). The two women who are the focus of this section both worked as prostitutes in Birmingham and were accused of murder along with male partners.

Veronica Collins

One August night in 1960, Veronica Collins, 21, was in the club room of the Victory Café in Birmingham City Centre with her boyfriend, Eamonn Hamilton, 23. A young man they knew informed them a fight was going on outside. Eamonn dashed out to join the fight, during which he stabbed and killed a 20-year old named Alexander Walton. Veronica also left the café and saw Eamonn stab Alexander. She and Eamonn ran from the scene and were driven home in the back of a van by a couple they knew.

Veronica had lived with Eamonn for 3 weeks before the stabbing. The police searched their flat the morning after. In her first statement, Veronica told the police that Eamonn did not own a knife and that she carried one for protection against a Maltese pimp. She gave Eamonn the knife 'on the spur of the moment' (DPP2/3153, Veronica's first statement, 20 August 1960) as he left the café. She retracted this in a later statement, claiming that she had merely borrowed the knife in the café to clean her nails, and that Eamonn snatched it back from her as he ran outside.

Neither Veronica nor Eamonn was officially employed. Veronica earned money working as a prostitute. Between the ages of 11 and 15, she lived in a council-run children's home in Herefordshire. She subsequently lived in different parts of the country and gave birth to a son when she was 19, whom she placed in the care of friends in Scotland.

Veronica stood trial for murder along with Eamonn. The case against her was that she gave him her knife knowing that he intended to cause grievous bodily harm and was therefore an accessory before the fact to murder. Her defence counsel argued that she had lied in her first statement in order to protect Eamonn and that her assertion the knife belonged to him was the truth. In his summing up, the judge stated that the prosecution had not proven its case as no evidence was presented that Veronica handed the knife to Eamonn. She was acquitted and Eamonn was found guilty of murder.

The trial exhibited two competing versions of Veronica's behaviour on the night Alexander Walton was stabbed and thus two different versions of the kind of young woman she was. The defence was able to draw on details of her past, and the assessment of the prison medical officer, to portray her as an innocent woman who simply wanted to help the man she loved. Her troubled past, which consisted of time spent in care, an itinerant lifestyle and childbirth outside of marriage, marked her as disreputable, as did her status as a prostitute.

These details were potentially damaging, but the defence employed a well established 'fallen woman' narrative, which sentimentally portrayed Veronica's past as tragic (see Mahood, 1990). When Veronica made her testimony, defence counsel began to build this narrative:

Defence: There are some very unhappy matters that I want to touch on lightly and pass from them. I think your mother was not married. That is right, is it not?
Veronica: Yes.
Defence: You were abandoned as a child and brought up by someone else?
Veronica: Yes.
Defence: Then you yourself, it appears from the statement, earned your living in a most unfortunate way?
Veronica: Yes. (J82/114, Veronica's testimony, 9 December 1960)

The defence deftly contextualised Veronica's work as a prostitute in terms of a tragic and unhappy life, making it a reason to pity, rather than disapprove of, her. The reference to prostitution is veiled as an 'unfortunate' way of making a living, understandable in the light of her illegitimate parentage and time spent in care. The barrister utilised a stock construction of prostitution as something to which young working-class women from 'bad' homes were vulnerable (see Finnegan, 1979).

In addition to sentimentality, Veronica's defence made its case through the romance genre. She was represented as besotted with, and loyal to, Eamonn, the only man who had ever treated her well. A female police officer conducted a lengthy interview with Veronica in which she spoke of her relationship with Eamonn. The defence cross-examined the WPC about this:

Defence: And in the course of the two hours and forty minutes you were getting quite a picture from this girl of the sort of life she had been leading and living?

WPC: Yes.

Defence: Was it apparent to you in the course of that two hours and forty minutes that she had developed an affection for this man Hamilton?

WPC: I was not aware of it.

Defence: Did you get the impression – that, as a change from her unhappy life, she found someone she was fond of?

WPC: I knew she was living with Hamilton; she told me.

Defence: Come. During that two hours and forty minutes she was telling you that, you being a woman, did you not get the impression that she was showing signs of him being a man who she had now got fond of?

WPC: Yes. (J82/114, Defence cross-examination of WPC Irene Pearson, 8 December 1960)

In this extract, Veronica's affection for Eamonn is implicitly suggested as a reason for her willingness to lie for him. Their story becomes a romance, in which Veronica attempts to seize her only chance of happiness. When asked why she wanted to protect Eamonn, Veronica replied 'Because I am very fond of him' (J82/114, Veronica's testimony, 9 December 1960).

This construction of Veronica as supportive and loving, wanting only to protect Eamonn, found favour with the judge. He was unimpressed by the scanty evidence offered by the prosecution and informed the jury:

You may take into consideration this, may you not, in her favour? Many a woman will make many a statement in order, as far as possible, to protect the man she is either married to or living with or in some way loves. So be very careful about Collins. You may think – it is a matter for you – that it would be a very different matter if Veronica Collins had been proved to be one of these viragos who rushed out from the café with the mob and who joined in screaming encouragement. That you may think would be a very different matter, but there is no such evidence here at all… might it be that, terrified for what sometimes is called 'her man', she handed it [the knife] to him so that he might have, at any rate, something to defend himself with if attacked? (J82/114, Judge's summing up, 13 December 1960)

Interestingly, the judge did not appear to disapprove of the fact that Veronica was not married to Eamonn, but was satisfied that she 'in some way' loved him, indicating the contemporary shifts that were taking place in relation to the norms of heterosexual relationships. The success of a romance narrative in Veronica's case was connected to her appropriately feminine behaviour. The judge noted that she was not a 'virago', a loud, boisterous woman. This perception of Veronica as recognisably feminine can also be found in the prison medical officer's report, which describes her as 'quiet and well behaved' (DPP2/3153, 21 November 1960). Veronica was not respectable, but as a young woman with a feminine demeanour, she could be viewed as redeemable. This was in keeping with the era's penal welfarism, which entailed a faith in the ability of offenders to rehabilitate (Garland, 2001), and chimes with the Wolfenden Report's (1957) construction of the young prostitute as reformable.

The story of romance and hardship told by the defence and endorsed by the judge won out, particularly as the prosecution's evidence was not strong. The prosecution narrative relied on portraying Veronica as a scheming femme fatale–type figure, complicit in the violence that occurred outside the café. This also depended on emphasising her lack of respectability and 'rough' background. The police report, in providing details of her past, represented Veronica from this perspective:

> She then secured employment in Herefordshire but later roamed the country and has led an unsavoury life. She is a single woman and has convictions for larceny and prostitution. At the time of her arrest she was following no regular employment and was living with HAMILTON [sic], her co-prisoner, as man and wife. (DPP2/3153, Police report, 16 September 1960)

The report succinctly outlines Veronica's departure from mid-twentieth-century respectability as a woman with criminal convictions, without legitimate employment and living with Eamonn 'as man and wife' without being married.

The construction of Veronica as threatening, rather than unfortunate, relied on identifying her as a member of a seedy underworld of all night cafes populated by Teddy Boys and their girlfriends. This portrayal drew on contemporary anxieties about the unruly, violent culture of working-class youth in Britain (see Fyvel, 1961). The 'Teddy Boy' exemplified these post-war fears about working-class young people, who had grown up under the welfare state and in a newly consumerist society. They had not imbibed the values of hard work and restraint. Nocturnal urban spaces, such as cafes, were the habitat of this new breed of young person (Jackson, 2008). The police report described the Victory Café in Birmingham, the scene of the stabbing, as 'a low class type of refreshment place...frequented in the main, by the "Teddy boy" and young female class of person' (DPP2/3153, 16 September 1960).

At the trial, the prosecution opening argument located Veronica and Eamonn within this urban milieu, referring to the Victory Café as somewhere 'which particularly catered for what are known as "teenagers" and young people generally', and emphasised that many of the witnesses and the two accused 'fall into that class' (J82/114, 8 December 1960). During his examination of a police officer, the prosecution counsel asked, 'Do a number of the so-called teddyboys or beatniks, or whatever you call them in this City, carry knives?' (J82/114, Prosecution examination of Detective Sergeant Merriman, 8 December 1960), highlighting the danger and violence associated with the way of life of certain modern, working-class 'young people'.

This depiction of after-hours danger was allied with a representation of Veronica that displayed elements of the femme fatale trope (see Doane, 1991). Some details of her physical appearance emerge from the case file material. An eye witness stated, 'I saw one dark-haired girl come from a Café and run towards the fight. She was about 5ft 6 dark hair wearing a bottle green costume' (DPP2/3153, Donald Clayton's deposition, 22 September 1960). Veronica's green suit was an important means of identifying her, but it also served as a visual marker of her dangerous femininity. Another witness, from inside the café, described Veronica handling the knife:

> She was wearing a green costume. I saw her lift the left-hand side of her jacket and pull a knife out. It looked as if it came from the waistband of her skirt. The knife was open when I saw it – it didn't look the sort of knife you could close, anyhow. She held the knife in her hand and ran her fingers up the blade. Then she put it back in her skirt. (DPP2/3153, Irene Smith's deposition, 21 September 1960)

The image of Veronica in her dark green suit, running her fingers up the side of a knife, is an arresting one and implies a scheming woman, hoping for the opportunity to encourage use of the weapon. The prosecution opening argument at the trial adopted this depiction:

> That was the knife which she was seen to take from under her jacket, apparently from her waistband, to run her fingers up the blade, and to put it back in her waistband still open. You may wonder why

she should keep a knife in her waistband – a knife of that sort still open – if it was not a knife which was designed for use in some sort of trouble, should any trouble arise. (J82/114, Prosecution opening argument, 8 December 1960)

Therefore, the trial offered two visions of Veronica: one an unfortunate, mistreated young woman who had been caught up in a murder case through her faith in true love, the other a dangerous, threatening woman, who was at home in the seedy landscape of Birmingham's nightlife and knew how to handle a knife.

Alice Fletcher

Like Veronica, Alice Fletcher lived in Birmingham. She was 51 and shared a room in a multi-occupied house in the Balsall Heath part of the city with Roy, who was 26. Alice and Roy were not married but she had adopted his surname. In the early hours of 29 May 1961, a room in the house where they lived was set on fire, killing its only occupant at the time, a 2-year old named Melvin Smith. The other residents managed to escape from the building and the fire brigade doused the fire. The police determined that it had been started by pouring petrol over the room's window sill and setting it alight. Melvin slept beneath the window. His mother, Lily Smith, and the man she lived with, Gus Richards, had been in the house's shared kitchen and were not harmed.

A stable narrative of the events leading up to the fire does not emerge from the case file material. Alice had recently had trouble with Lily and Gus. Gus had tried to force Alice out of her room, and she believed that this was because he wanted to sublet it to a prostitute who worked for him. Alice also worked as a prostitute in Balsall Heath. The argument between Alice and Gus had resulted in Gus, along with a group of friends, kicking in the door to Alice's room and beating her and Roy with an iron bar.

On the evening of 28 May, Boleslaw Ziminowodski, a friend of Alice and Roy's, bought some petrol and gave it to a woman standing outside the shop, who was probably Alice. After going out to work because Roy had 'asked for a pound' (ASSI13/509, Alice's first statement, 29 May 1961), Alice went to a party held in a flat in her street. She told some of the people present that she intended to set the house on fire because Gus had beaten her and Roy up, and because he wanted her room. She later went to a Maltese club in the city centre where she met Roy and Boleslaw. All three subsequently admitted they had planned to burn down the house, although they disagreed over who actually carried it out. It was probably Boleslaw who poured the petrol onto the window sill, although one eye witness claimed to have seen Alice do it.

Alice was born in Malta and grew up in Wales. In adulthood she moved to London. She married in 1937 and had four children with her husband. In 1957, she moved to Birmingham to live with Roy. In court, she claimed that she thought the plan to burn down the house was a joke. The prosecution argued that she was the dominant party in the plan, but the judge identified Boleslaw as the instigator. All three defendants were found guilty of murder.

Alice is constructed as the mastermind behind the fire in most of the case file documents. It was possible to portray her as dominant over two men because she was perceived as deeply unfeminine, and her domestic circumstances marked her as disreputable and poor. The house in which she lived was a residence that accommodated women who worked as prostitutes and men who worked as pimps. In a statement Roy later made for leave to appeal, he explicitly described the house as a 'brothel' (J82/152, Roy's statement, 8 December 1961) and this is how it would have been perceived. Alice's neighbourhood of Balsall Heath was identified as both a red light district and an area with a sizeable immigrant population. The Judgment from the Court of Criminal Appeal highlighted her disreputable living circumstances and, in particular, the multi-racial nature of the house:

> Alice Fletcher, who is a prostitute, was living with Roy Fletcher in a room on the ground floor of that house; and it is clear that for some time there had been rows between them and the landlord and his wife and one called Gus Richards, all coloured people. (J82/150, Judgment of the Court of Criminal Appeal, 21 December 1961)

Gus was Afro-Caribbean and the landlord and his wife were Indian. The Judgment frames the case as one which exemplifies the disorderly nature of immigrant communities, in contrast with the more 'civilised' tempo of British (i.e. white) life.

In 1950s and early 1960s Britain, appropriately feminine women were white and could be symbolically identified with home and hearth (Webster, 2001, 2007). Alice, a disreputable immigrant woman living apart from her husband and three children, could not be constructed in this way. At this time, Maltese people were considered 'coloured', rather than 'white' which would have added to negative views of Alice. They were understood to be associated with crime and prostitution (Gilroy, 1987) and were seen as a threat to 'domesticated', white British culture.

The powerful woman was a signifier of disreputable poverty. Mid-twentieth-century sociological studies construed female dominance as illustrative of the special way of life or culture of the poor, which was frequently perceived as anti-modern (Swanson, 2007). The 'mother centred' family was conceptualised as deviant, prevailing in urban slums in Britain as well as in countries such as Jamaica (see Kerr, 1958). The prosecution emphasised Alice's dominance in the opening argument by always mentioning her before the other two defendants:

> Alice Fletcher and Roy Fletcher were taken to hospital at about 3.45am in the early hours of Sunday morning
>
> ...
>
> At 5.15am Alice Fletcher was brought back from the hospital accompanied by Mr. Ziminowodski. (J82/150, Prosecution opening argument, 24 July 1961)

Witness depositions contain multiple examples of Alice's use of bad language and demonstrations of aggression. In mid-twentieth-century Britain, such behaviour from women was associated with disreputable poverty (see Spinley, 1953; Sprott et al., 1954). This meant Alice could be constructed as deeply unfeminine and also 'rough'. Lily, Melvin's mother, stated, 'I have heard Alice Fletcher use bad language to Gus Richards – she has called him a black bastard and a fucking cunt' (ASSI13/509, Lily Smith's deposition, 21 June 1961). A woman who spoke to Alice at the party she attended on the night of the fire said, 'Later she said she would set the house on fire. I told her not to do it. She said she didn't care a fuck' (ASSI13/509, June Pearson's deposition, 22 June 1961). In addition to use of threatening language, Alice had been involved in a fight with Gus, which formed an important part of the case as it suggested motive. A police officer's deposition described encountering Alice in the street after she was attacked by Gus:

> I was on duty... when I saw the accused Alice Fletcher walking along. She had a cut to her left thumb and smears of blood on her face. She said there had been a fight between herself, Roy Fletcher and Ziminowodski and a coloured party led by Gus Richards. (ASSI13/509, PC Peter Kain's deposition, 22 June 1961)

These depositions, which were partly shaped by the police and prosecution lawyers, constructed Alice as a deeply unladylike woman who worked as a prostitute, swore and fought. This made it possible to portray her as dominant and the mastermind of the fire that killed Melvin Smith. The prosecution made its case clear:

> Members of the jury, from what she was saying that day could you have any doubt that she was the principle [sic] instigator and actor in the whole plan... at her instigation and through her agreement and for her purposes that the Pole [Boleslaw] carried out the act. (J82/150, Prosecution opening argument, 24 July 1961)

The prosecution explicitly argued that Alice was the motivating force behind the fire, and that Boleslaw acted at her behest.

Alice was not represented as the victim or dupe of either of her two male co-defendants, and nor was she portrayed as having become involved in the plot through love. Alice was 25 years Roy's senior, which ruled out use of a romance narrative. The defence argued that she did not set fire to the house and regarded the 'plot' to burn it down as a joke. Her own testimony stressed the affection and concern she had for Melvin, the victim, and that she would never want to hurt him.

The judge did not adopt the prosecution's contention that Alice was the ringleader of the crime but rather focused on Boleslaw, who was Polish, describing him as 'a man of passion, vehement, a strong personality' (J82/150, Judge's summing up, 27 July 1961). In sentencing the defendants, the judge informed Boleslaw:

> Ziminowodski, on the other hand, I regard you as having played a dominant role. You are a man of strong personality; I have no doubt, as I said earlier, a man of passion. I regard your part in this dreadful offence as probably the most dominating one. (J82/150, Judge's sentencing remarks, 27 July 1961)

From the available material, the judge's interpretation was not based on the prosecution's case or the defences of Alice or Roy, as none of these argued Boleslaw was the driving force behind the crime. The judge may have been unconvinced that a woman could prevail over two men, or he may have been influenced by contemporary stereotypes which constructed displays of emotion by men as 'foreign' or 'un-British' (see Collins, 2002).

The representations of Veronica and Alice need to be understood in relation to mid-twentieth-century British views of criminal and deviant women, and in terms of the importance of age as an aspect of gendered identity. As a young woman who displayed at least some of the traits of appropriately feminine behaviour, Veronica could be seen as someone it was possible to reform. However, older women such as Alice were understood to symbolise the imperviousness of certain cultures of poverty to the modern interventions of the welfare state and were seen as beyond help, or as undeserving of it. Alice's relationship with Roy could not be framed as a romance, and as a woman of foreign birth, she was automatically further removed from normative womanhood than Veronica.

The discussion of the muse/mastermind dichotomy in Part I explored how in cases of murder involving women and their male sexual partners, the heterosexual relationship becomes a focus for contemporary anxieties and frustrations. The representations of Veronica and Alice, two women associated with the mid-twentieth-century urban underworld, demonstrate the cultural significance of hopes and anxieties concerning Britain as a modern nation. That they had both worked as prostitutes was significant as debates about vice were 'imbricated in the broader question of what kind of modern nation post-war Britain should be' (Swanson, 2007, p. 74). The negative portrayal of Veronica by the prosecution emphasised the urban landscape of the young, with its street fights and all night cafes, as a place of threat and danger, presenting a troubling outlook for the national character. The more positive construction of Veronica's femininity from the defence, and the version that triumphed, exhibits a sense of optimism about the enduring sanctity of the heterosexual partnership as symbolic of the continuation of the social order, even though Veronica and Eamonn were unmarried.

The criminal justice system's portrayal of Alice Fletcher was also intertwined with the question of the type of modern nation post-war Britain should be, but in her case, anxieties surfaced about putatively 'anti-modern' forces. By the end of the 1950s, 'coloured' immigration had been framed as a problem, and immigrants had replaced the white urban poor as the social group that represented slovenliness, disorder and a brake on modernisation (Webster, 2007). The construction of Alice, an immigrant woman and a prostitute, as the dominant party in the murder of a small child deployed stereotypes of the dominant woman as a symbol of poverty and 'backwardness'. This drew on a colonial narrative of the empire's 'others' as 'against British civilization and modernity' (ibid., p. 4), according to which, Balsall Heath, viewed as a locus of underworld vice and 'dark strangers' (Waters, 1997), was the type of urban area that threatened the boundaries of white British respectability.

The damaged personality

During the interwar period in Britain, psychological and eugenics approaches sought to explain faults of 'character' amongst the population and developed notions of the need for individuals to discipline the self in order produce healthy family and social relations (Miller, 1986; Rose, 1999; Swanson, 2007). The Second World War helped to increase interest in the 'psychology of everyday life', particularly in terms of understanding the weaknesses inherent in national cultures (Thomson, 2006, p. 249). Post war, eugenics-based theories declined in popularity before fading, but psychological explanations for human personality and behaviour continued to gain ascendancy (Rose, 1999). Psychology increased its role in the post-war British welfare system, although it was always contested and never enjoyed dominance as a guiding discourse or set of practices (Thomson, 2006). There was a plurality of approaches, and there was never one identifiable form of selfhood that constituted the ideal for the British citizen (Rose, 1999). However, certain traits and conditions perceived as necessary for development of the healthy or 'normal' personality can be delineated.

The high levels of employment in 1950s Britain, and the support available from the welfare state meant that those who did not thrive were open to construction as 'inadequate' and incorrigible. As part of the evidence it gave to the Royal Commission on Mental Illness and Mental Deficiency 1954–1957, the Royal Medico-Psychological Association suggested that a social inadequate was someone incapable of benefiting from measures taken by the state, and the British Medical Association suggested that adequacy should be judged according to whether a person could look after themselves without help from social workers. As Wootton (1959) observed, social competence was often judged in terms of economic independence.

A satisfactory family life was perceived as crucial to the development of psychologically normal citizens. 'Problem families', who dwelt in squalid living circumstances and had no interest in self-improvement, were likely to produce 'problem children' with psychological and behavioural difficulties (Welshman, 2006; Swanson, 2007). Bowlby's (1953) research into the deleterious effects of institutionalisation on children helped to cement the importance of parent/child relationships to healthy development, particularly through mothering. The Mental Health Act 1959 was passed in order to modernise and streamline the existing 'mosaic of outdated and complicated law and procedure' (Williams et al., 1960, p. 410). This superseded previous legislation on both mental disorder and mental deficiency. The three cases discussed in this section all took place before the passing of this Act, when the Mental Deficiency Act 1927 governed the treatment of people with 'arrested or incomplete development of mind' (Jones, 1960, p. 80).

Shirley Campbell

In April 1957, Shirley Campbell, 21, became the first person in England and Wales to successfully plead diminished responsibility under the Homicide Act, which had come into force in March of the same year (Walker, 1965). Two expert witnesses testified that she was 'in the lowest five percent of the population for intelligence' (*Yorkshire Post*, 27 April 1957) and that she was a psychopathic personality. She was found guilty of manslaughter and sentenced to life in prison.

Shirley was babysitting the 18-month-old daughter of her friend, Wendy Pickles, one evening in March 1957. She listened to the radio, and when her favourite song began to play, the child, Susan, started to scream. To stop her, Shirley submerged Susan's face in water and then strangled her with the belt from a raincoat that was hanging in the kitchen. She informed the police that she had left the house to go to the local shop and returned to find Susan dead. However, later the same evening she made a statement admitting that she had put the belt around Susan's neck. Shirley explained that she was frustrated by Susan crying and screaming, and also that she was angry because Wendy owed her money. When interviewed by the prison medical officer, she also stated that she was annoyed with Wendy for calling her a 'nigger' on a previous occasion (DPP2/2658, Prison medical officer's report, 25 April 1957).

Shirley was a black British woman who, from the age of three, grew up in two different children's homes in Yorkshire. Her maternal grandfather was a Jamaican man who settled in Britain and her grandmother was a white British woman. Her father was her grandfather's brother, who visited Britain and had a sexual relationship with his niece, Shirley's mother. He died shortly after she was born. Shirley was taken into a children's home after her mother was imprisoned for shoplifting offences. After leaving school, she had a variety of jobs in domestic service and the local mills. She remained under local authority supervision until the age of 18. By the time of the killing, she worked as a textile spinner and lived in lodgings.

Shirley was examined by the prison medical officer and a psychiatrist both of whom recommended that she came within the definition of diminished responsibility. The prison medical officer stated, 'she is a person of very unstable mentality due to gross personality defect and in my opinion she could be classified as a psychopathic personality' (DPP2/2658, Prison medical officer's report, 25 April 1957). Inappropriate, or absent, emotional responses were regarded by both medical professionals as significant, and as an indication of Shirley's damaged personality. In particular, perceived lack of remorse and an inability to understand that the crime was morally wrong were understood as signs of psychopathy. The prison medical officer commented that she showed 'a gross lack of moral sense and appreciation and expressed no regrets or remorse concerning the death of the child in question' (ibid.), and the psychiatrist noted:

> from her demeanour and absence of appropriate emotional response to the deed and to her present situation, [it appears] that she does not have anything like the capacity possessed by the average person to make proper judgments about right and wrong. (DPP2/2658, Psychiatrist's report, 15 April 1957)

In addition to lack of remorse, Shirley's perceived excessive emotional reactions were construed as pathological. The prison medical officer described her as 'an emotionally unstable person, subject to rapid mood swings, violent-tempered, impulsive, aggressive and immature' (DPP2/2658, Prison medical officer's report, 25 April 1957). The psychiatrist discussed her lack of forward planning and inability to consider that she would be punished and suggested she was unable to 'control sudden instinctive impulses' (DPP2/2658, Psychiatrist's report, 15 April 1957). Shirley's damaged personality was understood as an affective disorder. She was not incapable of demonstrating emotion, but unable to demonstrate it correctly.

An important feature of Shirley's case and trial was the emotional and psychological significance attached to her putative 'colour consciousness'. The police report notes that 'since leaving school Campbell has become increasingly conscious of her colour and that this may the main reason for her inability to settle' (DPP2/2658, undated). A large number of statements were collected from people who knew Shirley, or had known her in the past, such as work colleagues, landladies, teachers and personnel from the children's homes where she grew up. From these, it appears that they were asked to comment on Shirley's colour consciousness as many refer to this, even if it is to disagree that she was particularly aware of her colour.

Although some of the statements attest to the name-calling and prejudice that Shirley experienced as the only black child in her area, any awareness on Shirley's part that she was 'coloured' was interpreted by criminal justice personnel as a contributory factor to her pathology. These experiences were not labelled as racism, and although they were implicitly understood as unfortunate and undesirable, Shirley's 'colour consciousness' was framed as a further aspect of her abnormal, damaged personality. The prison medical officer honed in on this issue as the key to understanding why Shirley killed Susan:

> She was obviously deeply sensitive regarding her colour and when this matter was raised she became at once emotional and aggressive and then stated that the deceased child's mother had once called her a nigger and she had since then harboured a grievance against her and determined to have revenge and this she maintained was the reason for her criminal behaviour. (DPP2/2658, Prison medical officer's report, 25 April 1957)

This assessment needs to be treated with caution as it reflects the doctor's interpretation of Shirley's motives. The report does not provide details of his wider discussions with Shirley, and whether it was he or Shirley that raised this issue. Her statement to the police describes the annoyance she felt with Susan for screaming and crying, and that she was displeased with Wendy for owing her money. It does not mention whether Wendy had ever called her a 'nigger'.

The psychiatrist suggested that, 'Her illegitimacy and the fact that she was the only coloured child in her community imposed an extra emotional strain' (DPP2/2658, Psychiatrist's report, 15 April 1957). These medical judgments about colour consciousness as an emotional and psychological problem were important during Shirley's trial. The prison medical officer gave expert evidence that, 'There is in this case a very deep-seated mental conflict associated with her colour' (quoted in the *Yorkshire Post*, 27 April 1957) and the judge's summing up stated that 'the fact that she is terribly sensitive about the colour of her skin and people have said things about her colour' was one of the causes of 'a more or less permanent condition of one of mentality' (J82/28, Judge's summing up, 27 April 1957). This focus on 'colour consciousness' was in keeping with mid-twentieth-century views on black children in institutional care, who were believed to face particular cultural and psychological problems, and to have an exaggerated sense of difference due to preoccupation with their colour (Cox, 2002).

Shirley's perceived 'sensitivity' about being black was understood as a contributory factor to her damaged personality, although her supposedly heightened self-consciousness in this area seems at odds with the contemporary understanding of psychopathic personalities as able to experience only a simplified emotional life (see Part I, section 'The damaged personality'). The portrayal of Shirley's internal conflicts and feelings of alienation seem to suggest a complicated emotional existence, lending weight to the criticism that psychopathic personality was a 'wastebasket' category for people who appeared to be abnormal.

Further proof of Shirley's damaged personality was her perceived immaturity. This was central to the construction of psychopathy in the 1950s and 1960s. Shirley was understood as not only immature, but also 'mentally backward' (DPP2/2658, Counsel's opinion, 25 April 1957) and of 'subnormal intelligence' (DPP2/2658, Prison medical officer's report, 25 April 1957). As outlined in the section on the construction of psychopathy and severe personality disorder in Part I, low intelligence was generally not regarded as a feature of these conditions. However, there was some conceptual overlap in mid-twentieth-century Britain between the 'inadequate' psychopathic personality and notions of 'feeble-mindedness' and mental subnormality. The psychiatrist explained that Shirley felt Wendy Pickles had 'let her down' and 'reacted like a child, which intellectually and emotionally she is' (DPP2/2658, Psychiatrist's report, 15 April 1957). The closing speech of Shirley's defence counsel underlined this point about immaturity, stating, 'You may think it is really just like a case of a little girl who had broken someone else's doll' (quoted in the *Yorkshire Post*, 27 April 1957).

The discursive construction of Shirley as a damaged personality, unable to experience emotions appropriately or to appreciate the consequences of her actions, contributed to an understanding of her as dangerous. The judge, as quoted above, described her as having a 'permanent' condition of mentality in his summing up. In sentencing her, he stressed his responsibility to 'protect the public from the danger that you might commit such a crime again' (quoted in the *Yorkshire Post*, 27 April 1957). He imposed a life sentence in order that she would be 'kept in custody until such time as it is thought fit to release you' (ibid.).

Helen Sterry

Shortly after Christmas 1957, Helen, 25, arrived in Hereford, a small city in the English midlands, having spent the night in Worcester Bus Station, a city nearby. She took a pram from outside a shop, which contained Christopher Vincent, a 1-month-old baby. Helen pushed him along for a while, before abandoning the pram and carrying him instead. She started to find him heavy and sat on a bench by the river. When Christopher began to scream, Helen threw him over the railings and into the water. There was no one around to see her do this, but she was concerned that she would get into trouble for having taken him from outside the shop, and went to the central police station to inform them of what she had done.

Two weeks after she was born, Helen and her siblings were removed by an NSPCC inspector[2] from the caravan where they lived with their parents, who were not married. They were placed in children's homes, and Helen lived in homes until she was 15, when she went to work as a residential maid at a hospital. She had several residential jobs, although she was often dismissed from them. She had also spent time in borstal, prison and mental hospitals. Helen had previous convictions for larceny, house-breaking, criminal damage and breach of probation, and had been diagnosed as a psychopathic personality, schizophrenic and mentally defective. In 1957, she was certified insane and had left a mental hospital in November of that year. She had no job and was of no fixed abode.

At trial, the prosecution called no opposing medical evidence to Helen's defence of diminished responsibility and she was found guilty of manslaughter. Her defence counsel made a speech in mitigation, to be considered at the sentencing stage, and asked whether she could be dealt with under the Mental Deficiency Act 1927 and made the subject of a hospital order. The judge refused on the grounds that there was no hope of improvement through treatment. She was sentenced to life in prison.

Helen had been diagnosed as a psychopathic personality in 1950 during one of her periods spent in mental hospital and was therefore already perceived as a damaged personality. A report from Burghill Hospital, included in her prosecution file, states:

> she is a psychopathic personality of aggressive type, i.e., a person who is not insane in the generally accepted meaning of the word, but who, for constitutional reasons finds relationships with people and her environment so difficult that she is unable, at times, to conform to the ordinary rules of social behaviour. (DPP2/2767, Report from Burghill Hospital, 15 July 1950)

This particular report constructs psychopathic personality as 'constitutional' and as therefore having individualised causes. It also notes that

Helen was not likely 'to be amenable either to punishment or to medical treatment' (ibid.). Barghill Hospital also diagnosed Helen as being of low intelligence. Her prosecution file contains reports from mental hospitals, probation officers and the Central Aftercare Association,[3] all of which would have been read by the prison medical officer and the psychiatrist in her case so it is important to pay attention to how these earlier documents constructed her damaged personality.

The prison medical officer stated that Helen 'shows no remorse whatsoever and only giggles when asked about the alleged offence' (DPP2/2767, Prison medical officer's report, 12 February 1958). Helen's lack of remorse, understood as a key sign of psychopathy, was highlighted in the police report, which comments 'I feel certain that at no time since its commission does she appreciate the magnitude of her crime' (DPP2/2767, 4 January 1958). Similarly to Shirley, Helen's damaged personality was understood to be evinced by her lack of emotion at certain times, and excesses of emotion at others. Descriptions of Helen as 'aggressive', 'hysterical' and 'ungovernable' recur in the reports from her past, and were repeated in the prison medical officer and psychiatrists' reports. The psychiatrist who examined Helen summarised his impression of her stunted development:

> A perusal of the records in this case shows that the prisoner has never come up to a normal level, there being a history of tempers and aggressive reactions from her early days onwards. She has been emotionally unstable, being liable to noisy, abusive, and violent behaviour. She has been quite unable to make an adjustment to the reasonable demands of society, and her antisocial behaviour has included lying, stealing, larceny and breaking and entering. A feature has been her inability to profit by experience, and a lack of insight into the serious nature of her position. (DPP2/2767, Psychiatrist's report, 15 February 1958)

The psychiatrist highlights elements of Helen's behaviour that chime with a diagnosis of psychopathic personality such as being violent, anti-social and lacking self-insight. He represents her as abnormal and unable to meet the 'reasonable demands of society'. As demonstrated by the various assessments of Helen's condition, a damaged personality could be perceived as constitutional, emerging early in life and persisting stubbornly even after intervention through treatment. However, the psychiatrist's opinion of Helen implicitly acknowledges that normality is a social, rather than medical, standard, which she failed to meet.

Like Shirley, Helen's emotional inadequacies were understood to be compounded by immaturity and low intelligence. The prison medical officer described her manner as 'childish' and 'fatuous' (DPP2/2767, Prison medical officer's report, 12 February 1958) and the police report notes her 'vacant, childish and uncomprehending stare' (DPP2/2767, 4 January 1958). A police officer who knew her gave his interpretation of the killing: 'I envisaged a young and somewhat retarded child, casually discarding a broken and therefore irksome toy' (DPP2/2767, Past and present impressions of Helen Sterry, undated). This analogy recalls the one made about Shirley being like a little girl who had broken a doll, and constructs Helen as a long way from achieving normal, mature womanhood.

Her childishness was perceived as resulting from her mental defectiveness. The prison medical officer diagnosed Helen as 'feeble minded' and certifiable under the Mental Deficiency Act 1927. The psychiatrist who examined her agreed that she was mentally deficient and certifiable under the Act. He suggested that she was 'suffering from a form of mental defect which shows itself in the emotional and behaviour field even more than in the intellectual field' (DPP2/2767, Psychiatrist's report, 15 February 1958), indicating he felt her psychopathic disorder was more significant to her lack of responsibility for her actions. However, he concurred with previous assessments of Helen as being of subnormal intelligence and explained that her 'abnormality of mind' arose from 'a retarded development of mind' (ibid.).

Helen, like Shirley, was judged to be permanently damaged and imperfectible, and therefore dangerous. The judge emphasised her lack of rational motivation:

> She has no sense of property, and she steals without reason. You were told that this present offence could be regarded really in a way as stealing – stealing a child. Think of that. Stealing without reason.
> (J82/69, Judge's summing up, 19 February 1958)

This quotation can be analysed with reference to Foucault's (1978) conceptualisation of dangerousness as relating to crimes committed without motive (see Part I, section 'The damaged personality'). The judge cautioned that irrationality by itself was not enough to find diminished responsibility, but that Helen's retardation could also be considered. Helen's defence counsel requested that she be made the subject of a hospital order so that she could receive treatment, but the judge refused, stating, 'This is not a case, I was careful to elicit, where there is any hope of improvement through treatment' (J82/69, Judge's summing up, 19 February 1958). He gave her a life sentence, and explained, 'sad though it is that your mental condition is as it has been proved to be, I must see to it that you can never do this sort of thing again' (ibid.).

Doreen Baird

One evening in October 1958, in a small town in Yorkshire, northern England, Doreen Baird, 14, babysat for the Croft family. Winifred Croft spent the evening at a friend's house watching television and John Croft visited the pub. There were five Croft children, including a toddler and a baby. Doreen became frustrated with 'one and the other' (ASSI45/335, Detective Inspector Wolfinden's deposition, 4 November 1958) of the children crying and knotted a scarf tightly around 16-month-old June's neck. This stopped her crying so Doreen untied the scarf and returned downstairs. Later in the evening, she went back into the bedroom to fetch a book, and noticed that June was not breathing. After Winifred and John had both arrived home, Doreen had a cup of tea with them and left their house at 11.20 p.m. Winifred checked on June at around midnight and discovered that she was dead.

In 1957, Doreen's mother sought the help of a probation officer and in 1958 Doreen was referred to a child guidance clinic, where she was interviewed by an educational psychologist. He suggested that she was a psychopathic personality, due to her 'shallow emotion' and inability 'to feel for others or to make strong attachments' (ASSI45/335, Educational psychologist quoted in psychiatrist's report, 11 November 1958). As with the previous two cases, there was no opposing medical evidence offered at Doreen's trial, during which she was described as 'very disturbed' (Expert medical witness quoted in *The Times*, 28 November 1958), and was found guilty of manslaughter due to diminished responsibility. She was sentenced to approved school, which entailed a standard 3-year sentence.

Like Helen, Doreen had already been diagnosed as a psychopathic personality before she killed June. The educational psychologist who made this assessment noted that she was 'withdrawn' and 'showed little sign of disturbance on the surface' (ASSI45/335, quoted in the psychiatrist's report, 11 November 1958). The psychiatrist who interviewed Doreen after the killing drew on this earlier report in order to make recommendations about her state of mind. He argued that despite Doreen's assertions that she was afraid of what had happened to June, her behaviour after the killing was 'bland', 'callous' and bore 'no trace of fear or distress or even anxiety' (ibid.). He noted with disapproval that:

> On each occasion following my interview in which Doreen had appeared to be distressed by the discussion of her actions, her attitude changed almost instantaneously into that of a rather coy, happy, almost carefree girl as soon as I changed the subject and indicated that a meal was due or that her mother was waiting to see her. On the former occasion she immediately and cheerfully asked the staff what was for lunch, and being given this information she ate heartily. (Ibid.)

The psychiatrist's use of language indicates that he found Doreen's apparent lack of concern about June's death disturbing and that he saw any emotions she appeared to exhibit in relation to this as superficial. He suggested that her 'morbid personality development' was 'partly constitutional' but was exacerbated by environmental factors such as having a 'Psychopathic' father and experiencing 'maternal rejection' (ibid.). In arguing that Doreen was psychopathic, the psychiatrist compared her behaviour with that of an adult, male psychopath. It is worth quoting this section of his report at length:

> There is in the crime itself evidence of an indifference towards the feelings of others and a lack of any personal feeling of wrongness, remorse, or fear or apprehensiveness, and an almost complete inability to comprehend the consequences to herself; there is no guilt or horror – only a petulant dislike of any reference being made to the crime, of the same order as that expressed when her petty stealing is discussed. It is characteristic of the adult psychopathic criminal that after the commission of some bestial crime he will frequently behave as though nothing abnormal had occurred and may, for instance, go to a theatre or visit friends who can detect no sign of abnormality, tension, shock, or difference from normality. This girl betrays such features. (Ibid.)

The comparison the psychiatrist makes between Doreen and an adult who commits 'bestial' crimes imputes a greater degree of intention and pre-meditation to the strangling than the circumstances suggest. His characterisation of Doreen's behaviour does not allow for the possibility that she was overwhelmed by the situation and unable to know how to react, but suggests instead that she was calm and collected.

As a 14-year old, Doreen was not expected to have attained full maturity. However, like Shirley and Helen she was perceived to be emotionally immature. The psychiatrist stated:

> Doreen has written quite well-composed letters to her mother. These are mainly concerned with trivialities and show no depth of feeling in any particular direction. They might be the letters of a girl of 9 or 10 who had gone back to her Preparatory School after the summer holidays. (Ibid.)

The psychiatrist's use of middle-class reference points, such as preparatory school and evenings at the theatre in relation to the case of a working-class girl seem rather inappropriate and suggest that he held middle-class subjectivity as the normative standard. During the trial, the psychiatrist gave evidence that Doreen's emotional development was 'retarded' and 'not that of a girl of 14'. He also referred to her intellect as 'a little on the low side' (Psychiatrist's testimony quoted in *The Times*, 28 November 1958), making an association between low intelligence and emotional failings that was similar to those made in the cases of Shirley and Helen.

Although constructed as a damaged personality, the outcome of Doreen's trial did not represent her as dangerous. There are no surviving extracts from the transcript so it is necessary to rely on newspaper reports to gain an idea of how the trial unfolded. The discursive construction of Doreen was different from Mary Bell, who was described as wicked and evil. Notwithstanding the psychiatrist's report, it seems to have been accepted by the prosecution and defence that the case should be regarded as tragic for all concerned. Counsel for the prosecution described the case as 'wholly pitiful and pathetic' and noted that Doreen worked as a babysitter due to a 'sincere, legitimate, and loving interest in young children' (quoted in *The Times*, 28 November 1958). Her defence stated that June's death 'will live with her for always' (ibid.). After sentencing her to approved school, the judge informed the jury 'I entirely agree with the verdict. You can take it the girl will be well looked after' (ibid.).

In all three cases, inappropriate, inept or absent displays of emotion were understood to connote a damaged personality. This discourse constructed the women's femininity as unformed and underdeveloped. Unlike representations of madness that depict exaggerated and pathological versions of femininity, these cases are of women perceived to have failed to attain femininity. Gender is read from a number signs, which require performance. The lack of an appropriate repertoire of feminine emotion, such as tears, remorse or recognisable vulnerability, meant that Shirley, Helen and Doreen were not intelligible as females. They were either emotionless or performed the 'wrong' emotions, such as aggression. This interpretation arose from framing their behaviour and reactions selectively. As the discussion of the comparison the psychiatrist made between Doreen and an adult male psychopath demonstrates, the reactions of these women could have been understood differently.

The stress placed on immaturity exemplifies the gendering of the damaged, psychopathic personality in women as stunted womanhood. Maturity was an important aspect of the 1950s British 'new woman', who was in the vanguard of modernity (Geraghty, 2000). Maturity was necessary for successful marriage and motherhood, but also for success as an employee and a consumer. Immaturity meant failure in these areas and failure as a woman. It also indicated inability to participate in, and drive, society's modernisation. Women who could not achieve mature femininity, which was advocated in sources as diverse as sociological and educational studies, and popular magazines, were an anti-modern force (Geraghty, 2000).

The damaged personalities constructed in the cases of Shirley, Helen and Doreen contained elements and echoes of perceptions of 'feeble-mindedness' and 'mental deficiency', which informed British understandings of the inadequate psychopath. This demonstrates the influence of long-standing constructions of social class on conceptions of damaged personality, and echoes eugenics-inspired explanations for 'degenerative' traits. The subnormal, low-functioning individual unfit for modern society was iterated as an 'idiot' or 'imbecile' in the early twentieth century, and as a type of psychopathic personality in the 1950s (Wootton, 1959).

This highlights the importance of analysing intersectional identities in relation to the damaged personality discourse. The construction of damaged individuals unable to participate in the modern 'new Jerusalem' of post-war Britain, despite the provisions of the welfare state and improvements in living standards, individualised the vicissitudes of poverty and family instability that some people faced. This can be seen particularly clearly in the cases of Shirley and Helen. Their problems were attributed to their constitutional failings and little attention was paid to their backgrounds in institutional care, or in Helen's case to her experiences as a homeless woman, other than to further underline their failure to achieve normality. Shirley's presumed 'sensitivity' about being black was not understood as related to her social position and the experience of racism, but as a manifestation of her individual pathology. Certain features of the psychopathic personality such as abnormality, immaturity and aggression echoed racist, colonialist assumptions about black Africans (see McCulloch, 1995) and were aspects of a wider colonialist discourse of 'savage', 'irrational' colonial 'others', who existed in opposition to 'British civilization and modernity' (Webster, 2007, p. 4). As the result of a sexual relationship that would have been characterised in the mid-twentieth century as 'miscegenation' (Webster, 2007), Shirley was a racially liminal figure who traversed the boundaries between black and white, and British and not British.

Shirley and Helen were constructed as underdeveloped, failed women who remained overgrown, dangerous children from whom the public needed to be protected. Doreen had not reached womanhood by the time of her conviction for manslaughter and the outcome of her trial suggests that she was not regarded as seriously flawed to the same degree as Shirley and Helen. From what can be known of her trial, and the fact that she was sentenced to approved school, it seems that she was viewed as reformable. This was in keeping with the dominant approach to juvenile justice of the era, which sought to transform 'delinquents' into useful citizens (see Wills, 2005). Doreen was from a working-class background, but unlike Shirley and Helen did not have a history of institutionalisation and did not appear quite so removed from normality. However, the psychiatrist's report on Doreen demonstrates that her construction as a damaged personality could also result in a representation that portrayed her as disturbing and threatening.

The damaged personality, understood as manifest in conditions such as psychopathy, is a liminal category that collapses the boundary between sanity and insanity. In the context of mid-twentieth-century Britain, this made those judged psychopathic personalities both perplexing and threatening. They were individuals who could not govern themselves (or could not govern their 'selves' (Rose, 1999)) and therefore could not thrive in a modern, forward-looking society such as post-war Britain. Shirley, Helen and Doreen had all experienced high levels of state intervention in their lives (Shirley and Helen particularly so), and yet they still failed, indicating the persistence of those resistant to transformation. Their incorrect performances of gender did not trouble the boundaries between femininity and masculinity, as in the masculine woman discourse, but rather did not fulfil the rudiments of appropriate woman- or girlhood. They seemed curiously degendered, and not at all the capable, mature 'new women' idealised in the 1950s.

The respectable woman

The Second World War and the post-war era were pivotal times for British working-class respectability. The active engagement of working-class men and women in the war effort, coupled with the domestic strictures and dangers that fighting the 'People's War' entailed, incorporated the working class as legitimate and valuable members of the national community (Rose, 2003). Significantly, the white working class could now represent the British 'people'. The welfare settlement of the 'People's Peace' (Morgan, 1990) and the increased affluence and heightened standard of living experienced by many working-class families in the late 1950s and 1960s, exemplified by the availability of council housing, promised a better future (Giles, 2005). The white working class marked the boundaries of acceptable membership of the nation against the new Commonwealth (understood as non-white) immigration (Webster, 2007).

This increased acceptability and respectability was contingent upon the maintenance of certain standards, which were of course gendered. Modern working-class men provided financially for their families and also spent their leisure time with them, fulfilling the mid-twentieth-century ideal of the 'companionate marriage', in which the woman and man would be equal partners with different roles to perform (Collins, 2003). Respectable working-class women, if married with families, would be responsible for the family's consumption and keeping their home clean and tidy (Geraghty, 2000; Giles, 2005). Part-time employment was consistent with respectability, as it could be an effort to improve the family's living standards and enable the purchase of consumer goods (Wilson, 2006).

Working-class families who lived in dirty, chaotic homes and displayed an apparent disregard for norms of respectability were in the 1950s open to being labelled 'problem families', who rather than taking advantage of the 'better future' promised by the modern world 'lived in opposition to modernist principles' (Swanson, 2007, p. 34). These disreputable, or 'rough', members of the working class collapsed the boundaries between the orderly, clean, white working class and the noisy, disruptive and dirty immigrants settling in British cities at this time. As such, they surrendered the privileges of whiteness (and therefore belonging), becoming 'dark strangers' alongside the immigrants (Waters, 1997).

White working-class women were, therefore, important boundary markers of Britishness. They were also the focus for anxieties, as well as hopes, about the onward rush of modernity. Respectable working-class married women who were past youth could be constructed as archetypal 'Mum' figures, symbolic of reassuring tradition and continuity. Brooke (2001, p. 775) argues that '[a]t a moment when such stereotypes might have had less resonance in lived experience, nostalgia for traditional, more certain and more fixed stereotypes of femininity (such as the working class mother) became more intense'. 'Mum' was a sentimental, nostalgic construction of the strong, capable working-class woman who held her family together. She was above all hard working and self-sacrificing, with hard work in particular signifying working-class respectability. Crucially, as a woman past attractiveness, she was not glamorous or sexual and was therefore unthreatening (ibid.). She symbolised a world being lost to affluence and Americanisation (for articulation of these anxieties, see Hoggart (1957)). Although the mid-twentieth-century Mum was a sentimentalised and idealised figure, it was also recognised that strain and emotional tension could result from the domestic work that many women carried out (Langhamer, 2005).

A mid-twentieth-century opposite to Mum was the never married woman, or 'spinster'. As Holden (2007) argues, marital status is an important category for social analysis. Marriage is frequently conceptualised as a stage in the life course, with never married people being regarded as 'exceptions to the norm' (ibid., p. 1). In 1950s Britain, the married mother and the spinster represented different poles of femininity, with the spinster constituting a 'failed', unfulfilled woman. Post war, there were fewer young unmarried women and 'remaining unmarried became increasingly unacceptable' in comparison with the interwar period (ibid., p. 13). Persistent, negative stereotypes of spinsters as 'thwarted' women who led 'unnatural' lives (having missed out on marriage and motherhood) demonstrated the culturally devalued status of this subjectivity (Oram, 1992; Fink and Holden, 1999).

Despite constructions as 'superfluous', never married women were frequently family 'standbys' who played active roles in their families as daughters, sisters and aunts (Holden, 2007). Spinster representations were not uniformly negative – she could be a sensible, no nonsense figure who established and maintained order, and for women with a degree of financial independence spinsterhood could represent an alternative to the narrow confines of normative femininity (Joannou, 1994). Although they were often culturally reviled, spinsters were respectable women. Unmarried mothers, women who co-habited with men and unmarried women perceived as sexually promiscuous (all disreputable in the mid twentieth-century) were not spinsters, who were either pitied as celibate or suspected as lesbian (Oram and Turnbull, 2001; Holden, 2007). Both women whose cases are analysed in this section were represented as respectable, but they constitute two different poles of respectable mid-twentieth-century femininity.

Edith Chubb

In February 1958, in Broadstairs, an English town on the south east coast, Edith Chubb became irritated by her sister-in-law, Lilian Chubb, when she placed her teacup on the floor 'in a clean place' (*Daily Telegraph*, 2 May 1958). When Lilian was about to leave for work, Edith pulled on her scarf, causing her to gurgle. The postman's arrival at the door startled Edith, who placed her hand over Lilian's mouth and nose to stop her making a noise. When Edith removed her hand, she realised Lilian was dead.

Edith put the dead body in the coal shed until early the following morning. When her husband and children had left the house, she used an invalid chair covered with a blanket to dispose of it on a bank. Edith took the money that had been in Lilian's purse, before burning it along with Lilian's handbag. She used the money to pay off debts she owed on the rent and at a grocery store. A passer-by discovered the corpse later the same morning.

Edith lived with her husband, Ernest, their five children and Lilian, Ernest's unmarried sister. Until shortly before the killing, the household had also comprised Edith's mother, but she had gone into hospital. Until around 5 weeks before she killed Lilian, Edith had worked as a nursing assistant at a local hospital for three 12-hour night shifts per week. Ernest's new job as a plumber meant that she could give up her job, but she had been prescribed Dexedrine, an amphetamine, to overcome her exhaustion. Lilian had lived with the Chubbs for the 7 years since her mother had died. She worked as a buyer in the haberdashery section of a department store.

The police's suspicions centred on Edith because of the debts she settled on the day Lilian disappeared and because she appeared 'taut' when they visited the house (DPP2/2782, Police report, [day not specified] February 1958). Edith made two statements in which she denied any knowledge of the circumstances of Lilian's death, but made a third in which she admitted to pulling on her scarf and causing her death. She put forward defences of both diminished responsibility, because of her exhaustion and frayed nerves, and involuntary manslaughter on the grounds that she had not intended to hurt Lilian when she pulled her scarf. She was found guilty of involuntary manslaughter and sentenced to 4 years in prison.

Edith's defence developed a theme, which was also present in the prosecution documents, of representing her as over-worked and put upon. This depiction relied on perceiving Edith as respectable and as someone who had fulfilled her duties. In particular, she was identified as a working-class 'Mum', understood as the organiser and ruler of domestic space, and the archetypal emblem of 'home' (Brooke, 2001; Langhamer, 2005). Edith's statements to the police provided the basis for her portrayal through the Mum representation. These described her day of chores, which began at 4 A.M. when she made breakfast for her husband. She claimed that her family was 'very happy and united' (DPP2/2782, Edith's first statement, 7 February 1958) and that 'Lilian and I always got on well together and she had always promised to look after the children if anything happened to me' (DPP2/2782, Edith's third statement, 14 February 1958). Edith's former boss, a matron at the hospital where she had worked, framed Edith's professional life in terms of the sentimentalised Mum construction:

> she carried out her duties extremely well and was most reliable, most kind and considerate to all patients who came under her care. She was popular with the staff and the patients and was neat in her uniform and methodical in everything she did. I can't speak too highly of Mrs Chubb. I know that her children were always her first consideration. She was quite strong. (DPP2/2782, Evelyn Cook's statement, 17 February 1958)

The matron enumerates Edith's maternal qualities, such her reliability and kindness, and in keeping with the figure of the working-class Mum, describes her as 'strong'. She was called as a witness for the defence and testified that:

> As a nurse she is most efficient, and is an excellent nurse. As a person I like her very much, and so do her colleagues and the patients. She is called by the patients the 'ministering angel of the night'. (Evelyn Cook's testimony quoted in *The Times*, 2 May 1958)

This portrayal drew on a sentimental discourse of the devoted, attentive nurse and sought to establish a moral identity for Edith. Construction of a moral identity as a hard working mother and nurse[4] emphasised her value and therefore her respectability. This sentimentalised testimony from the matron recalls the conventions of melodrama, whereby events are constructed in emotional terms and the heroine's transgressions are recuperated (Landy, 1991).

Edith's moral subjectivity was constructed relationally by comparing her with Lilian, a spinster and therefore a failed woman. Edith, a wife and mother, could be constructed as having greater social value than Lilian against these pejorative assumptions about never married women. The social opprobrium attached to spinsterhood was indicated in the police report:

> The deceased appears to have been of a retiring nature and rather a dull sort of person. She had a number of business acquaintances but seems to have found no real friends. Occasionally she has been given a ride from her employment back to her home by commercial travellers, but apart from this has had no close association with men. (DPP2/2782, Police report, February 1958)

This extract was part of an explanation for why the police suspected Lilian had been killed by a family member, rather than a stranger or male acquaintance. However, the references to Lilian's 'retiring nature' and dullness serve as an implicit criticism, as does mention of her lack of friends or association with men. As a never-married woman, Lilian did not perform heterosexuality, a constituent part of appropriate femininity.

Edith was represented as an overburdened, respectable working-class woman stretched too far. The psychiatrist who examined her highlighted her hard work and exhaustion:

> Up to about five weeks before the crime the prisoner was working three nights a week from 8pm to 8am as night nurse at Haine Hospital. These were three consecutive nights... and, as she was running her home as well, she probably had insufficient sleep and became increasingly fatigued. I understand that she saw her doctor from time to time during this period and was helped to keep going by taking Dexedrine during the day. (DPP2/2782, Psychiatrist's report, 14 April 1958)

That she was willing to work so hard was an important aspect of her respectability, and differentiated her from 'rough' working-class women who failed to adequately care for their children or to keep their houses clean (see Spinley, 1953; Kerr, 1958). Despite her early assertions of family harmony, Edith's domestic life was constructed as a source of stress, as were her family relationships in themselves. The police report described Ernest, her husband, as 'a dull, unimaginative man' (DPP2/2782) whom they regarded as someone who would have been unable to disguise his role in the crime if he had taken part. This cast doubt on his masculinity, as the report suggests he was simply not up to committing or abetting a crime, and also constructed him as a rather substandard marriage partner.

Edith's self-sacrificial capacity for hard work was contrasted positively with Lilian's putative laziness. As will be discussed, the defence emphasised this difference during the trial, but similar views could be found in the prison medical officer's report. He commented on Edith's domestic responsibilities:

> Her mother was elderly and not in good health and her deceased sister-in-law a woman [to whom] she could speak little except about her work and tended to leave all the household chores to Mrs Chubb, who had to care for a household of eight and herself. (DPP2/2782, Prison medical officer's report, 2 April 1958)

This provided some basis for a defence of diminished responsibility which could avoid pathologising Edith. Rather, she was constructed as understandably overwrought and attempting to cope with little support. The family doctor appeared as a witness for the defence, as reported in *The Times*:

> All the years he had known Mrs Chubb she had been an exceptionally hard worker who lived on her nerves and was never able to relax. Last year, he formed the opinion that she was on the verge of a nervous breakdown. She felt she was 'between the devil and the deep blue sea.' (Dr Marshall's testimony reported in *The Times*, 2 May 1958)

The defence pursued this representation of Edith vigorously and contrasted it with Lilian's failures as a woman. Edith's identity as a respectable, hard-working wife and mother proved her moral worth. Her testimony in court stated that she had worked as a cleaner and then nurse to 'supplement the family income' (Edith's testimony reported in *The Times*, 2 May 1958) and had kept house for nine people. This industriousness was compared favourably with Lilian's laziness:

> Mr A P Marshall QC (defending): How much did your sister-in-law, Lilian, pay you for her board and lodgings? – [Edith's answer] 25s a week.
>
> Did seeing her sitting about placid and calm, and doing nothing, have any effect upon you? – It is a little irritating you know, to see her sitting around....
>
> 'I felt irritated by the way she had put her cup down' she explained. 'I followed her down the passage and pulled her scarf. I did not intend to hurt her: I intended to give her a shake up'...
>
> Mr Marshall: Why didn't you go to the police at once? – I knew I would have had to go away if I went to the police, and I did not want the children to be left on their own. (*The Times*, 2 May 1958)

Although it was argued that Edith did not mean to hurt her, Lilian's dirty teacup is almost offered as a justification for the attack upon her. Defence counsel and Edith also reminded the jury of her devotion to her children immediately after she outlined the killing. This framed hiding and disposing of Lilian's body, potentially disturbing facts, as measures taken to protect her children from the loss of their mother, rather than to save herself from detection. The defence discursively recuperated Edith as a fastidious housewife and good mother, which erased her use of violence.

In his closing speech, the defence barrister described the case as 'a story of human frailty... exasperation and not of hatred... basically the story of Martha and Mary. It is the story of sickness and exhaustion' (quoted in *Broadstairs and St Peters Mail*, 7 May 1958). The reference to the biblical story of two sisters visited by Christ identified Edith with Martha, the patron saint of housewives. This continued her sentimental portrayal and, although 'sickness' is mentioned, avoided pathological explanations for her actions. Edith was represented as an ordinary working-class woman pushed too far, not as an abnormal one.

The prosecution countered this sympathetic depiction of Edith by stressing the seeming intentionality of the killing. Summarising this argument, the judge reminded the jury:

> She held her hand over Lilian's face for two or three seconds to prevent the milkman [sic] from hearing the noise she was making. You will have to ask yourselves whether that is a true account of what happened. This woman is a trained nurse and you may think that the simplest thing in the world would have been for her to deal with

the situation and the deceased would have recovered quite quickly. (Judge's summing up quoted in *The Times*, 3 May 1958)

The judge suggested that Edith had lied about the circumstances of the killing and that she could be deceitful. He questioned whether there was any reason for Edith to have put her hand over Lilian's mouth and nose when she lay on floor, and also stated, 'While the deceased's body was in the coal house the accused woman was behaving as if she knew nothing about her' (Judge's summing up quoted in *Daily Telegraph*, 3 May 1958). This challenged the moral identity for Edith created by the defence, although it was the defence's version of events that ultimately succeeded as she was found guilty of involuntary manslaughter, the best outcome she could achieve.[5]

Renee Hargreaves

Renee Hargreaves, 54, called an ambulance one morning in January 1962 for Ernest Massey, 78, who lived with her and her friend, Clare Boston, in their home in Porkellis, Cornwall in south-west England. He had become violently ill and died soon after reaching hospital. It emerged that Ernest had died from sodium chlorate poisoning, an ingredient of weed killer, traces of which were found in his tea mug. Renee was the beneficiary of Ernest's will, had made recent inquiries arranging for him to live in a residential home (for which she needed his consent) and had, within the previous 6 months, asked her doctor if it was likely there would be an inquest if he died.

In her first statement to the police, Renee emphasised Ernest's 'peculiar habits' (ASSI26/262, 25 January 1962), which included drinking from bottles and pouring paraffin onto the fire. When interviewed for the second time by the police, and asked directly if she had poisoned Ernest, she admitted that she had put weed killer in his tea. However, she maintained that she had only intended to make him ill enough to go to hospital, and not to kill him. Her defence was involuntary manslaughter, as it was argued that she did not realise the weed killer was poisonous enough to cause death or serious injury, and it was not labelled as dangerous. This succeeded and she was found guilty of manslaughter, receiving an 18-month sentence.

Renee had lived in Porkellis for 4 years, but she had lived with Clare for a total of 20. Ernest moved in when his wife died in 1960, although he had not been invited to live with the two women. Renee had known him for many years, as his wife had been her nurse when she was a small child. Renee had three adult children in their 20s. She had left her husband between 20 and 23 years previously because he was a drunkard. After that time, she worked on farms and as a herdswoman. It appears that at the time of Ernest's death, neither she nor Clare was employed, but cared for him.

The discussion of Edith's case revealed the negative way in which Lilian, as a single woman, was represented. Renee had been married in the past, and may have never been divorced,[6] but she was referred to in newspaper stories as a 'spinster' (*Western Daily Press*, 27 January 1962; *The Times*, 28 January 1962), probably because it was not publicly known that she had been married and had children. Unlike Lilian, Renee was constructed as occupying a socially useful role. Her relationship with Clare was not viewed as abnormal, although the prison medical officer implied that it might be lesbian:

> She is fond of reading and has some rather masculine interests, in fact she is a very masculine person with her hair cut short and wearing trousers and a sweater. I did not probe into her sexual life. I did not consider it relevant... [she] lives in a cottage with Miss Boston who is aged 64. As I said they have been friends for 22 years and seem to have a close relationship. (ASSI26/262, Prison medical officer's report, 29 March 1962)

The prison medical officer refers to her as 'very masculine' and states the length of her friendship with Clare. However, he seems to have regarded further speculation as unseemly and did not 'probe' Renee about her sexuality. This contrasts with the cases of Yvonne Jennion, Norma Everson and Marilyn Bain, who were constructed through the masculine woman discourse, where perceived masculinity and lesbianism were regarded as having great importance. By the 1950s in Britain, close female friendships were increasingly likely to be perceived as lesbian, although female couples could also be seen as non-sexual (Oram and Turnbull, 2001).

The difference between Renee's case and those discussed in relation to the masculine woman discourse is partly due to age. As a woman in her late 50s living with a woman in her 60s, her relationship may have been understood as a sensible, second best alternative to relationships with men. Her sexuality was less contentious than that of younger women, as she and Clare were likely to be perceived as past heterosexual attractiveness or availability. The prison medical officer's report describes Renee as 'co-operative and friendly' and states that she 'was interesting to me for of all the persons that I have examined in similar situations, she appeared by far the most normal' (ASSI26/262, 29 March 1962). The prison medical officer did not disapprove of Renee leaving her husband two decades previously, but accepted that he was a 'drunkard' (ibid.).

Not all mid-twentieth-century medical understandings of lesbianism perceived it as pathological or abnormal (Jennings, 2008). However, in cases of unusual killings by women, the pathological masculine woman has been a recurrent image. In Renee's case, there may have been less need to provide an explanation for the killing beyond her own justifications. Use of poison was more conventionally feminine than use of a knife or gun and Renee did not kill Ernest violently. Significantly, her life was not unconventional, chaotic or connected to the underworld. She lived quietly in Cornwall with Clare, and in this sense she was respectable. Therefore, a pathological representation of female homosexuality was not a useful means of telling her story. Her lifestyle was marginal to, rather than in opposition with, normative mid-twentieth-century ideals of marriage and motherhood.

As with Edith's case, a sympathetic portrayal of Renee was partly achieved by viewing Ernest, the man she poisoned, as a nuisance who had foisted himself upon her. Although she had known him nearly all her life, he was not a biological relative and this limited her perceived obligation to him. Her first statement to the police outlined some of the difficulties of living with, and caring for, Ernest:

> Mr Massey was also very peculiar in that he was very reluctant to wash himself or to keep himself clean. Miss Boston and I thought that he had become flea-ridden and eventually it became necessary for me to bath him... At one time he grew a beard because he would not shave himself and as he got so dirty and I thought his hair had fleas in it, I shaved his beard off myself, after he had protested very strongly. (ASSI26/262, Renee's first statement, 25 January 1962)

From Renee's description, it appears that Ernest was quite confused and unable to look after himself. Recognition that he was a hard person to care for made Renee's actions seem comprehensible. Depositions and statements from other witnesses reflected this attitude. Under cross-examination at the committal hearing, Renee's doctor stated, 'Miss Hargreaves did a very good job of looking after this old man. His condition was one of general debility. He was a frail old man' (ASSI26/262, Charles Clapham's deposition, 27 February 1962). A welfare officer who had visited the home described her as 'a kindly soul especially with regard to the old man's interest' (ASSI26/262, John Clemo's statement, 31 January 1962) and a friend suggested that Ernest 'was playing on the nerves of both women who were extremely friendly and his presence made it impossible for them to go out' (ASSI26/262, Ethel Abbott's statement, 31 January 1962).

As with the construction of Edith and Lilian, Renee was represented as someone of greater social worth than Ernest, a very old man perceived as having little contribution to make to society. By the early 1960s, interwar anxieties about the social burden of an aging population had disappeared, as the post-war baby boom and Commonwealth immigration swelled the working age population (Thane, 2000). However, needy 'elderly' people as a burden on individual female family members was a theme raised in mid-twentieth-century social studies (ibid.). Like Edith, Renee had performed an undesirable and stressful caring role and was perceived to have succumbed to its pressure. Her performance of care, a central element of mid-twentieth century appropriate femininity, also made it possible to recognise her as a respectable, dutiful woman. Newspaper reports of the judge's summing up indicate that the defence strategy utilised the representation of Renee as severely tested by caring for Ernest, and the judge appeared to concur:

> He told the jury that there seemed little doubt that in the 15 months he lived with Miss Hargreaves and Miss Boston this man of 78 had become nosey, dirty, and rather a nuisance.
>
> 'You may think he was getting on the nerves of both ladies looking after him.' (Judge's summing up quoted in *The Guardian* 6 April 1962)

He informed the jury that sodium chlorate was not marked as a poison and if the jury believed that Renee did not know it would do Ernest grave harm, its verdict should be manslaughter, and this is the verdict they delivered.

Viewing Renee as put upon by Ernest, a man for whom she had successfully cared for 2 years, helped to erase the more troubling aspects of the case, such as the fact she was the sole beneficiary of his will and had made inquiries about whether his death would be likely to be investigated. The pathologist testified that it was unlikely that Ernest was fatally poisoned with a single dose of weed killer, but over 2 or 3 days. In addition to the tea mug, the police also found a beer glass with traces of sodium chlorate in it. Of course, this does not mean that Renee knew she was fatally poisoning Ernest, and the pathologist may have been wrong about the dosage. However, as with Edith's case, quite a high degree of intent to harm could be read from the evidence, but

Renee was successfully recuperated as a respectable woman with a moral subjectivity.

The defence's alignment of Edith Chubb with a nostalgic, sentimental construction of the self-sacrificing working-class mother needs to be understood in relation to the new inscription of the white working class as the British 'people'. Edith's hard work and selflessness meant that she could be implicitly constructed as a paragon of 'traditional' white, maternal femininity in an era when better living standards and immigration threatened to transform the working-class population. In Edith's case, the respectable woman discourse articulated these fears about the effects of post-war modernity on the British people, as they were perceived to move from warm, tightly knit communities to the anonymity of new housing estates, where they could take advantage of consumer goods, but perhaps lose their vital humanity (see Young and Willmott, 1957). This represents another strand of the complex and competing notions of modern British society that shaped the discourses of femininity in these mid-twentieth-century cases. We have examined modernity as threat in terms of the sexual and urban pleasures that it could offer, and we have also explored the revulsion and frustration that shaped the construction of the 'anti-modern', who could not be improved by the advantages modern Britain had to offer. From Edith's case, we can read a representation of modernity as a threat to the British people's integrity.

This portrayal of Edith was complicated by the stress placed on her hard life and financial struggles, introducing ambiguity to the nostalgic 'Mum' symbol. Although her performance of traditional working-class womanhood granted Edith moral worth, as the put upon 'Mum' to a large household comprising five children and wider family members, especially as one who 'snapped', the case highlighted undesirable aspects of traditional working-class life. Edith's case was a venue for anxieties about modernity, but also demonstrated its potential advantages, in the form of smaller, more contained families. This is perhaps why it had wider cultural resonance – the *Daily* and *Sunday Mirror* newspapers, which were aimed at a working-class readership, mounted a campaign for her release from prison a year after her conviction that displayed a similar tension between elegiac sentimentality and emphasis of the burdens placed on Edith (for a full discussion see Seal, 2009a).

Lilian, although respectable, embodied a non-normative femininity in relation to Edith's married motherhood. She provided the contrast which enabled an idealised image of Edith to emerge. However, the construction of Renee demonstrates that mid-twentieth-century women perceived as 'spinsters' were not automatically denigrated, underlining the importance of close attention to the dynamics of particular cases. Renee's relationship with Clare, even if understood as lesbian, did not pose a threat to the contemporary norm of marriage and motherhood. Their relationship could be viewed as a 'second best' adopted later in life, rather than as a destabilising challenge to normative sexual relations. Renee, a woman in her 50s, could be represented as a familiar and recognisable figure, the spinster, rather than as the more disruptive and confusing sexual 'deviant' explored in the masculine woman section. Rather than signalling the potential threat of modernity's sexual pluralism, her quiet lifestyle could be interpreted as making do with an inferior alternative to a life with her husband and children. It is also significant that like Edith, she was constructed positively in relation to her victim, a demanding old man.

The witch

The iteration of the witch discourse in two mid-twentieth-century cases needs to be understood through constructions of 'disreputable' poverty as they applied to older women. The analysis of Alice Fletcher's case through the muse/mastermind dichotomy explored her construction as a poor woman associated with Birmingham's sleazy urban underworld, and the section on damaged personalities discussed the mid-twentieth-century concept of 'social inadequacy', whereby individuals were perceived to be incapable of adjusting to modern society. Unlike Alice Fletcher, the two women whose cases are decoded in this section did not live in big cities, and unlike the 'damaged personalities', they were not assessed as psychologically abnormal. However, the case file material demonstrates that they were viewed as socially marginal, poor women of bad character.

In late 1950s and early 1960s Britain, there was a widespread belief that poverty had been eradicated by full employment and the helping hand of the welfare state (Coates and Silburn, 1973). Those who stubbornly remained in reduced living circumstances did so either because of immorality, profligacy or inadequacy. 'Rough' women were unable to get by financially with what they had and were seen as likely to 'misspend' their money on fripperies such as cream cakes and tinned peaches (Sprott et al., 1954). They had to resort to degrading measures, such as pawning their possessions (Roberts, 1986). Low morals were a constitutive feature of socially marginal, disreputable women. Co-habiting with men without being married and bearing illegitimate children were markers of sexual immorality that could result in a bad reputation and women's ostracism from their local communities. Unmarried mothers had a 'potentially contaminating presence' and were perceived as bearers of shame (Holden, 2007, p. 117). Having left a husband, or having been deserted by one, was also construed as an indication of working-class women's lack of respectability (see Spinley 1953; Kerr, 1958). These categories of disreputable working-class womanhood can be contrasted with both the sentimentalised 'Mum' figure and the 'spinster' representations, which established the parameters of respectable femininity for working-class women past youth.

The two women whose cases are discussed in this section were suspected of multiple killings and both were well over 60 years of age. As explained in the section in Part I outlining the witch discourse, this representation did not mean that the women in question were actually believed to be witches. Rather, the witch is a socially marginal older woman, often poor and with a bad reputation in her community.

Sarah Harvey

Thomas Harvey and his wife were clearing out the house of his mother, Sarah, in Rhyl, North Wales, one day in May 1960. Sarah, 65, was ill with bladder cancer and was in hospital at the time. There was a cupboard on the landing, which Thomas had never seen unlocked. Sarah had always told him that it contained the belongings of a woman who had lodged in her house 20 years previously. Thomas broke the cupboard open to discover that it contained a corpse, which he immediately reported to the police. The corpse was identified as the remains of Frances Knight, the woman whose possessions Sarah had said were in the cupboard. It emerged that Sarah had been claiming Frances' maintenance money, paid by her husband due to their separation, for the preceding two decades. While in the cupboard, Frances' corpse had not decomposed, but had naturally mummified.

Before the body had been identified, Sarah told the police that she had no knowledge of it. When confronted with the information that it was Frances Knight, the woman whose maintenance money she had been claiming, Sarah explained that Frances had died from natural causes and that she had hidden the body in the cupboard, but kept up the pretence that Frances was alive in order to collect the money. Frances' mummified corpse had the remains of ligature made from a stocking around its neck. A blanket had been placed between the legs, seemingly to absorb the discharge of putrefaction. The Solicitor General and the Director of Public Prosecutions decided that Sarah could be charged with murder.

Sarah had been married twice. Her first husband divorced her in 1932, 11 years after they had separated. She gave birth to Thomas, who was not her husband's child, in 1931. She remarried in 1936, and her second husband died 2 years later 'apparently of cancer' (DPP2/3098, Preliminary police report, 7 May 1960). Sarah earned a living by taking in lodgers. This included short-term holiday makers, as well as longer-term residents, who were usually older people, or people with chronic illnesses. In 1955, she stopped boarding lodgers and took a job in a hotel as a still room maid. She performed this role until becoming ill with cancer.

The police discovered that in addition to Sarah's second husband and Frances Knight, a further six people had died in her house. These included an aunt, from whom she inherited tenancy of the house, and her mother, from whom she inherited what had been her aunt's investments. There were also elderly residents who had deceased in the house, including a woman who died 2 days after making Sarah the sole executrix and beneficiary of her will. However, it was decided that there was not enough evidence to warrant exhumations.

Sarah's trial began, but the case against her collapsed when an expert forensic witness passed out whilst under cross-examination by the defence. The judge ordered that the murder charge should be withdrawn because the prosecution could not prove that Sarah was responsible for Frances' death or for the ligature around her neck. Frances had been ill with disseminated sclerosis (multiple sclerosis) and there was insufficient evidence that she had been killed by someone else. Sarah pleaded guilty to two counts of obtaining money by false pretences and was sentenced to 15 months in prison.

Throughout his childhood, Sarah eked out a living for herself and Thomas by running her boarding house. The case file material echoes the 'beggar witch' stereotype of an impecunious older woman who causes harm to others (see Part I, section 'The witch'). One of the police reports[7] comments that, 'From the persons interviewed one is able to draw a picture of Mrs Harvey as being a thief, continually incurring debts and a hard and mercenary woman' (DPP2/3098, Second police report, 1 June 1960). A pawnbroker's list is included in her file (DPP2/3098, Pawnbroking transactions since 1936, Exhibit 12), which shows that she mainly pawned her wedding ring (other items included cutlery and an alarm clock). The police also took a statement from Sarah's pawnbroker, who described her as a 'frequent visitor' since the early 1920s (DPP2/3098, William Smout's statement, 23 May 1960). Several former residents attested that Sarah had stolen possessions from them, and this probably accounted for the police's interest in the pawnbroker. However, the inclusion of a list of pawned items underlined Sarah's status as an economically marginal woman, and recalls the image of the witch as a poor, older woman. Sarah emerges from the case file material as a 'rough' working-class woman, who needed to resort to the pawnshop in order to get by.

The police reports stressed that Sarah was known as disreputable in her local community. The third police report informs personnel at the office of the Director of Public Prosecutions that, 'Some statements from persons interviewed are attached and again, whilst of no evidential value, they provide the background of this woman and an indication of her reputation and character' (DPP2/3098, Third police report, 20 June 1960). These statements include one from Sarah's first husband, which alleges that she stole some of his sister's wedding presents and on one occasion pawned all his clothes, leaving him 'only what I stood in' (DPP2/3098, William Williams' statement, 10 May 1960). He also claims that Sarah once set his bed on fire while he was still in it. One of Sarah's neighbours stated that, 'When I rented my house I was told by the owner of the property that my neighbours on one side were undesirable – meaning Mrs Harvey, who was a widow living with her only son' (DPP2/3098, Peter Griffiths' statement, 9 May 1960). Other witnesses described her as 'moody', 'hard' and 'mysterious'. Not all of the statements disparage Sarah. Others refer to her as 'decent', 'ordinary' and 'kind'. However, the police reports drew from the negative representations in their portrayal of her.

As the 20 June police report acknowledged, the information from these witness statements did not carry legal weight as it did not count as evidence. However, that Sarah was a disreputable woman of bad character and regarded with suspicion in her community is offered as a wider explanation for why she committed the crimes of which she was suspected. It also signals unease about the case, and an assumption that Sarah's behaviour was only explicable if she was both evil and socially marginal – in other words, witch-like.

Sarah's marginality was highlighted by her status as the mother of an illegitimate child. This detail is seemingly irrelevant to the case, but reference to Thomas' illegitimacy recurs in the case file material. A timeline of events notes that the body was discovered by the 'Accused's illegitimate son, Thomas Harvey' (DPP2/3098, 7 June 1960). The preliminary police report states that Thomas' birth certificate 'does not give particulars of his father' and a progress report from the police relates that Sarah 'has persistently refused to disclose the identity of the child's father' (DPP2/3098, 1 June 1960). However, it was by no means unusual in interwar and post-war Britain for unmarried mothers to keep the details of their children's paternity secret (Davidoff et al., 1999). Steedman (1986, p. 67) describes the experience of being an illegitimate child in 1950s Britain as an existence marked by 'illegality and impropriety', and one that placed social distance between illegitimate children and 'respectable' families. Stressing that Sarah had a child outside of marriage also suggested that she was sexually deviant, another element of the witch discourse (and of other discourses of transgressive femininity). Her 'refusal' to name Thomas' father was read as uncooperative, but also deceitful, which was characteristic of the witch. As a woman who had been a lone mother, Sarah challenged the normative gender roles of male provider and domestic female and, like the witch, turned the social order upside down.

The deception involved in hiding the fact of Frances' death and collecting her maintenance money also contributed to the witch discourse in relation to Sarah's case. She claimed that she put Frances' body in the cupboard in a moment of panic, which was disputed by the prosecution during the trial. Sir Jocelyn Simon, the Solicitor General, acted for the prosecution, indicating the seriousness with which Sarah's case was regarded and the perceived difficulties in proving that she had killed Frances.[8] He pointed out that Sarah had put flypapers and disinfectant in the cupboard and had placed the absorbent bedspread between the body's legs. He argued that this indicated her guilt:

> The taking of precautions against the natural consequences of hiding the body, precautions which are irreconcilable with panic but were cold-blooded, calculated acts. The clear action of Mrs Harvey once she had Mrs Knight's maintenance money, and week after week for 20 years drawing the money which should have come to the dead woman. (quoted in *The Times*, 14 October 1960)

Claiming the maintenance money involved Sarah in the pretence that Frances was still alive, but housebound. This entailed answering questions about the state of Frances' health and temper. Perhaps most significant was the successful hiding of the body for 20 years. The second police report notes, 'The fact that during the course of a day she [Sarah] and very many other persons who have lived at this address, would pass the cupboard on many occasions, gives one an idea of her character' (DPP2/3098, 1 June 1960).

Unsurprisingly, some of the case file material on Sarah employs elements of the gothic. A letter from the Chief Constable to one of the Assistant Directors of Public Prosecutions states, 'an alarmingly high number of people have died in this house' (DPP2/3098, 3 June 1960). The centrality of Sarah's house, with its 20-year secret of a locked cupboard containing a body, chimes with the gothic conventions of mysterious houses and locked doors (see D'Cruze, 2006). The discovery of Frances Knight's body in Sarah Harvey's locked cupboard is reminiscent of ghost stories by writers such as Le Fanu (1923), where the plot hinges around similar discoveries of long dead victims (see, for example, *Madam Crowl's Ghost*). Notes at the beginning of the prosecution file warn, 'This may turn into a female "Christie" case before it is finished' (DPP2/3098, Handwritten notes on file, 9 May 1960). This statement compares Sarah with John Christie, executed in 1953 after the bodies of six women, including his wife, were found in the wall, under the floorboards and buried in the garden of his flat in London. The notes acknowledge the macabre nature of the case and also its capacity to become a sensation. The seemingly gothic elements of Sarah's case contributed to her witch-like representation.

The details of a case involving a mummified corpse, discovered after 20 years on the landing of a boarding house, provided scope for media representations to exploit it as a horror story. In his deposition, the pathologist highlighted some fictive elements of the press reporting: 'The headline in a National Daily Newspaper [*sic*] of the 17th May "Woman deliberately turned into Mummy" is complete nonsense' (DPP2/3098, Gerald Evans' deposition, 11 October 1960). The American current affairs magazine, *Time*, ran a story about the case headlined 'A Mummy in the Closet' (19 October 1960). At Sarah's committal hearing, her defence counsel raised the issue of sensationalist media reporting:

> Hardly a day has gone by when the searchlight of the press has not been turned on this case, and some suggestions which have been made in certain organs of the press are quite irresponsible and will be shown to be completely without foundation. (Quoted in *The Times*, 1 July 1960)

In particular, the barrister criticised a newspaper, which he did not name, for suggesting Sarah had been involved in 'ritual orgies and ghoulish practices' (ibid.). There was no indication that she participated in orgies or rituals, but these allegations hinted at witchcraft, showing that Sarah was associated with the supernatural in certain popular representations of the case. The prosecution process required that events were articulated in a fashion which adhered to bureaucratic conventions and legal procedural rules. Despite this, invocations of the gothic did appear in the criminal justice process.

Mary Wilson

In 1958, Mary Wilson became the last woman to be reprieved from the death penalty in England and Wales before its effective abolition in 1965. She was a 68-year-old widow (although the newspapers reported her age as 66) resident in County Durham, north-east England, and was found guilty of murdering two of her husbands by poisoning them with phosphorous, which at the time could be found in rat and beetle poison. She received a death sentence because she had committed murder on two separate occasions, which made her liable for the death penalty under the Homicide Act 1957.

On the 20 September 1956, Mary married 75-year-old Oliver Leonard, who died on 3 October. Just over a year later, on 28 October 1957, she married 76-year-old Ernest Wilson, who died on 12 November. The bodies of Oliver and Ernest were exhumed due to suspicion that they had not died of natural causes. Traces of phosphorous and bran were found in their intestines, which suggested they had been poisoned with Rodine beetle poison. Mary inherited some money from Oliver and was paid from Ernest's life insurance policies. She also attempted, unsuccessfully, to withdraw £100 from an account of Ernest's.

Mary was born in 1890 and worked in domestic service before she married her first husband, John Knowles, a chimney sweep, in 1914. They had six children, four of whom survived into adulthood. John Knowles died in 1955. She had been legally separated from him since 1945, although they lived in the same house, which was not unusual for working-class people at the time. She had worked as a daily housekeeper for a painter and decorator, John Russell, since the Second World War and continued to do so after John Knowles' death. John Russell died in January 1956, aged 65. The bodies of both these men were also exhumed. No phosphorous was recovered, although the pathologist believed that they died from 'some noxious substance' (J92/195, Summary, 13 May 1958).

Mary became the first and only woman to be sentenced to death after the Homicide Act 1957 restricted the application of capital punishment in cases of murder. She was reprieved by the Home Secretary of the time, Rab Butler, on the grounds that the execution of a woman of her age would be 'a shock to public opinion' (HO291/241, Conditional Pardon, 29 May 1958). Issues related to public opinion about her case and reprieve are discussed in greater detail in Seal (2008).

Echoes of the witch discourse appeared in relation to Mary because she was an older woman who seemed to have killed for acquisition. The unusual and macabre aspects of the story also contributed to its scope for sensationalism. Mary was found guilty of two murders, but a further two bodies were also exhumed. *The Times* reported that the solicitor for the prosecution acknowledged the unusualness of her case at her committal hearing:

> 'This is one of those cases,' he said, 'that in the ordinary way one would associate more with the realm of fiction rather than real life, save that cases of this kind do appear from time to time in the annals of crime. Within a space of little more than a year the accused murdered two husbands by poisoning.' (Quoted 11 February 1958)

Traditionally, poisoning (or in more recent iterations, drugging) victims is considered especially witch-like. Witchcraft is secret harm done by apparently ordinary women, although they may have certain characteristics that indicate their natures. A letter by Rab Butler in Mary's Home Office file explains that, 'Murder by poisoning has always been regarded as one of the worst forms of murder, being always deliberate and often difficult to detect' (HO291/241, 22 May 1958). He also notes that the female poisoners Charlotte Bryant, Dorothea Waddingham and Louisa Merrifield were executed in the twentieth century (on these cases, see Ballinger, 2000).

Mary's apparent financial motives for killing her husbands contributed to her representation as a woman who was evil and mercenary, prepared to do harm for meagre rewards. The prosecuting barrister described her as 'a wicked woman who married in succession two men, and then deliberately poisoned them in order to get the paltry benefits that she hoped she might obtain by their deaths' (quoted in *The Guardian*, 25 March 1958). Butler understood the case as 'one of cold-blooded and petty murder for petty gain, in which it would ordinarily be difficult to justify interference with the due course of law' (HO291/242, Conditional Pardon, 29 May 1958).

When Mary first met Oliver Leonard, one of the men she was convicted of murdering, she asked a friend of his, Mrs Connolly, 'has that old bugger any money?' (J92/195, Summary, 13 May 1958). After being informed that he had a little money, she had a 20-minute conversation with him, after which she announced they were to be married. Three days later, she asked Mrs Connolly to 'get the old bugger out; that he would not leave her the money until she had married him, and until he had put the ring on her finger' (J92/195, Judge's summing up, 29 March 1958). As discussed in relation to the muse/mastermind discourse, women perceived as dominant can become monstrous if they seem to exercise power or influence over men. This upsets the heteronormative matrix of male authority and female submission. In mid-twentieth-century Britain, the dominant woman was also a symbol of the 'rough' working class and bore the stigmatised culture of the poor (see Kerr, 1958).[9]

This picture of Mary as both malign and mercenary contributed to the witch representation. It is worth comparing her portrayal with that of Renee Hargreaves. Renee was considerably younger than Mary, but also a woman past youth, who killed an old man with poison, from whom she stood to inherit some money. Renee was perceived as more respectable than Mary, and was understood to have cared for Ernest, the old man, well. Mary's lack of attention to both social niceties and the caring duties of working-class womanhood, coupled with an undisguised interest in Oliver's finances, marked her as disreputable and unpleasant.

Like Sarah, Mary's portrayal is reminiscent of the beggar witch stereotype of the poor old woman who harms others for gain and both women were also widows, a further characteristic of the witch. The discursive framing of these women as witch-like expressed social disapproval for their suspected crimes and for their status as poor and socially marginal. The Judgment of the Court of Criminal Appeal states that after Oliver's death, Mary 'then waited for a year and at the end of October, 1957, she married another old man, and in a fortnight he was dead' (J92/195, 19 May 1958). Use of the verb 'waited' implies that Mary was biding her time until she could snare another victim. This interpretation constructs Mary's crimes as calculated far in advance and requiring intense malevolence, rather than as opportunistic.

Given the witch's supposed sexual insatiability and ability to drain the life out men, it was perhaps unfortunate that Mary's defence suggested Oliver and Leonard may have had phosphorous in their organs due to taking Damiana aphrodisiac pills. A private detective established that the pills were on sale locally and could have been bought by both men. In his summing up, the judge gave this explanation short shrift, stating:

> The suggestion that I think is put forward is that Leonard in 1956, and Wilson in 1957 – both of them in their middle seventy's [sic],

may have taken these pills as a sex stimulant. Well, if that suggestion was made, give it such weight as you think it deserves. (J92/195, Judge's summing up, 29 March 1958)

Along with implied sexual voracity, Mary's association with a range of men, despite her age, indicated her low morals and 'rough' nature.

As with Sarah Harvey, the more dramatic accounts of Mary's case could be found in the press discourse, rather than the bureaucratic, institutional language of the criminal justice system. The unusual nature of Mary's case made it newsworthy and interest was further enhanced by her defence counsel, Rose Heilbron, QC. Along with Helena Normanton, Rose was one of the first women to be made a Queen's Counsel and became a household name in the 1950s (*The Guardian*, 13 December 2005).[10] Newspapers dubbed Mary the 'Widow of Windy Nook' (see, for example, *Daily Mirror*, 25 March 1958; *News of the World*, 30 March 1958), an appellation which recalls the 'Wicked Witch of the West' from *The Wizard of Oz* (1939), and draws on long-standing stereotypes of the witch as an older, widowed woman.

Sarah Harvey and Mary Wilson were older, working-class women who had profoundly violated the normative carer role, and were believed to have killed the very people they should have been looking after. Analysis of Edith Chubb's case demonstrated the nostalgia that could endow working-class femininity with value, but also how this was contingent on performance of respectability, which entailed hard work and self-sacrifice. Sarah and Mary appeared to have killed for financial gain and to have led lives contrary to mid-twentieth-century working-class respectability. Sarah had divorced and given birth to a child outside of marriage – and was perceived with suspicion and disapproval in her local community. Mary had been involved with a range of men, seemingly as a means of income, and did not fit the self-denying 'Mum' representation. Rather than being worthy members of the British 'people', they were disreputable others – 'rough' older women whose lives showed the bad old habits of poverty that in modern Britain would be extinguished. In particular, the perceived acquisitive nature of their crimes was constructed as profoundly distasteful.

As older women from poor backgrounds, Sarah and Mary exercised very limited social power and would ordinarily be assumed to pose no threat to others. The discovery that they may have killed several people, and possessed a secret, malevolent power, therefore inverted the social order, rendering them witch-like.

3
Conclusion to Part II

Part II has involved undertaking a two-stage analysis of unusual cases of women accused of murder, which focuses on regulatory constructions of gender and the wider symbolic meanings attached to femininity. It has employed this analysis to examine 12 empirically researched cases from a specific context, that of mid-twentieth-century England and Wales. This has enabled a discussion of gender construction in a particular time and place and an exploration of how these representations of women accused of murder articulated cultural anxieties about the nature of post-war British society. They became sites of contested meaning, particularly in relation to understandings of Britain as a 'modern' society.

Gender regulation

The utilisation of the typology of five discourses of womanhood in relation to women who kill provides insights into constructions of normative and deviant femininity as they appeared in the mid-twentieth-century criminal justice system. These discourses were not specific to representations of criminal women, but participated in the wider regulation of femininity. The five discourses share some overlapping themes, which chime with those highlighted in previous feminist research on representations of women who kill (Nicolson, 1995; Ballinger, 2000; Frigon, 2006). The focus on unusual cases of women accused of murder allows themes of sexuality, pathology, duty/care and family life to be analysed in relation to women who occupied a variety of social positions, and provides access to a range of representations. This includes women who were constructed as outside of, or in opposition to, heterosexual subjectivity and, significantly, women who were perceived as single.

Conclusion to Part II 165

Continuing to expand the feminist analysis of gender representations of women who kill is important in order to examine how themes of normative gender arise in cases of where women were not necessarily positioned as wives or mothers, or, as in the case of Edith Chubb how being a wife and mother was central in a case where a woman did not kill a male partner or her own child. This helps to extend the feminist analysis of gender constructions of women who kill to examples where the subject for feminist consideration may have carried out acts inconsistent with feminist ethics, such as having killed another woman. The value of these cases is in what they can reveal about representations of gender and the symbolic meanings attached to femininity.

Sexuality is an important component of the masculine woman, muse/mastermind and witch representations. Constructions of deviant sexuality are integral to the masculine woman and witch discourses, and the negotiation of the muse/mastermind dichotomy revolves around conceptualisations of acceptable and unacceptable heterosexual relationships. The absence of negative constructions of a woman's sexuality is important to the respectable woman representation. Pathology is a key element of the damaged personality discourse, and also appears in the masculine woman construction, particularly in Yvonne Jennion's case, where schizophrenia, psychopathic personality and 'female homosexuality' were explicitly linked. However, as the analysis of Marilyn Bain's case highlighted, construction of female masculinity as deviant did not rely on notions of pathology, but could also arise from explanations that focused on licentiousness and immorality.

The adequate performance of care and duty cuts across most of the discourses and demonstrates how essential this was to normative constructions of mid-twentieth-century femininity. The section on the respectable woman explored how this representation was largely made possible in the cases of Edith Chubb and Renee Hargreaves because they were portrayed as having met their caring obligations and having behaved dutifully. In both cases, perceptions of duty stretched too far were significant to understandings of their respectability. Conversely, the perceived violations of care by Sarah Harvey and Mary Wilson contributed to their representation through the witch discourse, especially as they were accused of killing the very people they should have cared for.

Another important theme that runs like a thread throughout the discourses of womanhood is positioning within families. Marginality to the normative nuclear family contributed to discursive construction as deviant or unintelligible, showing how deeply mid-twentieth-century representations of femininity were intertwined with understandings of family life. The three women whose cases were analysed as exhibiting the masculine woman discourse lived in all female households, which challenged the norm of the family based on the heterosexual partnership. In Yvonne Jennion's case, this was not because she lived with another woman who could be construed as a sexual partner, but because she lived with her mother and daughter. The significance given to the illegitimacy of Sarah Harvey's son underlined her representation as a disreputable, witch-like older woman, as her family situation was marginal to the socially acceptable formation. For Shirley Campbell and Helen Sterry, women constructed as damaged personalities, their backgrounds of growing up in institutional care contributed to placing them beyond intelligible femininity as they did not perform the roles of daughter, mother or even spinster aunt, which would help to position them within a recognisable discourse of womanhood.

Of the 12 mid-twentieth-century women accused of murder, Edith Chubb occupied the family position most associated with contemporary appropriate femininity, the married mother. This made her culturally intelligible and enabled the respectable woman representation, especially in comparison with her victim, Lilian, a never-married woman. Renee Hargreaves, also constructed as respectable, lived with a close female companion, but as an older woman, could be perceived as having settled for 'second best', rather than as having resisted or rejected the normative ideal. The negative portrayals of women who existed in marginal relation to the normative family demonstrate the anxiety that possible alternatives could generate. On the one hand, this highlights fear of the potential for the feminine to disrupt the social order (Heberle, 2001) and the use of derogatory discourses as part of the exertion of social control. However, these anxieties can also be read as resulting from the lack of fixity to existing social relations and as fear of impending change. This point will be developed further in the section on 'murder and meanings' below.

Out of the five discourses of womanhood explored in the typology of unusual cases of women who kill, three of them construct deviant or unintelligible femininity, one is dichotomous and one is a representation of acceptable womanhood. The deviant constructions illuminate the point that the transgressive is often symbolically central because it exposes the boundaries of the normative (Stallybrass and White, 1986; Cresswell, 1996; Butler, 1999). Analysis of gender representations of mid-twentieth-century women accused of murder helps to make clear the constitution of, and the limits to, contemporary appropriate femininity. The boundaries between femininity and masculinity, approved and unacceptable heterosexual relationships, normality and abnormality, are thrown into sharp relief. The masculine woman discourse exposes the limits to femininity as an intelligible gendered performance, and the mastermind and witch representations highlight how characteristics such as perceived dominance and sexual assertiveness became elements of deviant or abject femininity. Like the masculine woman, the damaged personality lays bare the borders of intelligible femininity, but also of gendered performance itself. Whereas female masculinity appeared in opposition to femininity, women such as Shirley Campbell and Helen Sterry were portrayed as almost falling outside of gender. Their lack of family relationships, of a stable home and absence of recognisable emotional display de-gendered them.

An intersectional analysis demonstrates the importance of attention to the multiple nature of subjectivity, and how this contributes to discursive constructions of womanhood. Female masculinity is not dependent on representations of working-class subjectivity, but the already symbolic distance of working-class women from 'ladylike' femininity can contribute to masculinisation. The three women whose cases were analysed in the section on the masculine woman violated understandings of acceptable mid-twentieth-century working-class femininity in terms of their physical appearance and lifestyle. In different ways, the damaged personality and the witch discourses relied on portrayals of the social and economic marginalisation of the women they constructed. Intersections between gender, class and 'race'/ethnicity can be seen in the construction of Shirley Campbell as a damaged personality, where racist, colonialist assumptions shaped her portrayal as a psychopathic personality.

The dichotomous muse/mastermind construction is not inherently related to a particular class subjectivity, but in the two cases explored, Veronica Collins and Alice Fletcher, class helped to shape the women's representation through this discourse. The defence's depiction of Veronica as an unfortunate young woman deployed well-established representations of the vulnerability of working-class women to the depredations of vice. The portrayal of Alice as a 'mastermind' utilised notions of female dominance as an aspect of the 'deviant' culture of poverty, and was exacerbated by the fact that she was a Maltese woman who lived in an immigrant area.

Age was also significant to these women's representation, whereby Veronica's youth made a more 'forgiving' depiction possible. Although the construction of Doreen Baird contained many elements of the damaged personality discourse, as a 14-year old, she was ultimately judged as open to rehabilitation rather than as permanently defective. Age was also fundamental to the witch discourse, which was a representation of disreputable, poor older women. Edith Chubb's portrayal as a respectable woman relied on a number of intersections. The 'Mum' representation symbolised respectable, as opposed to 'rough' working-class female subjectivity. It was also conditional upon whiteness, and could only be embodied by a woman who was past youth and disruptive sexual attractiveness.

The three women who were constructed through non-derogatory representations, Veronica, Edith and Renee, did not fully inhabit mid-twentieth-century appropriate femininity, but rather could be identified with aspects of it. Edith attained the closest approximation as she could be identified with married motherhood. However, as a working-class woman with a large family, she did not occupy a socially powerful position and did not completely meet ideal womanhood. This exemplifies Butler's (1993, 2004) argument that normative versions of gender are hyperbolic and never fully embodied by social agents, which ultimately exposes their constructed nature. Certainly in the cases of Veronica and Edith, the contingency of their more positive representation is highlighted by alternative interpretations of their subjectivities. Veronica was depicted by the prosecution during her trial as a scheming femme fatale and newspaper reports of the judge's summing up of Edith's case reveal that he suggested she was calculating and deceitful. These alternative stories of these women's cases demonstrate the lack of fixity to portrayals of gendered subjectivity, and the importance of analysing differences within women as well as between them (Braidotti, 1994).

None of the empirically researched cases involved women positioned as middle class. This is not surprising, as women who kill are disproportionately socio-economically disadvantaged (Jones, 1996; Ballinger, 2000). Much of the reason for the enduring high profile of a case such as Lizzie Borden, explored in Part I, is the unusualness of a socially and economically privileged woman being tried for murder (especially axe murder). This illustrates Fraser's (1995) point that the politics of representation are not neatly separable from the politics of redistribution. The 12 women whose cases were analysed in Part II were not privileged and several of them were poor. The analysis has highlighted how construction through a recognisable subjectivity as a respectable working-class woman could offer some restricted advantages in terms of positive representation, and that had the potential to affect criminal justice outcomes.

For Edith Chubb and Renee Hargreaves, this partly resulted from their greater social value relative to their victims, a spinster and an old man. However, both women were of limited social power and position overall. The potentially greater advantages that might accrue to a more socially and economically privileged mid-twentieth-century woman if she could be constructed as embodying constituent elements of appropriate femininity cannot be known from this research. However, this serves to underline the poststructuralist feminist argument that it is necessary to appreciate the power differences between women, and the complexities of discursive representation (Cornell, 1995; Mouffe, 2005). The disciplinary, social control aspects of the five discourses of femininity as they appeared in the cases of 12 mid-twentieth-century women from England and Wales had uneven implications for different social groups.

Murder and meanings

The five discourses of womanhood in cases of women accused of murder contributed to gender regulation and the constitution of appropriate femininity in mid-twentieth-century Britain. However, they also generated wider cultural meanings about contemporary British society, which included, but also went beyond, issues of criminal justice, murder and gender. The analysis in Part II shares many of the characteristics of microhistory as it provides a window on a short, tightly defined period, 1957–62 and, although it is not an examination of one case, confines itself to a small number of examples. Microhistories aim to explore the wider social and cultural resonances of particular cases (Berenson, 1993), and as Phillips and Gartner (2003) argue, violent crimes, which are instances of the rending of the social fabric, are especially likely to reveal clashes and struggles over meaning. Cases of women accused of murder present fertile examples, due to the shocking nature of women's perpetration of violent crime and to the especially symbolic nature of femininity (Shapiro, 1996). Constructions of femininity become signs around which other meanings circulate.

Microhistories have tended to focus on high-profile examples, as have other historical and sociological cultural analyses of cases of murder and violent crime. The cases that received the most public attention and contemporary cultural representation can be particularly telling about the major aspirations, rifts and social problems of the day (Chancer, 2005; Srebnick, 2005). However, the same type of cultural analysis can be performed in relation to cases that received limited attention beyond the criminal justice system (D'Cruze et al., 2006; Bakken and Farrington,

2009). These were also products of their time, and the institutional discourses that constructed them incorporated wider cultural meanings. Of the 12 empirically researched cases, those of Sarah Harvey, Mary Wilson and Edith Chubb were the most high profile at the time, and the cases of Sarah and Mary were reported internationally.[1]

Others, such as Yvonne Jennion, Shirley Campbell, Veronica Collins and Alice Fletcher, were the subject of more than one story in the national press. Norma Everson and Marilyn Bain received scant media attention, but analysis of their case files demonstrates that they are no less evocative of mid-twentieth-century meanings.

The chosen time period was a pivotal one, during which British society was undergoing transformation (Sandbrook, 2005; Hennessey, 2007). Mid-twentieth-century debates about the type of society Britain should be were shaped by processes and perceptions of accelerating modernity. This had attractions, as it could appear to promise greater prosperity, opportunity and the relaxation of stultifying conventions and moralities. For the same reasons, the hurly burly of modernisation could induce anxieties and fears about loss of certainty, moral decline and potential disturbance of the social order. In particular, the possible deleterious effects on working-class citizens of loosening social strictures were cause for concern from elites. It was feared that working-class people would not manage to deal with new found freedoms and opportunities responsibly, or that the tacky baubles of the new consumer society would distract them from traditional, collectivist values.

Part II explored how these cultural tensions relating to the attractions and dangers of modernity emerged from the cases of women accused of unusual murder. If we return to the key themes that circulated between the five discourses of femininity – sexuality, pathology, care/duty and family life – it becomes clear that they were imbricated in competing perceptions of modernity. Norma Everson and Marilyn Bain, both portrayed as 'masculine women', could be interpreted as belonging to London's emerging post-war lesbian subculture (see Jennings, 2006).[2] Marilyn, who met her flatmate Jan, the woman she stabbed, at the Gateways Club was constructed as a member of the seedy, urban underworld. Criminal justice representations of both women were derogatory; constructions of Norma were framed in language that equated female masculinity with pathology and representations of Marilyn stressed her moral dissolution. These constructions reflect anxieties about not only transformations in sexual behaviours and subjectivities, but also metropolitan lifestyles. They signal fears that modernity could mean decline in sexual morals and changes to the established social order, which was based on the heterosexual partnership and the nuclear family.

The temptations of the city, an emblem of modernity (Swanson, 2007), and its potential threat to the stability of sexual morality, arises as an issue in the case of Veronica Collins. In the prosecution narrative of the events that occurred on the night her boyfriend, Eamonn, stabbed another young man, Veronica was located in the milieu of Birmingham's urban underworld, which revolved around the all night haunts of working-class young people. According to this reading of her subjectivity, she was a symbol of both feminine danger and, as a prostitute, the tawdry pleasures of the city. The judge's summing up of the case presented a different version of Veronica that emphasised instead the heterosexual conventionality of her wish to protect 'her man'. This was despite the fact that she and Eamonn cohabited without being married, indicating the beginnings of a shift in sexual mores to include a wider range of heterosexual formations.

Fears of impending modernity as a threat to tradition can be divined from the representation of Edith Chubb as a respectable woman and bulwark of traditional working-class femininity. The sentimentalised portrayal of Edith as a self-sacrificing 'Mum' figure articulated nostalgia for the British working class as representative of community, decency and authenticity (on nostalgia, see Brooke, 2001). It expressed anxiety that consumerism and modern living would corrupt working-class values. Paradoxically, the narrative of Edith as an overburdened woman stretched too far hinted at the benefits of modern family life in smaller units with fewer children and fewer obligations to wider relatives. Renee Hargreaves, although represented as a respectable woman, was not portrayed with the same symbolic intensity. However, her insertion into a well-established representation of British womanhood, the spinster, meant that she did not threaten boundaries of gender and sexuality, or signal new, plural subjectivities.

Analysis of unusual cases of mid-twentieth-century women accused of murder uncovers a variety of cultural constructions of modernity. In addition to hopes and fears about the changes modernisation would bring, there were also anxieties that British society would fail to properly modernise. These can be connected to wider disquiet concerning Britain's relative loss in status as world power, which was linked to its new position as a post-imperial nation (Black and Pemberton, 2004). The damaged personality and witch discourses constructed femininities conceived as a drag on modernity. In an era when women symbolised the modern (Geraghty, 2000), those perceived as 'anti-modern' forces were open to negative representation. Damaged personalities such as Shirley Campbell and Helen Sterry had not responded to the new interventions of the welfare state, and had not managed to work sufficiently on their own subjectivities to achieve acceptable expressions of emotion and behaviour (see Rose, 1999). They represented the persistence of certain social problems, which expert knowledge could not solve.

The witch discourse was also a construction of anti-modernity. Its mid-twentieth-century iteration as poor, disreputable womanhood highlighted another social group seemingly impervious to modern transformations. It is particularly significant that the witch is an older woman, as she can symbolise failure to modernise. Sarah Harvey and Mary Wilson stood for the bad old ways of poverty – scraping by, low morals and female domination. Poverty had supposedly been eradicated by the post-war welfare reforms (Coates and Silburn, 1973). Those who failed to escape its grasp failed to participate in new, forward-looking Britain, in which standards of living had risen and consumer goods were available to all. Similarly to Sarah and Mary, Alice Fletcher was also constructed in relation to disreputable poverty, although in her case this was linked to the seedy landscapes of the inner city and the disorder of immigrant areas, another drag on modernity.

The mid-twentieth-century iterations of discourses of femininity in relation to women accused of murder demonstrate the ambiguous and ambivalent cultural understandings of post-war modernity and its impact on British society. Fears of the possible damaging effects of modernisation jostled with anxieties that certain sections of the population would act as a brake on modernity. The gender constructions that emerge from the cases show how these different interpretations of Britain as a modern society also involved negotiation of whom British society should include. Analysis of discourses of womanhood reveal how femininity becomes a symbol for a variety of issues, which relate to the appropriate behaviour of members of the collective, and how these members should conduct themselves (Anthias et al., 1992). Constructions of belonging and non-belonging should be understood as matters for dispute, as they entail cultural struggles over where these boundaries should be drawn.

In late 1950s and early 1960s Britain, the contestations over who 'belonged' as valuable members of the collective circled around important social shifts, such as changes to gender and sexual relations, the heightened status of the respectable working class and the arrival of immigrants from the Commonwealth. As explored in relation to Edith Chubb, white working-class British people could hold the status of valued citizen if they could be identified with attributes such as duty and respectability. The symbolic belonging of working-class people was, however, conditional. Those perceived as unruly, licentious and 'rough' were not examples of the 'people'. Another important component of belonging was whiteness. In the mid-twentieth century the British working class was symbolically constructed as 'white', which was part of its new status as representative of Britishness (Bonnett, 1998). This drew a boundary around the attainment of Britishness, which automatically excluded those who were not constructed as white. The significance of 'race'/ethnicity can seen in the construction of Shirley Campbell as a damaged personality, and Alice Fletcher as a dominant 'mastermind' and rough woman.

Appropriate sexual behaviour was a further element of respectable British citizenship. Sexuality is frequently a key aspect of normative national identity (Mosse, 1985), particularly in terms of the sexual behaviour of women (Yuval-Davis, 1997). The cases of Yvonne Jennion, Norma Everson and Marilyn Bain show how in late 1950s and early 1960s Britain, 'belonging' required perceived heterosexuality (or a lifestyle that did not threaten hegemonic heterosexuality, as in the case of Renee Hargreaves). The negative portrayal of Lilian Chubb, Edith Chubb's victim, as a worthless spinster also demonstrates the power of heterosexuality, and appropriate femininity as connoting married motherhood, to assemble the boundaries of mid-twentieth-century belonging. It also highlights the contingency of gender representations, as spinsterhood was figured very differently in relation to Renee and Lilian. The symbolic exclusion of certain groups and identities from valued citizenship highlights the conditional and contingent nature of cultural recognition in late 1950s and early 1960s Britain.

A 'murder and meanings' approach enables us to identify mid-twentieth-century cultural anxieties around which the contours of Britishness were being reshaped. In keeping with this approach, it is also important to acknowledge the porousness of cultural boundaries as social changes occur (Walkowitz, 1992; Shapiro, 1996). Although perceived as preceding the wider-ranging social shifts of the later 1960s, 1957–62 is a critical era that adumbrated the major transformations in post-war British life. Sexual norms were shifting, as were the definitions of what constituted an ideal marriage. The boundaries of women's acceptable roles were also in flux, with the increased acceptability of married mothers performing paid work outside the home. Cultural boundaries and norms of gender were not fixed. Analysis of unusual cases of mid-twentieth-century women accused of murder reveals the tensions and anxieties that the permeability of these frontiers could induce.

Appendix – Two Further Cases from the Sample

Hilde Adames (DPP2/3098)

Late one evening in September 1960, Hilde, 38, arrived at the bungalow in Bedfordshire where her husband and son lived. She had been away in Europe for several months, having visited Spain, France, Belgium and subsequently Germany, the country of her birth. Through the window of the bungalow, she could see them sat on the sofa watching television along with a woman Hilde did not know. Hilde had bought a Mauser pistol whilst in Germany, and she entered the bungalow, stood in the living room doorway, and shot the woman. No one had been aware of her presence until they heard the explosion from the gun. Francis, Hilde's husband, wrestled the gun from her and then checked the pulse of Phyllis Shields, his friend who had been staying with him for a few days. She was dead.

Hilde and Francis met while he was stationed in Germany with the United Nations Relief and Rehabilitation Administration. They began a relationship, married and had a child. In 1947, Francis was discharged from the UNRRA and returned to England. Hilde and their son, Arthur, remained in Germany until she could get a passport in 1948, when they moved to Britain. Three days later, she attempted suicide and was certified insane. Hilde was diagnosed with paranoid schizophrenia and admitted to mental hospital. She was again admitted to mental hospital in 1956, and remained there until 1958. Upon release, she went to live with her husband and son. When she made another suicide attempt in November 1959, Francis asked her to leave. Although Hilde came back for a couple of months in 1960, Francis again asked her to leave.

After being remanded to Holloway prison, Hilde was certified insane and was removed to a mental hospital. She claimed to have shot Phyllis because she didn't think her husband should have another woman in the house, but she also claimed that it was a mistake and she had been aiming for Francis. The initial committal hearing at a Magistrate's Court had to be abandoned due to Hilde struggling with women police officers and a nurse in the dock. A short committal was held in a mental hospital at which she was found unfit to plead to the charge of capital murder (defined as such under the Homicide Act 1957, as she had used a gun), and was detained at Her Majesty's pleasure.

Alice Louisa Lyons (DPP2/3020)

One night in October 1959, Alice Louisa, 39, hauled her 71-year-old mother, Alice Amelia, out of the bed they shared, threw her onto the floor, bit her on the arms and jumped up and down on her with her bare feet. Their neighbour below, Sydney Simmonds, heard thumps and the noise of Alice Amelia moaning, and called the police. Alice Amelia had a broken hip and was taken to hospital. Alice

Louisa was charged with grievous bodily harm. Ten days later, Alice Amelia died from a pulmonary embolism (blood clot) resulting from her fracture. Alice Louisa was initially charged with her mother's manslaughter, but this was changed to murder.

Alice Louisa had lived in London with both of her parents all her life, until her father died in 1957. At this time, she started to share her mother's bed. Alice Louisa had been in receipt of disabled persons' benefit since 1949, when she had had a stroke. This left her subject to epileptic fits and with restricted mobility. Since July 1959, four assaults by Alice Louisa on her mother had been reported to the police, and three of them had resulted in Alice Amelia being treated in hospital for cuts and bruises. She had refused to take action against her daughter until an assault that happened around a week before the one that caused her death, after which she applied for a summons to the Magistrate's Court. Alice Louisa's fatal attack on her mother happened during an argument about the summons.

The prison medical officer recommended that Alice Louisa was suffering from diminished responsibility at the time of the attack on Alice Amelia. However, it appears that Alice Louisa's defence at trial was involuntary manslaughter (it is possible both defences were offered), and this was the verdict delivered by the jury. She was sentenced to 3 years in prison.

Notes

Introduction: Women, Murder and Femininity

1. Not all of the cases in this book are of women found guilty of murder – some were convicted of manslaughter. I have chosen to mainly adopt the term 'murder', rather than 'homicide' (which incorporates manslaughter) as 'murder' is more prevalent in everyday cultural representations, which do not necessarily draw legal distinctions, and as such it carries greater symbolic weight.
2. Statistics from Australia (Verhoeven, 1993), England and Wales (Chan, 2001) and the United States (Jensen, 2001) indicate that women perpetrate around 10 per cent of homicides.
3. In full, the six stories are: Madonna/whore; sexual passion/love as an 'excuse' for crime; reproduction and madness; figure of evil – witch or monster; criminal woman as 'not woman'; and female as devious and manipulative (Naylor, 1995, p. 81).
4. The full eight narratives: sexuality and sexual deviance; (absence of) physical attractiveness; bad wives; bad mothers; mythical monsters; mad cows; evil manipulators; and non-agents (Jewkes, 2004, p. 113).

Five Gender Representations of Women Who Kill

1. This phenomenon is not exclusive to the contemporary United States. See Ballinger (2000) on the executions of masculine women in twentieth-century England and Wales.
2. 'Prostitute' is Aileen Wuornos' own description of how she earned money (Hart, 1994).
3. The term 'race'/ethnicity is employed to explore both how entrenched stereotypes and beliefs about racial difference encode certain 'racial' identities as subordinate, and how ethnicity is figured as perceived cultural differences between groups. Social understandings of ethnic groups and differences are implicated in relations of power, but the term 'ethnicity' does not carry the same associations of perceived biological traits that 'race' does. See Fenton (1999).
4. The 'muse/mastermind' is my own designation, but other feminist writers have highlighted the dichotomous construction of women involved in killing with male partners. See Cameron and Frazer (1987) on the 'Pygmalion/Lady MacBeth' representations of Myra Hindley, Kilty and Frigon (2007) on the construction of Karla Homolka as either 'in danger' or 'dangerous' and Morrissey (2003) on women who kill as either manipulators or dupes.

5. Clytemnestra is a queen from classical Greek mythology, who along with her lover, Aegisthus, kills her husband, Agamemnon. Her character represents subversive female power.
6. Mary Bell's case remains well known in Britain. In 1993, two 10-year-old boys, Robert Thompson and John Venables, killed 3-year-old James Bulger in Bootle, northern England. This drew comparisons with Mary, and is the only other case of children killing children in twentieth-century Britain to generate so much notoriety. On the Bulger case, see James and Jenks (1996) and Haydon and Scraton (2000).
7. *The Bad Seed* is a novel by William March published in 1954 and made into a film in 1956. The plot concerns an 8-year-old female child who murders several people for trivial reasons.
8. The Altamont Festival was a large rock festival held in California. While the Rolling Stones were on stage, an audience member was stabbed and kicked to death by Hell's Angels bikers, who provided security for the event. The 'Manson Family murders' refers to the murders of Sharon Tate, actress and wife of film director, Roman Polanski, and three others who were at her house the evening four members of the 'Manson Family' broke in and stabbed them to death, and to the murder of a further two people the following night. The 'Family' was a commune/cult that formed in California around Charles Manson, an aspiring musician. Although these are American examples, they were widely reported in Britain.
9. This is not to suggest that the regulation of masculine sexuality, particularly in relation to homosexuality, is insignificant. See Mosse (1985) and Foucault (1990).
10. The Bluebeard legend is about a woman who marries an aristocrat, only to discover a blood-filled room in his house, which contains the dead bodies of his previous wives mounted on hooks.
11. A woman on a train bound for New York was arrested on 9 May 1908 on suspicion of being Belle. She was released after questioning (*New York Times*, 10 May 1908).
12. 'European' was the Census definition of white South Africans used in 1921, 1936 and 1946 and was the state's official designation of whiteness. It was one of four racial classifications. The others were 'Native', 'Mixed and Other Coloured' and 'Asiatic' ('Indian' in 1946). Racial classification was administered by the white elite as part of its system of control over the majority. See Christopher (2002).
13. Daisy was not universally perceived as ugly. The South African *Sunday Times* described her as 'a dapper little woman dressed in black' (23 October 1932, reproduced in Dreyer, 2006).

1 Gender, Murder and Mid-Twentieth-Century England and Wales

1. The publisher, Penguin, was tried for obscenity when they issued a full version of the novel. The new Act enabled the argument that *Lady Chatterley's Lover* should be published on the grounds of literary merit, and Penguin won the case.

2. As explored in Part II, section 'The muse/mastermind dichotomy', its recommendations on prostitution were not liberalising.
3. In a 1957 speech, Macmillan stated, 'most of our people have never had it so good'. He discussed the new found prosperity of the British people, but warned that measures would need to be taken in order to maintain growth (Hennessey, 2007, p. 533).
4. In practice, 40 per cent of men and 90 per cent of women found guilty of murder 1900–49 were reprieved and therefore went to prison (Christoph, 1962). However, death was the only sentence that could be given by the judge in this period.

2 Gender Representations of Twelve Mid-Twentieth-Century Women Accused of Murder

1. Approved schools were for young people judged as delinquent by the courts and entailed a 3-year sentence. See Cox (2003) on girls and approved schools in mid-twentieth-century Britain.
2. National Society for the Prevention of Cruelty to Children, a children's welfare organisation.
3. This organisation provided supervision to individuals after they were released from prison.
4. Although referred to as a 'nurse', Edith was not fully qualified and was a nursing assistant.
5. Complete acquittal was not an option as Edith had admitted to causing Lilian's death.
6. It does not state in Renee's file whether or not she was divorced. Most working-class people who separated before legal aid for divorce cases became available in 1950 did not formally divorce (McGregor, 1957).
7. Due to the complexity of the case, there were four police reports and an additional progress report from the police.
8. The Solicitor General is deputy to the Attorney General, the chief legal advisor to the British Government. The Attorney and Solicitor General oversee the Director of Public Prosecutions.
9. This construction was the deviant flipside to the respectable 'Mum' depiction, which was explored in relation to Edith Chubb in the previous chapter.
10. At the time, Queen's Counsel were barristers recognised as experts in their field of law. Heilbron was actually appointed as King's Counsel in 1949.

3 Conclusion to Part II

1. On Sarah Harvey, see *New York Times*, 14 October 1960; *Chicago Tribune*, October 1960; *Time*, 31 October 1960, on Mary Wilson, see *Miami News*, 29 March 1958; *Modesto Bee*, 12 December 1957; *Hartford Courant*, 10 December 1957, on Edith Chubb, see Seal (2009a) on the *Mirror* and *Sunday Mirrors'* campaign to have her released from prison.

2. This point is complicated by both women's denial of a lesbian subjectivity, particularly in the case of Norma, who stated that she did not experience sexual feelings at all. However, the case file material indicates that she and Gladys, the woman with whom she lived, were members of a supportive all female community in their area of London.

Bibliography

The national archives

ASSI13/509
ASSI26/262
ASSI45/335
CRIM1/3700
DPP2/2658
DPP2/2767
DPP2/2782
DPP2/2834
DPP2/3020
DPP2/3098
DPP2/3153
HO291/242
HO301
J82/28
J82/69
J82/114
J82/150
J82/152
J82/160
J82/195

Books, articles and websites

'A Mummy in the Closet', *Time*, 19 October 1960.
Alcoff, L and Gray, L (1993) 'Survivor Discourse: Transgression or Recuperation?', *Signs*, 18 (2) 260–290.
Alford, R P (2006) 'Appellate Review of Racist Summations: Redeeming the Promise of Searching Analysis', *Michigan Journal of Race and Law*, 11 (2) 325–365.
Allen, C (2004) *Practical Guide to Evidence*, London: Cavendish.
The Allitt Inquiry (1994) London: HMSO.
Amnesty International (2000) 'Death Penalty/Legal Concern – Wanda Jean Allen', UA 355/00, http://asiapacific.amnesty.org/library/index/ENGAMR511772000?open&of=ENG-USA. Accessed 6 October 2008.
Anderson, T and Twining, W (1991) *Analysis of Evidence: How to Do Things With Facts*, London: Weidenfield and Nicolson.
Anthias, F (2002) 'Beyond Feminism and Multiculturalism: Locating Difference and the Politics of Location', *Women's Studies International Forum*, 25 (3) 275–286.

Anthias, F, Yuval-Davis, N and Cain, H (1992) *Racialized Boundaries: Race, Nation, Gender, Colour, and Class in the Anti-Racist Struggle*, London: Taylor and Francis.

Arieti, S (1963) 'Psychopathic Personality: Some Views on its Psychopathology and Psychodynamics', *Comprehensive Psychiatry*, 4, 301–312.

Arieti, S (1967) *The Intrapsychic Self*, New York: Basic Books.

Arrigo, B A and Shipley, S (2001) 'The Confusion Over Psychopathy (I): Historical Considerations', *International Journal of Offender Therapy and Comparative Criminology*, 45 (3) 325–344.

Arrigo, B A and Williams, C R (2006) *Philosophy, Crime and Criminology*, Urbana, IL: University of Illinois Press.

Atwood, M (1997) *Alias Grace*, New York: Anchor.

Bailey, P (1999) 'Jazz at the Spirella: Coming of Age in Coventry in the 1950s', B Conekin, F Mort and C Waters (eds), *Moments of Modernity: Reconstructing Britain 1945–1964*, London: Rivers Oram.

Bailey, V (2000) 'The Shadow of the Gallows: The Death Penalty and the British Labour Government, 1945–52', *Law and History Review*, 18 (2) 305–349.

Baker, D V (2008) 'Black Female Executions in Historical Context', *Criminal Justice Review*, 33 (1) 64–88.

Bakhtin, M M (1986) *Speech Genres and Other Late Essays*, Austin: University of Texas Press.

Bakken, G M and Farrington, B (2009) *Women Who Kill Men: California Courts and the Press*, Lincoln, NE: University of Nebraska Press.

Ballinger, A (2000) *Dead Woman Walking: Executed Women in England and Wales 1900–1965*, Aldershot: Ashgate.

Ballinger, A (2007) 'Masculinity in the Dock: Legal Responses to Male Violence and Female Retaliation in England and Wales, 1900–1965', *Social and Legal Studies*, 16 (4) 459–481.

Barnett, B (2006) 'Medea in the Media: Narrative and Myth in Newspaper Coverage of Women Who Kill Their Children', *Journalism*, 7 (4) 411–432.

Basilio, M (1996) 'Corporal Evidence: Representations of Aileen Wuornos', *Art Journal*, 55 (4) 56–61.

Bauman, Z (1991) *Modernity and Ambivalence*, Cambridge: Polity Press.

Beck, R B (2000) *The History of South Africa*, Westport, CT: Greenwood.

Beck, U (1992) *Risk Society: Towards a New Modernity*, London: Sage.

Beinart, W (2001) *Twentieth-Century South Africa*, 2nd edition, Oxford: Oxford University Press.

Bell, C and Fox, M (1996) 'Telling Stories of Women Who Kill', *Social and Legal Studies*, 5 (4) 471–494.

Berenson, E (1993) *The Trial of Madame Caillaux*, Berkeley, CA: University of California Press.

Bergler, E (1958) 'D H Lawrence's "The Fox" and the Psychoanalytic Theory on Lesbianism', *Journal of Nervous and Mental Disease*, 126 (5) 488–491.

Beukes, L (2004) *Maverick: Extraordinary Women From South Africa's Past*, Cape Town: Oshun.

Bhabha, H K (1996) 'Culture's In-Between', S Hall and P Du Gay (eds) *Questions of Cultural Identity*, London: Sage.

Bibbings, L (2004) 'Heterosexuality as Harm: Fitting In', P Hillyard, C Pantazis, S Tombs and D Gordon (eds) *Beyond Criminology: Taking Harm Seriously*, London: Pluto Press.

Biggs, J (1955) *The Guilty Mind*, New York: Harcourt, Brace and Co.
Binder, G and Weisberg, R (2000) *Literary Criticisms of Law*, Princeton, NJ: Princeton University Press.
Birch, H (1993) 'If Looks Could Kill: Myra Hindley and the Iconography of Evil', H Birch (ed.) *Moving Targets: Women, Murder and Representation*, London: Virago.
Black, L and Pemberton, H (2004) 'Introduction – The Uses (and Abuses) of Affluence', L Black and H Pemberton (eds) *An Affluent Society?: Britain's Post-war 'Golden Age' Revisited*, Aldershot: Ashgate.
Bland, L (2002) *Banishing the Beast: Feminism, Sex and Morality*, London: I B Tauris.
Block, B P and Hostettler, J (1997) *Hanging in the Balance: A History of the Abolition of Capital Punishment in Britain*, Winchester: Waterside Press.
Blom-Cooper, L and Morris, T (2004) *With Malice Aforethought: A Study of the Crime and Punishment for Homicide*, Oxford: Oxford University Press.
Bonnett, A (1998) 'How the British Working Class Became White: The Symbolic (Re)formation of Racialized Capitalism', *Journal of Historical Sociology*, 11 (3) 316–340.
Bools, C, Neale, B and Meadow, R (1994) 'Munchausen Syndrome by Proxy: A Study of Psychopathology', *Child Abuse and Neglect*, 18 (9) 773–788.
Borowitz, A (2002) *Blood and Ink: An International Guide to Fact-Based Crime Literature*, Kent, OH: Kent State University Press.
Borowitz, A (2005) 'The Snows on the Moors: C P Snow and Pamela Hansford Johnson on the Moors Murder Case', *Legal Studies Forum*, 29 (2) 571–588.
Bourdieu, P (1984) *Distinction: A Social Critique of the Judgement of Taste*, Cambridge, MA: Harvard University Press.
Bowlby, J (1953) *Child Care and the Growth of Love*, London: Penguin.
Braidotti, R (1994) *Nomadic Subjects: Embodiment and Sexual Difference in Contemporary Feminist Thought*, New York: Columbia University Press.
Broadstairs and St Peters Mail, 7 May 1958.
Bronte, C ([1847] 2004) *Jane Eyre*, Whitefish: Kessinger.
Brooke, S (2001) 'Gender and Working Class Identity in Britain During the 1950s', *Journal of Social History*, 34 (4) 773–795.
Broomfield, N (1992) *Aileen: The Selling of a Serial Killer* [Motion Picture], United Kingdom: Channel 4 Television Corporation.
Broomfield, N (2003) *Aileen: Life and Death of a Serial Killer* [Motion Picture], United States: Lafayette Films.
Brown, A D (2000) 'Making Sense of Inquiry Sensemaking', *Journal of Management Studies*, 37 (1) 45–75.
Burgess-Proctor, A (2006) 'Intersections of Race, Class, Gender and Crime: Future Directions for Feminist Criminology', *Feminist Criminology*, 1 (1) 27–47.
Buring, D (1997) *Lesbian and Gay Memphis: Building Communities Behind the Magnolia Curtain*, London: Taylor and Francis.
Burton, A M (1994) *Burdens of History: British Feminists, Indian Women and Imperial Culture*, Chapel Hill, NC: University of North Carolina Press.
Butler, J (1993) *Bodies That Matter: On the Discursive Limits of 'Sex'*, London: Routledge.
Butler, J (1997) *Excitable Speech: A Politics of the Performative*, London: Routledge.
Butler, J (1999) *Gender Trouble: Feminism and the Subversion of Identity*, 2nd edition, London: Routledge.

Butler, J (2000) 'Agencies of Style for a Liminal Subject', S Hall, P Gilroy, L Grossberg and A McRobbie (eds) *Without Guarantees: Essays in Honour of Stuart Hall*, London: Verso.
Butler, J (2004) *Undoing Gender*, London: Routledge.
Byrne, C F and Trew, K J (2008) 'Pathways Through Crime: The Development of Crime and Desistance in the Accounts of Men and Women Offenders', *The Howard Journal of Criminal Justice*, 47 (3) 238–258.
Cameron, D (1996) 'Rosemary West: Motives and Meanings', *The Journal of Sexual Aggression*, 4 (2) 68–80.
Cameron, D and Frazer, E (1987) *The Lust to Kill: A Feminist Investigation of Sexual Murder*, Cambridge: Polity Press.
Canning, K (2006) *Gender History in Practice: Historical Perspectives on Bodies, Class and Citizenship*, Ithaca, NY: Cornell University Press.
Caprio, F (1957) *Female Homosexuality: A Psychodynamic Study of Lesbianism*, London: Peter Owen.
Carlen, P (1983) *Women's Imprisonment: A Study in Social Control*, London: Routledge and Kegan Paul.
Carline, A (2005a) 'Women Who Kill Their Abusive Partners: From Sameness to Gender Construction', *Liverpool Law Review*, 26 (1) 13–44.
Carline, A (2005b) 'Zoora Shah: "An Unusual Woman"', *Social and Legal Studies*, 14 (2) 215–238.
Castle, T (1993) *The Apparitional Lesbian: Female Homosexuality and Modern Culture*, New York: Columbia University Press.
Chan, W (2001) *Women, Murder and Justice*, Basingstoke: Palgrave Macmillan.
Chancer, L S (2005) *High-Profile Crimes: When Legal Cases Become Social Causes*, Chicago: University of Chicago Press.
Chesler, P (1993) 'Women in the Criminal Justice System: A Woman's Right to Self Defence, the Case of Aileen Wuornos', *St John's Law Review*, 66 (4) 933–977.
Chesney-Lind, M (2006) 'Patriarchy, Crime and Justice', *Feminist Criminology*, 1 (1) 6–26.
Chesney-Lind, M and Eliason, M (2006) 'From Invisible to Incorrigible: The Demonization of Marginalized Women and Girls', *Crime Media Culture*, 2 (1) 29–47.
Chesney-Lind, M and Pasko, L (2004) *The Female Offender: Girls, Women and Crime*, Thousand Oaks: Sage.
Chicago Tribune, 19 October 1960.
Choi, P, Henshaw, C, Baker, S, Tree, J (2005) 'Supermum, Superwife, Supereverything: Performing Femininity in the Transition to Motherhood', *Journal of Reproductive and Infant Psychology*, 23 (2) 167–180.
Christoph, J B (1962) *Capital Punishment and British Politics*, London: Allen and Unwin.
Christopher, A J (2002) '"To Define the Indefinable": Population Classification and the Census in South Africa', *Area*, 34 (4) 401–408.
Cleckley, H (1941) *The Mask of Sanity*, St Louis: The C V Mosby Company.
Coates, K and Silburn, R (1973) *Poverty: The Forgotten Englishmen*, London: Penguin.
Codd, H (1998) 'Older Women, Criminal Justice, and Women's Studies', *Women's Studies International Forum*, 21 (2) 183–192.
Cohen, A K (1955) *Delinquent Boys: The Culture of the Gang*, New York: Free Press.

Collins, M (2002) 'The Fall of the English Gentleman: The National Character in Decline c. 1918–1970', *Historical Research*, 75 (187) 90–111.

Collins, M (2003) *Modern Love: An Intimate History of Men and Women in Twentieth-Century Britain*, London: Atlantic Books.

Comaroff, J and Comaroff, J (2004) 'Criminal Obsessions, after Foucault: Postcoloniality, Policing, and the Metaphysics of Disorder', *Critical Inquiry*, 30 (4) 800–824.

Conekin, B, Mort, F and Waters, C (1999) 'Introduction', B Conekin, F Mort and C Waters (eds) *Moments of Modernity?: Reconstructing Britain, 1945–64*, London: Rivers Oram.

Connell, R W (1987) *Gender and Power: Society, the Person, and Sexual Politics*, Cambridge: Polity Press.

Conrad, P and Angell, A (2004) 'Homosexuality and Remedicalization', *Society*, 41 (5) 32–39.

Cook, H (2004) *The Long Sexual Revolution: English Women, Sex and Contraception 1800–1975*, Buckingham: Open University Press.

Cornell, D (1995) 'What is Ethical Feminism?', S Benhabib, J Butler, D Cornell and N Fraser (eds) *Feminist Contentions: A Philosophical Exchange*, London: Routledge.

Cowie, J, Cowie, V and Slater, E (1968) *Delinquency in Girls*, London: Heinemann.

Cox, P (2002) 'Race, Delinquency and Difference in Twentieth Century Britain', P Cox and H Shore (eds) *Becoming Delinquent: British and European Youth, 1650–1950*, Aldershot: Ashgate.

Cox, P (2003) *Gender, Justice and Welfare*, Basingstoke: Palgrave Macmillan.

Cresswell, T (1996) *Out of Place: Geography, Ideology and Transgression*, Minneapolis: University of Minnesota Press.

Cruikshank, M (1992) *The Gay and Lesbian Liberation Movement*, London: Routledge.

D'Cruze, S (2001) ' "A Little Decent Looking Woman": Violence Against Nineteenth-Century Working Women and the Social History of Crime', A M Gallagher, C Lubelska and L Ryan (eds) *Re-presenting the Past: Women and History*, Harlow: Pearson Education Limited.

D'Cruze, S (2006) ' "The Damned Place was Haunted": The Gothic, Middlebrow Culture and Inter-war "Notable" Trials', *Literature and History*, 15 (1) 37–58.

D'Cruze, S, Walklate, S and Pegg, S (2006) *Murder: Social and Historical Approaches to Understanding Murder and Murderers*, Cullompton: Willan.

Daily Mirror, 25 March 1958.

Daily Telegraph, 2 May 1958.

Daily Telegraph, 3 May 1958.

Daly, K (1997) 'Different Ways of Conceptualizing Sex/Gender in Feminist Theory and their Implications for Criminology', *Theoretical Criminology*, 1 (1) 25–51.

Davidoff, L, Doolittle, M, Fink, J and Holden, K (1999) *The Family Story: Blood, Contract and Intimacy, 1830–1960*, London: Longman.

Davies, O (1999) *Witchcraft, Magic and Culture, 1736–1951*, Manchester: Manchester University Press.

Davies, O (2001) 'Newspapers and Witchcraft', B P Levack (ed.) *New Perspectives on Witchcraft, Magic and Demonology*, London: Taylor and Francis.

Davis, K (2008) 'Intersectionality as Buzzword', *Feminist Theory*, 9 (1) 67–85.

De Lauretis, T (1987) *Technologies of Gender: Essays on Theory, Film and Fiction*, Basingstoke: Macmillan.

Demos, J P (1983) *Entertaining Satan: Witchcraft and the Culture of Early New England*, Oxford: Oxford University Press.

Dennis, N, Henriques, F and Slaughter, C (1956) *Coal is Our Life: An Analysis of a Yorkshire Mining Community*, London: Eyre and Spottiswoode.

Derrida, J (1994) 'Spectres of Marx', *New Left Review*, 205, 31–58.

Devlin, P (1960) *The Criminal Prosecution in England*, London: Oxford University Press.

Dillinger, J (2004) 'Terrorists and Witches: Popular Ideas of Evil in the Early Modern Period', *History of European Ideas*, 30 (2) 167–182.

Doane, J and Hodges, D (1992) *From Klein to Kristeva: Psychoanalytic Feminism and the Search for the 'Good Enough' Mother*, Ann Arbor, MI: University of Michigan Press.

Doane, M A (1991) *Femmes Fatales: Feminism, Film Theory, Psychoanalysis*, London: Routledge.

Dodson, L (2007) 'Wage-Poor Mothers and Moral Economy', *Social Politics*, 14 (2) 258–280.

Dolan, F (1994) *Dangerous Familiars: Representations of Domestic Crime in England, 1550–1700*, Ithaca, NY: Cornell University Press.

Douglas, M (1966) *Purity and Danger: An Analysis of Concepts of Pollution and Taboo*, London: Routledge and Kegan Paul.

Dreiser, T ([1925] 2000) *An American Tragedy*, London: Penguin.

Dreyer, N (2006) *A Century of Sundays: 100 Years of Breaking the News in the Sunday Times, 1906–2006*, Cape Town: Zebra.

Duggan, L (1993) 'The Trials of Alice Mitchell: Sensationalism, Sexology, and the Lesbian Subject in Turn-of-the-Century America', *Signs*, 18 (4) 791–814.

Earle, N (1961) *What's Wrong with the Church?*, London: Penguin.

Edwards, J (1957) 'The Homicide Act, 1957: A Critique', *British Journal of Delinquency*, 8 (1) 49–61.

Einhorn, B (1996) 'Links Across Difference: Gender, Ethnicity and Nationalism', *Women's Studies International Forum*, 19 (1/2) 1–3.

Elkind, P (1990) *The Death Shift: Nurse Genene Jones and the Texas Baby Murders*, New York: Onyx.

Ellis, H ([1897] 1937) *Studies in the Psychology of Sex, Volume 2: Sexual Inversion*, New York: Random House.

Epstein, D, Johnson, R and Steinberg, D L (2000) 'Twice Told Tales: Transformation, Recuperation and Emergence in the Age of Consent Debates 1998', *Sexualities*, 3 (1) 5–30.

Ewick, P and Silbey, S S (1995) 'Subversive Stories and Hegemonic Tales: Toward a Sociology of Narrative', *Law and Society Review*, 29 (2) 197–226.

Faludi, S (1991) *Backlash: The Undeclared War Against Women*, London: Vintage.

Farr, K A (1999) 'Defeminizing and Dehumanizing Female Murderers: Depictions of Lesbians on Death Row', *Women and Criminal Justice*, 11 (1) 49–66.

Fenton, S (1999) *Ethnicity: Racism, Class and Culture*, Basingstoke: Palgrave Macmillan.

Ferrell, J, Hayward, K, Morrison, W and Presdee, M (2004) 'Fragments of a Manifesto: Introducing Cultural Criminology Unleashed', J Ferrell, K Hayward,

W Morrison and M Presdee (eds) *Cultural Criminology Unleashed*, London: The GlassHouse Press.

Filetti, J S (2001) 'From Lizzie Borden to Lorena Bobbitt: Violent Women and Gendered Justice', *Journal of American Studies*, 35 (3) 471–484.

Finch, J and Summerfield, P (1991) 'Social Reconstruction and the Emergence of Companionate Marriage, 1945–59', D Clark (ed.) *Marriage, Domestic Life and Social Change*, London: Routledge.

Fink, J (2000) 'Natural Mothers, Putative Fathers, and Innocent Children: The Definition and Regulation of Parental Relationships Outside Marriage in England, 1945–1959', *Journal of Family History*, 25 (2) 178–195.

Fink, J and Holden, K (1999) 'Pictures from the Margins of Marriage: Representations of Spinsters and Single Mothers in the Mid-Victorian Novel, Inter-war Hollywood Melodrama and British Film of the 1950s and 1960s', *Gender and History*, 11 (2) 233–255.

Finnegan, F (1979) *Poverty and Prostitution: A Study of Victorian Prostitutes in York*, Cambridge: Cambridge University Press.

FitzGerald, S A and Muszynski, A (2007) 'Negotiating Female Morality: Place, Agency and Ideology in the Red River Colony', *Women's History Review*, 16 (5) 661–680.

Fleming, V (1939) *The Wizard of Oz* [Motion Picture] United States: Metro-Goldwyn-Meyer.

Flood, G F (1963) 'The Model Sentencing Act: A Higher Level of Penal Law', *Crime and Delinquency*, 9 (4) 370–380.

Flowers, R B and Flowers, H L (2004) *Murders in the United States: Crimes, Killers and Victims*, Jefferson, NC: McFarland.

Foertsch, J (2008) *American Culture in the 1940s*, Edinburgh: Edinburgh University Press.

Foucault, M (1978) 'About the Concept of the "Dangerous Individual" in 19th Century Legal Psychiatry', *International Journal of Law and Psychiatry*, 1 (1) 1–18.

Foucault, M (1979) *Discipline and Punish: The Birth of the Prison*, London: Penguin.

Foucault, M (1989) *The Archaeology of Knowledge*, London: Routledge.

Foucault, M (1990) *The History of Sexuality, Volume 1*, London: Penguin.

Fox, J A and Levin, J (2005) *Extreme Killing: Understanding Serial and Mass Murder*, London: Sage.

Francis, M (2002) 'The Domestication of the Male? Recent Research on Nineteenth- and Twentieth-Century Masculinity', *The Historical Journal*, 45 (3) 637–652.

Fraser, N (1995) 'From Redistribution to Recognition? Dilemmas of Justice in a "Post-Socialist" Age', *New Left Review*, 1, 68–93.

Fraser, N (2000) 'Rethinking Recognition', *New Left Review*, 3, 107–120.

Fraser, N (2007) 'Feminist Politics in the Age of Recognition: A Two-Dimensional Approach to Gender Justice', *Studies in Social Justice*, 1 (1) 23–35.

Freedman, E B (1987) ' "Uncontrolled Desires": The Response to the Sexual Psychopath, 1920–1960', *The Journal of American History*, 74 (1) 83–106.

Freedman, E B (1996) 'The Prison Lesbian: Race, Class and the Construction of the Aggressive Female Homosexual, 1915–1965', *Feminist Studies*, 22 (2) 397–423.

Frigon, S (2006) 'Mapping Scripts and Narratives of Women Who Kill Their Husbands in Canada 1866–1954', A Burfoot (ed.) *Killing Women: The Visual Culture of Gender Violence*, Waterloo, ON: Wilfrid Laurier Press.

Furbee, R B (2006) 'Criminal Poisoning: Medical Murderers', *Clinics in Laboratory Medicine*, 26 (1) 255–273.
Fyvel, T R (1961) *The Insecure Offenders: Rebellious Youth in the Welfare State*, London: Chatto and Windus.
Garland, D (2001) *The Culture of Control: Crime and Social Order in Contemporary Society*, Oxford: Oxford University Press.
Gaskill, M (2008) 'The Pursuit of Reality: Recent Research into the History of Witchcraft', *The Historical Journal*, 51 (4) 1069–1088.
Gatens, M (2002) 'The Politics of "Presence" and "Difference": Working Through Spinoza and Eliot', S James and S Palmer (eds) *Visible Women: Essays on Feminist Legal Theory and Political Philosophy*, Oxford: Oxford University Press.
Geraghty, C (2000) *British Cinema in the Fifties: Gender, Genre and the 'New Look'*, London: Routledge.
Gibson, D C (2006) *Serial Murder and Media Circuses*, Westport, CT: Greenwood.
Gibson, M (2007) *Witchcraft Myths in American Culture*, London: Routledge.
Gilbert, P G (2006) *Violence and the Female Imagination: Quebec's Women Writers Reframe Gender in North American Cultures*, Montreal: McGill-Queen's University Press.
Giles, J (1992) ' "Playing Hard to Get": Working-Class Women, Sexuality and Respectability in Britain, 1918–40', *Women's History Review*, 1 (2) 239–255.
Giles, J (2005) 'Good Housekeeping: Professionalising the Housewife, 1920–1950', K Cowman and L A Jackson (eds) *Women and Work Culture, Britain c. 1850–1950*, Aldershot: Ashgate.
Gilligan, C (1982) *In a Different Voice: Psychological Theory and Women's Development*, Cambridge: Harvard University Press.
Gilroy, P (1987) *There Ain't No Black in the Union Jack: The Cultural Politics of Race and Nation*, London: Hutchinson Education.
Glueck, S and Glueck, E L (1934) *Five Hundred Delinquent Women*, New York: Alfred A. Knopf.
Grant, C (2004) *Crime and Punishment in Contemporary Culture*, London: Routledge.
Graycar, R (1996) 'Telling Tales: Legal Stories about Violence Against Women', *Cardozo Studies in Law and Literature*, 8 (2) 297–315.
Greener, M R (1991) 'Social Security Administration's Representative Payee Program: An Act of Benevolence or Cruelty', *Cardozo Law Review*, 12 (6) 2025–2058.
Griggers, C (1995) 'Phantom and Reel Projectors', J Halberstam and I Livingston (eds) *Posthuman Bodies*, Bloomington, IN: Indiana University Press.
The Guardian, 25 March 1958.
The Guardian, 6 April 1962.
The Guardian, 18 May 1993.
The Guardian, 6 December 2007.
Guttmacher, M S (1963) 'Dangerous Offenders', *Crime and Delinquency*, 9 (4) 381–390.
Halberstam, J (1998) *Female Masculinity*, Durham, NC: Duke University Press.
Hall, L A (2000) *Sex, Gender and Social Change in Britain Since 1800*, Basingstoke: Palgrave Macmillan.
Halmari, H and Ostman, J O (2001) 'The Soft-Spoken, Angelic Pickax Killer: The Notion of Discourse Pattern in Controversial News Reporting', *Journal of Pragmatics*, 33 (6) 805–823.

Halttunen, K (1998) *Murder Most Foul: The Killer and the American Gothic Imagination*, Cambridge, MA: Harvard University Press.

Hare, D (1980) 'A Research Scale for the Assessment of Psychopathy in Criminal Populations', *Personality and Individual Differences*, 1 (1) 111–119.

Hare, D (1993) *Without Conscience: The Disturbing World of the Psychopaths Among Us*, London: The Guilford Press.

Harley, D (1990) 'Historians as Demonologists: The Myth of the Midwife-witch', *The Society for the Social History of Medicine*, 3 (1) 1–26.

Hart, L (1994) *Fatal Women: Lesbian Sexuality and the Mark of Aggression*, London: Routledge.

Hartford Courant, 10 December 1957.

Hartman, M S (1995) *Victorian Murderesses: A True History of Thirteen Respectable French and English Women Accused of Unspeakable Crimes*, 2nd edition, London: Robson.

Haydon, D and Scraton, P (2000) ' "Condemn a Little More, Understand a Little Less": The Political Context and Rights Implications of the Domestic and European Rulings in the Venables-Thompson Case', *Journal of Law and Society*, 27 (3) 416–448.

Heberle, R (1999) 'Disciplining Gender, or, Are Women Getting Away with Murder?', *Signs*, 24 (4) 1103–1112.

Heberle, R (2001) 'Law's Violence and the Challenge of the Feminine', *Studies in Law, Politics and Society*, 22, 49–73.

Heidensohn, F (1996) *Women and Crime*, 2nd edition, Basingstoke: Macmillan.

Henderson, D K (1939) *Psychopathic States*, New York: W W Norton and Company.

Hendin, J G (2004) *Heartbreakers: Women and Violence in Contemporary Culture and Literature*, New York: Palgrave.

Hendley, N (2007) *Bonnie and Clyde: A Biography*, Westport, CT: Greenwood.

Hennessy, P (2007) *Having it So Good: Britain in the Fifties*, London: Penguin.

The Herald, 29 May 1993.

Herve, H (2007) 'Psychopathy Across the Ages: A History of the Hare Psychopath', H Herve and J Yuille (eds) *The Psychopath: Theory, Research and Practice*, London: Routledge.

Hill, A and Whichelow, A (1964) *What's Wrong with Parliament?*, London: Penguin.

Hinton, P (1999) ' "The Unspeakable Mrs Gunness": The Deviant Woman in Early-Twentieth-Century America', M A Bellesiles (ed.) *Lethal Imagination: Violence and Brutality in American History*, New York: New York University Press.

Hirschfeld, M ([1913] 2000) M A Lombardi-Nash (trans.) *The Homosexuality of Men and Women*, Amherst: Prometheus.

Hoggart, R (1957) *The Uses of Literacy*, London: Chatto and Windus.

Holden, K (2007) *The Shadow of Marriage: Singleness in England, 1914–1960*, Manchester: Manchester University Press.

Holmes, C (1993) 'Women: Witnesses and Witches', *Past and Present*, 140 (1) 45–78.

Howard, A and Smith, M (2004) *River of Blood: Serial Killers and Their Victims*, Parkland, FL: Universal Publishers.

Howarth, J W (2002) 'Executing White Masculinities: Learning from Karla Faye Tucker', *Oregon Law Review*, 81 (1) 183–230.

Hubback, J (1957) *Wives Who Went to College*, London: William Heinemann.

Hubbard, P (1998) 'Sexuality, Immorality and the City: Red-light Districts and the Marginalisation of Female Street Prostitutes', *Gender, Place and Culture*, 5 (1) 55–72.

Hudson, K (2005) *Offending Identities: Sex Offenders' Perspectives on their Treatment and Management*, Cullompton: Willan.

Hughes, G (1959) 'The English Homicide Act of 1957: The Capital Punishment Issue, and Various Reforms in the Law of Murder and Manslaughter', *The Journal of Criminal Law, Criminology and Police Science*, 49 (6) 521–532.

Hughes, K (2001) *The Victorian Governess*, 2nd edition, London: Continuum.

Hunt, A (1998) 'The Great Masturbation Panic and the Discourses of Moral Regulation in Nineteenth and Early Twentieth-Century Britain', *Journal of the History of Sexuality*, 8 (4) 575–615.

Hunt, L (2002) 'Witchcraft and the Occult', S Chibnall and J Petley (eds) *British Horror Cinema*, London: Routledge.

Jackson, L A (2008) '"The Coffee Club Menace": Policing Youth, Leisure and Sexuality in Post-War Manchester', *Cultural and Social History*, 5 (3) 289–308.

Jackson, S (1999) *Heterosexuality in Question*, London: Sage.

Jackson, S and Scott, S (1999) 'Risk Anxiety and the Social Construction of Childhood', D Lupton (ed.) *Risk and Sociocultural Theory*, Cambridge: Cambridge University Press.

James, A and Jenks, C (1996) 'Public Perceptions of Childhood Criminality', *British Journal of Sociology*, 47 (2) 315–331.

Jarvis, M (2005) *Conservative Governments, Morality and Social Change in Affluent Britain, 1957–64*, Manchester: Manchester University Press.

Jenkins, P (2003) *Monster* [Motion Picture], United States: Media 8 Entertainment.

Jenkins, P (1994) *Using Murder: The Social Construction of Serial Homicide*, New York: Aldine de Gruyter.

Jennings, R (2004) 'Lesbian Voices: The Hall Carpenter Oral History Archive and Post-war British Lesbian History', *Sexualities*, 7 (4) 430–444.

Jennings, R (2006) 'The Gateways Club and the Emergence of a Post-Second World War Lesbian Subculture', *Social History*, 31 (2) 206–225.

Jennings, R (2007a) 'From "Woman-Loving Woman" to "Queer": Historiographical Perspectives on Twentieth-Century British Lesbian History', *History Compass*, 5 (6) 1901–1920.

Jennings, R (2007b) *Tomboys and Bachelor Girls: A Lesbian History of Post-War Britain, 1945–71*, Manchester: Manchester University Press.

Jennings, R (2008) '"The Most Uninhibited Party They'd Ever Been To": The Postwar Encounter Between Psychiatry and the British Lesbian, 1945–1971', *Journal of British Studies*, 47 (4) 883–904.

Jensen, V (2001) *Why Women Kill: Homicide and Gender Equality*, London: Lynne Rienner.

Jewkes, Y (2004) *Media and Crime*, London: Sage.

Joannou, M (1994) '"Nothing is Impracticable for a Single, Middle-Aged Woman with an Income of her Own": The Spinster in Women's Fiction of the 1920s', S Oldfield (ed.) *This Working-Day World: Women's Lives and Culture(s) in Britain 1914–1945*, London: Taylor and Francis.

Johnson, P H (1967) *On Iniquity: Some Personal Reflections Arising Out of the Moors Murder Trial*, London: Macmillan.

Johnstone, G (1996) *Medical Concepts and Penal Policy*, London: Cavendish.

Jones, A (1996) *Women Who Kill*, Boston: Beacon Press.
Jones, K (1960) *Mental Health and Social Policy, 1845–1959*, London: Routledge and Kegan Paul.
Jones, J P (2001) 'Forums for Citizenship in Popular Culture', R P Hart and B H Sparrow (eds) *Politics, Discourse, and American Society: New Agendas*, Lanham, MD: Rowman and Littlefield.
Kahn, E (1960) 'Crime and Punishment 1910–1960: Reflections on Changes Since Union in the Law of Criminal Punishment and its Application', *Acta Juridica*, 209, 191–222.
Kandiyoti, D (1991) 'Identity and its Discontents: Women and the Nation', *Millennium – Journal of International Studies*, 20 (3) 429–443.
Karpman, B (1941) 'On the Need of Separating Psychopathy into Distinct Clinical Types: The Symptomatic and Idiopathic', *Journal of Criminal Psychopathology*, 3, 112–137.
Karpman, B (1946) 'Psychopathy in the Scheme of Human Typology', *Journal of Nervous and Mental Disease*, 103 (3) 276–288.
Karpman, B (1948) 'The Myth of the Psychopathic Personality', *American Journal of Psychiatry*, 104 (9) 523–534.
Karpman, B (1951) 'The Sexual Psychopath', *The Journal of Criminal Law, Criminology, and Police Science*, 42 (2) 184–198.
Kemshall, H (2004) 'Risk, Dangerousness and Female Offenders', G McIvor (ed.) *Women Who Offend*, London: Jessica Kingsley Publishers.
Kemshall, H and Maguire, M (2001) 'Public Protection, Partnership and Risk Penality', *Punishment and Society*, 3 (2) 237–264.
Kendall, K (1991) 'The Politics of Premenstrual Syndrome: Implications for Feminist Justice', *Critical Criminology*, 2 (2) 77–98.
Kendall, K (2005) 'Beyond Reason: Social Constructions of Mentally Disordered Female Offenders', R Menzies, D E Chunn and W Chan (eds) *Women, Madness and the Law*, London: Routledge.
Kerr, M (1958) *The People of Ship Street*, London: Routledge and Kegan Paul.
Kilty, J M and Frigon, S (2007) 'Karla Homolka – From a Woman in Danger to a Dangerous Woman', *Women and Criminal Justice*, 17 (4) 37–61.
Kinsey, A (1948) *Sexual Behaviour in the Human Male*, London: Saunders.
Kinsey, A (1953) *Sexual Behaviour in the Human Female*, London: Saunders.
Klein, D (1973) 'The Etiology of Female Crime', *Issues in Criminology*, 8 (2) 3–30.
Knox, S L (1998) *Murder: A Tale of Modern American Life*, Durham, NC: Duke University Press.
Knox, S L (2001) 'The Productive Powers of Confessions of Cruelty', *Postmodern Culture*, 11 (3) 1–19.
Kobil, D T (2003) 'How to Grant Clemency in Unforgiving Times', *Capital University Law Review*, 31 (2) 219–241.
Kocsis, R N and Irwin, H J (1998) 'The Psychological Profile of Serial Offenders and a Redefinition of the Misnomer of Serial Crime', *Psychiatry, Psychology and Law*, 5 (2) 197–213.
Kohn, S (2001) 'Greasing the Wheel: How the Criminal Justice System Hurts Gay, Lesbian, Bisexual and Transgendered People and Why Hate Crime Law Won't Save Them', *New York University Review of Law and Social Change*, 27 (3) 257–280.
Korobkin, L H (1998) *Criminal Conversations: Sentimentality and Nineteenth-Century Legal Stories of Adultery*, New York: Columbia University Press.

Kozol, H L, Boucher, R J and Garofalo, R F (1972) 'The Diagnosis and Treatment of Dangerousness', *Crime and Delinquency*, 18 (4) 371–392.

Krafft-Ebing, R von (1894), C G Chaddock (trans.) *Psychopathia Sexualis, with Especial Reference to Contrary Sexual Instinct: A Medico-Legal Study*, Philadelphia: F A Davis.

Kramar, K J and Watson, W D (2006) 'The Insanities of Reproduction: Medico-Legal Knowledge and the Development of Infanticide Law', *Social and Legal Studies*, 15 (2) 237–255.

Kramer, R and Mitchell, T (2002) *Walk Towards the Gallows: The Tragedy of Hilda Blake, Hanged 1899*, Toronto: University of Toronto Press.

Kristeva, J (1982) *Powers of Horror: An Essay on Abjection*, New York: Columbia University Press.

Kruttschnitt, C (1982) 'Respectable Women and the Law', *The Sociological Quarterly*, 23 (2) 221–234.

Laclau, E and Mouffe, C (2001) *Hegemony and Socialist Strategy: Towards a Radical Democratic Politics*, 2nd edition, London: Verso.

Landy, M (1991) *Imitations of Life: A Reader on Film and Television Melodrama*, Detroit: Wayne State University Press.

Langhamer, C (2005) 'The Meanings of Home in Postwar Britain', *Journal of Contemporary History*, 40 (2) 341–362.

Langlois, J L (1983) 'Belle Gunness, the Lady Bluebeard: Symbolic Inversion in Verbal Art and American Culture', *Signs*, 8 (4) 617–634.

Le Fanu, J S ([1923] 1994) *Madam Crowl's Ghost and Other Stories*, London: Wordsworth.

Lenzenweger, M F and Clarkin, J F (2004) 'The Personality Disorders: History, Classification and Research Issues', M F Lenzenweger and J F Clarkin (eds) *Major Theories of Personality Disorder*, New York: The Guilford Press.

Leonard, E D (2002) *Convicted Survivors: The Imprisonment of Battered Women Who Kill*, Albany, NY: State University of New York Press.

Lewis, J (1992) *Women in Britain Since 1945*, Oxford: Blackwell.

Lewis, J (1999) 'Rethinking Social Policy: Gender and Welfare Regimes', *IWM Working Paper No. 6*, Vienna: Institute for Human Sciences, 1–22.

Light, A (1991) *Forever England: Femininity, Literature and Conservatism Between the Wars*, London: Routledge.

Lindquist, L J (1995) 'Images of Alice: Gender, Deviancy and a Love Murder in Memphis', *Journal of the History of Sexuality*, 6 (1) 30–61.

Lipkin, R J (2000) 'Impeachment and the War Over the Democratization of American Culture', *Widener Law Symposium Journal*, 5, 213–248.

Logan, A (2008) *Feminism and Criminal Justice: A Historical Perspective*, Basingstoke: Palgrave Macmillan.

Lombroso, C and Ferrero, G (2004) N H Rafter and M Gibson (trans.) *Criminal Woman, the Prostitute and the Normal Woman*, Durham, NC: Duke University Press.

Lucy, D and Aitken, D (2002) 'A Review of the Role of Roster Data and Evidence of Attendance in Cases of Suspected Excess Deaths in a Medical Context', *Law, Probability and Risk*, 1 (2) 141–160.

Magee, M and Miller, D C (1992) ' "She Foreswore her Womanhood": Psychoanalytic Views of Female Homosexuality', *Clinical Social Work Journal*, 20 (1) 67–87.

Maher, L (1992) 'Reconstructing the Female Criminal: Women and Crack Cocaine', *Southern Californian Review of Law and Women's Studies*, 2 (1) 131–154.
Mahood, L (1990) *The Magdalenes: Prostitution in the Nineteenth Century*, London: Routledge.
March, W (1954) *The Bad Seed*, New York: Rinehart.
Marwick, A (1998) *The Sixties: Cultural Revolution in Britain, France, Italy and the United States, 1958–74*, Oxford: Oxford University Press.
Mason, T (2005) 'An Archaeology of the Psychopath: The Medicalization of Evil', T Mason (ed.) *Forensic Psychiatry: Influences of Evil*, Totowa, NJ: Humana Press.
Mason, T, Richman, J and Mercer, D (2002) 'The Influence of Evil on Forensic Clinical Practice', *International Journal of Mental Health Nursing*, 11 (2) 80–93.
McClintock, A (1993) 'Family Feuds: Gender, Nationalism and the Family', *Feminist Review*, 44, 61–80.
McClintock, A (1995) *Imperial Leather: Race, Gender and Sexuality in the Colonial Contest*, London: Routledge.
McCord, M and McCord, J (1964) *The Psychopath: An Essay on the Criminal Mind*, Princeton, NJ: Van Nostrand.
McCulloch, J (1995) *Colonial Psychiatry and the 'African Mind'*, Cambridge: Cambridge University Press.
McDonagh, J (1997) 'Infanticide and the Nation: The Case of Caroline Beale', *New Formations*, 32, 11–21.
McDonagh, J (2003) *Child Murder and British Culture, 1720–1900*, Cambridge: Cambridge University Press.
McGregor, O R (1957) *Divorce in England: A Centenary Study*, London: Heinemann.
McKibbin, R (1998) *Classes and Cultures: England 1918–1951*, Oxford: Oxford University Press.
Meadow, R (1977) 'Munchausen Syndrome by Proxy: The Hinterland of Child Abuse', *Lancet*, 2, 343–345.
Melossi, D (2008) *Controlling Crime, Controlling Society*, Cambridge: Polity Press.
Merton, R K (1946) *Mass Persuasion: The Social Psychology of a War Bond Drive*, New York: Harper.
Merton, R K (1949) *Social Theory and Social Structure*, Glencoe, IL: The Free Press.
Meyer, C L and Oberman, M (2001) *Mothers Who Kill Their Children*, New York: New York University Press.
Miami News, 29 March 1958.
Millard, R (2008) 'One Day as a Perfect 1950s Wife', *The Times*, 9 March.
Miller, P (1986) 'Psychotherapy of Work and Unemployment', P Miller and N Rose (eds) *The Power of Psychiatry*, Cambridge: Polity Press.
Miller, T (2005) *Making Sense of Motherhood: A Narrative Approach*, Cambridge: Cambridge University Press.
Miller, V (2004) ' "The Last Vestige of Institutionalized Sexism"? Paternalism, Equal Rights and the Death Penalty in Twentieth and Twenty-First Century Sunbelt America: The Case for Florida', *Journal of American Studies*, 38 (3) 391–424.
Millin, S (1934) *Three Men Die*, London: Chatto and Windus.
Millin, S (1941) *The Night is Long*, London: Faber and Faber.
Minkes, J and Vanstone, M (2005) 'Gender, Race and the Death Penalty: Lessons from Three 1950s Murder Trials', *Howard Journal of Criminal Justice*, 45 (4) 403–420.

Modesto Bee, 12 December 1957.
Mogul, J L (2005) 'The Dykier, the Butcher, the Better: The State's Use of Homophobia and Sexism to Execute Women in the United States', *New York City Law Review*, 8 (2) 473–494.
Moran, P (1999) 'Should Psychiatrists Treat Personality Disorders?', *Maudsley Discussion Paper No. 7*, London: Institute of Psychiatry.
Morgan, K O (1990) *The People's Peace*, Oxford: Oxford University Press.
Morris, T and Blom-Cooper, L (1964) *A Calendar of Murder*, London: Michael Joseph.
Morrissey, B (2003) *When Women Kill: Questions of Agency and Subjectivity*, London: Routledge.
Mort, F (1999) 'Social and Symbolic Fathers and Sons in Postwar Britain', *The Journal of British Studies*, 38 (3) 353–384.
Mosse, G L (1985) *Nationalism and Sexuality: Respectability and Abnormal Sexuality in Modern Europe*, New York: Howard Fertig.
Mouffe, C (1995) 'Feminism, Citizenship, and Radical Democratic Politics', L J Nicholson and S Seidman (eds) *Social Postmodernism: Beyond Identity Politics*, Cambridge: Cambridge University Press.
Mouffe, C (2005) *The Return of the Political*, 3rd edition, London: Verso.
Mullen, P E (1999) 'Dangerous People with Severe Personality Disorder', *British Medical Journal*, 319, 1146–1147.
Murphy, T and Whitty, N (2006) 'The Question of Evil and Feminist Legal Scholarship', *Feminist Legal Studies*, 14 (1) 1–26.
Murray, C (1984) *Losing Ground: American Social Policy, 1950–80*, New York: Basic Books.
Myrdal, A and Klein, V (1956) *Women's Two Roles: Home and Work*, London: Routledge and Kegan Paul.
Naffine, N (1985) 'The Masculinity-Femininity Hypothesis: A Consideration of Gender-Based Personality Theories of Female Crime', *British Journal of Criminology*, 25 (4) 365–381.
Naffine, N (1987) *Female Crime: The Construction of Women in Criminology*, Sydney: Allen and Unwin.
Naffine, N (1997) *Feminism and Criminology*, Cambridge: Polity Press.
Naylor, B (1995) 'Women's Crime and Media Coverage: Making Explanations', R E Dobash, R P Dobash and L Noaks (eds) *Gender and Crime*, Cardiff: University of Wales Press.
New York Times, 10 May 1908.
New York Times, 14 June 1908.
New York Times, 27 March 1914.
New York Times, 14 October 1960.
New York Times, 18 November 1988.
New York Times, 8 August 1993.
New York Times, 27 August 1993.
New York Times, 14 October 1993.
New York Times, 11 December 1993.
News of the World, 30 March 1958.
Newton, E (1994) 'The Myth of the Mannish Lesbian: Radclyffe Hall and the New Woman', *Signs*, 9 (4) 557–575.

Nickerson, C R (1999) ' "The Deftness of Her Sex": Innocence, Guilt and Gender in the Trial of Lizzie Borden', M A Bellesiles (ed.) *Lethal Imagination: Violence and Brutality in American History*, New York: New York University Press.
Nicolson, D (1995) 'Telling Tales: Gender Discrimination, Gender Construction and Battered Women Who Kill', *Feminist Legal Studies*, 3 (2) 186–206.
Noddings, N (1984) *Caring, a Feminist Approach to Ethics and Moral Education*, Berkeley, CA: University of California Press.
O'Shea, K A (1999) *Women and the Death Penalty in the United States, 1900–1998*, Westport, CT: Praeger.
Oberman, M and Meyer, C (2008) *When Mothers Kill: Interviews from Prison*, New York: New York University Press.
'Obituary: Dame Rose Heilbron', *The Guardian*, 13 December 2005.
Oram, A (1992) 'Repressed and Thwarted, or Bearer of the New World? The Spinster in Inter-war Feminist Discourses', *Women's History Review*, 1 (3) 413–433.
Oram, A (2007) *Her Husband was a Woman!: Women's Gender-Crossing in Modern British Popular Culture*, London: Routledge.
Oram, A and Turnbull, A (2001) *The Lesbian History Sourcebook: Love and Sex Between Women in Britain, 1780–1970*, London: Routledge.
Paget, R, Silverman, S and Hollis, C (1953) *Hanged – And Innocent?* London: Gollancz.
Parsons, T (1947) 'Certain Primary Sources and Patterns of Aggression in the Social Structure of the Western World', *Psychiatry*, 10 (2) 167–181.
Pearson, K (2007) 'The Trouble with Aileen Wuornos, Feminism's First Serial Killer', *Communication and Critical/Cultural Studies*, 4 (3) 256–275.
Pearson, P (1998) *When She Was Bad: Violent Women and the Myth of Innocence*, London: Virago.
Peiss, K (1987) *Cheap Amusements: Working Women and Leisure in Turn of the Century New York*, Philadelphia: Temple University Press.
Penn, A (1967) *Bonnie and Clyde* [Motion Picture], United States: Tatira-Hiller Productions.
Phillips, L and Jorgensen, M W (2002) *Discourse Analysis as Theory and Method*, London: Sage.
Phillips, J and Gartner, R (2003) *Murdering Holiness: The Trials of Franz Creffield and George Mitchell*, Vancouver: University of British Columbia Press.
Philofsky, R (2008) 'The Lives and Crimes of African-American Women on Death Row: A Case Study', *Crime, Law and Social Change*, 49 (4) 289–302.
Pierrepoint, A (1998) *Executioner: Pierrepoint*, Philadelphia: Coronet.
Pinel, P (1806) *A Treatise on Insanity*, Sheffield: W. Todd.
Poovey, M (1988) *Uneven Developments: The Ideological Work of Gender in Mid-Victorian England*, Chicago: University of Chicago Press.
Potter, C B (1998) *War on Crime: Bandits, G-Men and the Politics of Mass Culture*, New Brunswick, NJ: Rutgers University Press.
Powell, D (2002) *Nationhood and Identity: The British State Since 1800*, London: I B Tauris.
Pratt, J (2000) 'Dangerousness and Modern Society', M Brown and J Pratt (eds) *Dangerous Offenders*, London: Routledge.

Presdee, M (2000) *Cultural Criminology and the Carnival of Crime*, London: Routledge.
Presdee, M (2004) 'Cultural Criminology: The Long and Winding Road', *Theoretical Criminology*, 8 (3) 275–285.
Press Association, 28 May 1993.
Prevezer, S (1957) 'The English Homicide Act: A New Attempt to Revise the Law of Murder', *Columbia Law Review*, 57 (5) 624–652.
Primeau, R (1996) *Romance of the Road: The Literature of the American Highway*, Madison, WI: University of Wisconsin Press.
Prins, H (2002) 'Incapacitating the Dangerous in England and Wales: High Expectations, Harsh Reality', *Journal of Mental Health Law*, 6, 5–20.
Prior, L (2003) *Using Documents in Social Research*, London: Sage.
Pritchard, J C (1835) *A Treatise on Insanity and Other Disorders Affecting the Mind*, London: Sherwood, Gilbert and Piper.
Purkiss, D (1996) *The Witch in History: Early Modern and Twentieth-Century Representations*, London: Routledge.
Quinn, T (2008) 'The Conservative Party and the "Centre Ground" of British Politics', *Journal of Elections, Public Opinion and Parties*, 18 (2) 179–199.
Radford, J (1993) 'Pleading for Time: Justice for Battered Women Who Kill', H Birch (ed.) *Moving Targets: Women, Murder and Representation*, London: Virago.
Rafter, N (2007) 'Crime, Film and Criminology: Recent Sex-Crime Movies', *Theoretical Criminology*, 11 (3) 403–420.
Rafter, N H and Gibson, M (2004) 'Introduction', N H Rafter and M Gibson (eds) *Criminal Woman, the Prostitute and the Normal Woman*, Durham, NC: Duke University Press.
Rafter, N H (1997) 'Psychopathy and the Evolution of Criminological Knowledge', *Theoretical Criminology*, 1 (2) 235–259.
Raman, S (1986) 'The Category of Psychopathy: Its Professional and Social Context in Britain', P Miller and N Rose (eds) *The Power of Psychiatry*, Cambridge: Polity Press.
Rapaport, E (2000) 'Equality for the Damned: The Execution of Women on the Cusp of the 21st Century', *Ohio Northern University Law Review*, 26 (3) 581–600.
Rapaport, E (2006) 'Mad Women and Desperate Girls: Infanticide and Child Murder in Law and Myth', *Fordham Urban Law Journal*, 33 (2) 527–569.
Renzetti, C (1999) 'The Challenge to Feminism Posed by Women's Use of Violence in Intimate Relationships', S Lamb (ed.) *New Versions of Victims: Feminists Struggle with the Concept*, New York: New York University Press.
Report of the Committee on Homosexual Offences and Prostitution, 1953–1957 (Wolfenden Report) (1957) Cmnd. 247, London: HMSO.
Report of the Royal Commission on Capital Punishment, 1949–1953 (1953) Cmnd. 8932, London: HMSO.
Rich, A (1980) 'Compulsory Heterosexuality and Lesbian Experience', *Signs*, 5 (4) 631–660.
Riehle, A (1996) 'Canada's "Barbie and Ken" Murder Case: The Death Knell of Publication Bans?', *Indiana International and Comparative Law Review*, 7 (1) 193–222.
Riley, D (1983) *War in the Nursery: Theories of the Child and Mother*, London: Virago.

Riley, D (1988) *'Am I that Name?': Feminism and the Category of 'Women' in History*, Basingstoke: Macmillan.

Ringrose, J (2006) 'A New Universal Mean Girl: Examining the Discursive Construction and Social Regulation of a New Feminine Pathology', *Feminism and Psychology*, 16 (4) 405–424.

Roberts, E (1984) *A Woman's Place: An Oral History of Working-Class Women, 1890–1940*, Oxford: Blackwell.

Roberts, E (1986) 'Women's Strategies, 1890–1940', J Lewis (ed.) *Labour and Love: Women's Experiences of Home and Family 1850–1940*, Oxford: Basil Blackwell.

Roberts, E (1995) *Women and Families: An Oral History, 1940–1970*, Oxford: Blackwell.

Roberts, M L (2002) 'True Womanhood Revisited', *Journal of Women's History*, 14 (1) 150–155.

Robertson, C W (1996) 'Representing "Miss Lizzie": Cultural Convictions in the Trial of Lizzie Borden', *Yale Journal of Law and the Humanities*, 8 (2) 351–416.

Robertson, P R (2000) 'The Importance of an "Escape Valve for Mercy"', *Capital University Law Review*, 28 (3) 579–583.

Robertson, S (2005) 'What's Law Got to Do with It? Legal Records and Sexual Histories', *Journal of the History of Sexuality*, 14 (1/2) 161–185.

Robson, R (1997) 'Convictions: Theorizing Lesbians and Criminal Justice', M B Duberman (ed.) *A Queer World: the Center for Gay and Lesbian Studies Reader*, New York: New York University Press.

Rock, P (1993) *The Social World of an English Crown Court*, Oxford: Oxford University Press.

Rodger, J (1995) 'Family Policy or Moral Regulation?', *Critical Social Policy*, 15 (43) 5–25.

Roggenkamp, K (2005) *Narrating the News: New Journalism and Literary Genre in Late Nineteenth-Century American Newspapers and Fiction*, Kent, OH: Kent State University Press.

Romero, D, Chavkin, W, Wise, P H and Smith, L A (2003) 'Low-Income Mothers' Experience with Poor Health, Hardship, Work and Violence', *Violence Against Women*, 9 (10) 1231–1244.

Roper, L (1991) 'Witchcraft and Fantasy in Early Modern Germany', *History Workshop Journal*, 32 (1) 19–43.

Rose, J (1988) 'Margaret Thatcher and Ruth Ellis', *New Formations*, 6 (3) 3–29.

Rose, N (1999) *Governing the Soul: The Shaping of the Private Self*, 2nd edition, London: Free Association Books.

Rose, N (2000) 'The Biology of Culpability: Pathological Identity and Crime Control in a Biological Culture', *Theoretical Criminology*, 4 (5) 5–34.

Rose, S O (2003) *Which People's War? National Identity and Citizenship in Britain 1939–1945*, Oxford: Oxford University Press.

Rosenberg, D A (2003) 'Munchausen Syndrome by Proxy: Medical Diagnostic Criteria', *Child Abuse and Neglect*, 27 (4) 421–430.

Rowlands, A (2001) 'Witchcraft and Old Women in Early Modern Germany', *Past and Present*, 173 (1) 50–89.

Royal College of Psychiatrists (2007) *Personality Disorders Leaflet*, London: Royal College of Psychiatrists, http://www.rcpsych.ac.uk/mentalhealthinfo/problems/personalitydisorders/pd.aspx. Accessed 11 December 2008.

Ruffles, J (2004) 'Diagnosing Evil in Australian Courts: Psychopathy and Antisocial Personality Disorder as Legal Synonyms of Evil', *Psychiatry, Psychology and Law*, 11 (1) 113–121.

Rush, B (1812) *Medical Inquiries and Observations Upon the Diseases of the Mind*, Philadelphia: Kimber and Richardson.

Russell, B L and Melillo, L S (2006) 'Attitudes Toward Battered Women Who Kill: Defendant Typicality and Judgments of Culpability', *Criminal Justice and Behavior*, 33 (2) 219–240.

Saggar, S (1999) 'Immigration and Economics: The Politics of Race in the Postwar Period', H Fawcett and R Lowe (eds) *Welfare Policy in Britain: The Road from 1945*, Basingstoke: Macmillan.

Samuels, A (1964) 'Criminal Appeal Act, 1964', *The Modern Law Review*, 27 (5) 568–573.

Sandbrook, D (2005) *Never Had it So Good: A History of Britain from Suez to the The Beatles*, London: Little, Brown.

Sayer, A (2005a) *The Moral Significance of Class*, Cambridge: Cambridge University Press.

Sayer, A (2005b) 'Class, Moral Worth and Recognition', *Sociology*, 39 (5) 947–963.

Schone, J M (2000) 'The Hardest Case of All: Myra Hindley, Life Sentences and the Rule of Law', *International Journal of the Sociology of Law*, 28 (4) 273–289.

Schuller, R A, McKimmie, B M and Janz, T (2004) 'Trials of Battered Women Who Kill: The Impact of Expert Testimony on Jurors' Decisions', *Psychiatry, Psychology and Law*, 11 (1) 1–12.

Schultz, A R (1994) *Ethnicity on Parade: Inventing the Norwegian American Through Celebration*, Amherst, MA: University of Massachusetts Press.

Scott, D M (1997) *Contempt and Pity: Social Policy and the Image of the Damaged Black Psyche, 1880–1996*, Chapel Hill, NC: University of North Carolina Press.

Scott, G G (2007) *American Murder*, Westport, CT: Greenwood.

Scott, J W (1986) 'Gender: A Useful Category of Historical Analysis', *The American Historical Review*, 91 (5) 1053–1075.

Seal, L (2008) 'Public Reactions to the Case of Mary Wilson, the Last Woman to be Sentenced to Death in England and Wales', *Papers from the British Criminology Conference*, 8, 65–84.

Seal, L (2009a) 'Issues of Gender and Class in the *Mirror* Newspapers' Campaign for the Release of Edith Chubb', *Crime, Media, Culture*, 5 (1) 57–78.

Seal, L (2009b) 'Discourses of Single Women Accused of Murder: Mid Twentieth-Century Constructions of "Lesbians" and "Spinsters" ', *Women's Studies International Forum*, 32 (3) 209–218.

Seitz, T N (2005) 'The Wounds of Savagery: Negro Primitivism, Gender Parity and the Execution of Rosanna Lightner Phillips', *Women and Criminal Justice*, 16 (1/2) 29–64.

Self, H J (2003) *Prostitution, Fallen Women and the Misuse of the Law: The Fallen Daughters of Eve*, London: Frank Cass.

Sereny, G (1995) *The Case of Mary Bell: A Portrait of a Child Who Murdered*, London: Pimlico.

Sereny, G (1998) *Cries Unheard: The Story of Mary Bell*, London: Macmillan.

Shapiro, A (1996) *Breaking the Codes: Female Criminality in Fin de Siecle Paris*, Stanford, CA: Stanford University Press.

Shapiro, A (1999) ' "Stories More Terrifying Than the Truth Itself": Narratives of Female Criminality in Fin-de-Siècle Paris', M L Arnot and C Usborne (eds) *Gender and Crime in Modern Europe*, London: UCL Press.

Shapiro, A (2000) 'Unequal Before the Law: Men, Women and the Death Penalty', *American University Journal of Gender, Social Policy and Law*, 8 (2) 427–470.

Shaw, S B (1997) 'New England Gothic by the Light of Common Day: Lizzie Borden and Mary E Wilkins Freeman's "The Long Arm" ', *New England Quarterly*, 70 (2) 211–236.

Shipley, S L and Arrigo, B A (2004) *The Female Homicide Offender: Serial Murder and the Case of Aileen Wuornos*, Saddle River, NJ: Prentice Hall.

Shipman, M (2002) *The Penalty is Death: US Newspaper Coverage of Women's Executions*, Columbia, MO: University of Missouri Press.

Shortnacy, M B (2001) 'Guilty and Gay, A Recipe for Execution in American Courtrooms: Sexual Orientation as a Tool for Prosecutorial Misconduct in Death Penalty Cases', *American University Law Review*, 51 (2) 309–365.

Shotwell, A M (1946) 'A Study of Psychopathic Delinquency', *American Journal of Mental Deficiency*, 51, 57–62.

Silvio, H, McCloskey, K and Ramos-Grenier, J (2006) 'Theoretical Consideration of Female Sexual Predator Serial Killers in the United States', *Journal of Criminal Justice*, 34 (4) 251–259.

Simon, J (1993) *Poor Discipline: Parole and the Social Control of the Underclass, 1890–1990*, Chicago: University of Chicago Press.

Simon, J (2007) *Governing Through Crime*, Oxford: Oxford University Press.

Skeggs, B (1997) *Formations of Class and Gender Becoming Respectable*, London: Routledge.

Skeggs, B (2005) 'The Making of Class and Gender through Visualizing Moral Subject Formation', *Sociology*, 39 (5) 965–982.

Smart, C (1995) *Law, Crime and Sexuality: Essays in Feminism*, London: Sage.

Smith, D E (1990) *Texts, Facts and Femininity: Exploring the Relations of Ruling*, London: Routledge.

Smith-Rosenberg, C (1986) *Disorderly Conduct: Visions of Gender in Victorian America*, Oxford: Oxford University Press.

Snow, C P (1968) *The Sleep of Reason*, London: World Books.

Spelman, E (1988) *Inessential Woman: Problems of Exclusion in Feminist Thought*, London: Women's Press.

Spinley, B M (1953) *The Deprived and the Privileged: Personality Development in English Society*, London: Routledge and Kegan Paul.

Sprott, W J H, Jephcott, P and Carter, M P (1954) *The Social Background of Delinquency*, Research Report, Nottingham: University of Nottingham.

Srebnick, A G (2005) 'Does the Representation Fit the Crime? Some Thoughts on Writing Crime History as Cultural Text', A G Srebnick and R Levy (eds) *Crime and Culture: An Historical Perspective*, Aldershot: Ashgate.

Stallybrass, P and White, A (1986) *The Politics and Poetics of Transgression*, Ithaca, NY: Cornell University Press.

Stanko, E and Scully, A (1996) 'Re-telling the Tale: The Emma Humphreys Case', A Wight and S Myers (eds) *No Angels: Women Who Commit Violence*, London: Pandora.

Starr, K (2005) *California: A History*, New York: Modern Library.

Steedman, C (1986) *Landscape for a Good Woman: A Story of Two Women*, London: Virago.
Stoler, A L (1989) 'The Politics of Race and Sexual Morality in 20th-Century Colonial Cultures', *American Ethnologist*, 16 (4) 634–660.
Storrs, E (2004) ' "Our Scapegoat": An Exploration of Media Representations of Myra Hindley and Rosemary West', *Theology and Sexuality*, 11 (1) 9–28.
Storrs, E (2006) 'Mothers, Mothering and Christianity: Exploring the Connections Between the Virgin Mary, Myra Hindley and Rosemary West', *Feminist Theology*, 14 (2) 237–254.
Strange, C (1999) 'Murder and Meanings in US Historiography', *Feminist Studies*, 25 (3) 679–697.
Streib, V L (2002) 'Gendering the Death Penalty: Countering Sex Bias in a Masculine Sanctuary', *Ohio State Law Journal*, 63 (1) 433–474.
Stubbs, J and Tolmie, J (1995) 'Race, Gender, and the Battered Woman Syndrome: An Australia Case Study', *Canadian Journal of Women and Law*, 8 (1) 122–158.
Summerfield, P (1998) *Reconstructing Women's Wartime Lives*, Manchester: Manchester University Press.
Sutherland, E E (2006) 'Undue Deference to Experts Syndrome?', *Indiana International and Comparative Law Review*, 16 (2) 375–421.
Swanson, G (2007) *Drunk with the Glitter: Space, Consumption and Sexual Instability in Modern Urban Culture*, London: Routledge.
Taylor, B (1999) ' "Coming Out" as a Life Transition: Homosexual Identity Formation and its Implications for Health Care Practice', *Journal of Advanced Nursing*, 30 (2) 520–525.
Tebbutt, M (1995) *Women's Talk? A Social History of 'Gossip' in Working-Class Neighbourhoods, 1880–1960*, Aldershot: Ashgate.
Thane, P (2000) *Old Age in English History*, Oxford: Oxford University Press.
Thomas, D A (1964) 'Theories of Punishment in the Court of Criminal Appeal', *Modern Law Review*, 27 (5) 546–567.
Thomas, K (2005) 'Imagining Lesbian Legal Theory', *New York City Law Review*, 8 (2) 505–510.
Thomas, W I (1923) *The Unadjusted Girl*, Boston: Little Brown and Company.
Thomson, M (2006) *Psychological Subjects: Identity, Culture and Health in Twentieth-Century Britain*, Oxford: Oxford University Press.
Thornborrow, J (2002) *Power Talk: Language and Interaction in Institutional Discourse*, London: Longman.
Threadgold, T (1997) 'Narratives and Legal Texts: Telling Stories about Women Who Kill', *UTS Review: Cultural Studies and New Writing*, 3 (1) 56–73.
Thunder, J M (2002) 'Quiet Killings in Medical Facilities: Detection and Prevention', *Issues in Law and Medicine*, 18 (3) 211–237.
The Times, 10 July 1858.
The Times, 18 October 1932.
The Times, 19 October 1932.
The Times, 21 October 1932.
The Times, 24 October 1932.
The Times, 11 February 1958.
The Times, 2 May 1958.
The Times, 3 May 1958.
The Times, 28 November 1958.

The Times, 1 July 1960.
The Times, 14 October 1960.
The Times, 28 January 1962.
The Times, 22 April 1966.
The Times, 6 December 1968.
The Times, 14 December 1968.
The Times, 18 December 1968.
Tinkler, P (2006) *Smoke Signals: Women, Smoking and Visual Culture in Britain*, Oxford: Berg.
Tronto, J C (1987) 'Beyond Gender Difference to a Theory of Care', *Signs*, 12 (4) 644–663.
Uelman, G F (1998) 'Lizzie Borden Meets O J Simpson: The Trials of Two Centuries', *Litigation*, 24 (2) 57–58, 70–71.
Valverde, M (2003) *Law's Dream of a Common Knowledge*, Princeton, NJ: Princeton University Press.
Van Hamel, J A (1911) 'The International Union of Criminal Law', *Journal of the American Institute of Criminal Law and Criminology*, 2 (1) 22–27.
Verhoeven, D (1993) 'Biting the Hand that Breeds: The Trials of Tracey Wigginton', H Birch (ed.) *Moving Targets: Women, Murder and Representation*, London: Virago.
Vicinus, M (1992) ' "They Wonder to Which Sex I Belong": The Historical Roots of the Modern Lesbian Identity', *Feminist Studies*, 18 (3) 467–497.
Walker, N (1965) *Crime and Punishment in Britain*, Edinburgh: Edinburgh University Press.
Walker, N and McCabe, S (1973) *Crime and Insanity in England*, Vol. 2, Edinburgh: Edinburgh University Press.
Walkowitz, J (1992) *City of Dreadful Delight: Narratives of Sexual Danger in Late Victorian London*, Chicago: University of Chicago Press.
Wallinga, J V (1959) 'The Probation Officer's Role in Psychiatric Cases', *The Journal of Criminal Law, Criminology and Police Science*, 50 (4) 364–367.
Warf, B and Waddell, C (2002) 'Heinous Spaces, Perfidious Places: The Sinister Landscapes of Serial Killers', *Social and Cultural Geography*, 3 (3) 323–345.
Waters, C (1997) ' "Dark Strangers" in Our Midst: Discourses of Race and Nation in Britain, 1947–1963', *The Journal of British Studies*, 36 (2) 207–238.
Waters, C (1999) 'Disorders of the Mind, Disorders of the Body: Peter Wildeblood and the Making of the Modern Homosexual', B Conekin, F Mort and C Waters (eds) *Moments of Modernity: Reconstructing Britain, 1945–1964*, London: Rivers Oram Press.
Webster, W (2001) ' "There'll Always Be An England": Representations of Colonial Wars and Immigration, 1948–1968', *The Journal of British Studies*, 40 (4) 557–584.
Webster, W (2007) *Englishness and Empire 1939–1965*, Oxford: Oxford University Press.
Weeks, J (1985) *Sexuality and Its Discontents: Meanings, Myths and Modern Sexualities*, London: Routledge and Kegan Paul.
Weeks, J (1989) *Sex, Politics and Society: The Regulation of Sexuality Since 1800*, 2nd edition, Harlow: Longman.
Weeks, J (2007) *The World We Have Won: The Remaking of Erotic and Intimate Life*, London: Routledge.

Welshman, J (2006) *Underclass: A History of the Excluded, 1880–2000*, London: Hambledon Continuum.
West, D A and Lichtenstein, B (2006) 'Andrea Yates and the Criminalization of the Filicidal Maternal Body', *Feminist Criminology*, 1 (3) 173–187.
Western Daily Press, 27 January 1962.
Wheedon, C (1997) *Feminist Practice and Poststructuralist Theory*, 2nd edition, Oxford: Blackwell.
Whitehead, A (2005) 'Man to Man Violence: How Masculinity May Work as a Dynamic Risk Factor', *The Howard Journal of Criminal Justice*, 44 (4) 411–422.
Whorton, J (2001) 'The Solitary Vice: The Superstition that Masturbation Could Cause Mental Illness', *Western Journal of Medicine*, 175 (1) 66–68.
Widom, C S (1979) 'Female Offenders: Three Assumptions about Self-Esteem, Sex-Role Identity, and Feminism', *Criminal Justice and Behavior*, 6 (4) 365–382.
Wilczynski, A (1997) 'Mad or Bad?: Child Killers, Gender and the Courts', *British Journal of Criminology*, 37 (3) 419–436.
Williams, J E H (1960) 'Sex Offenses: The British Experience', *Law and Contemporary Problems*, 25 (2) 334–360.
Williams, J E H, Gibbens, T C N and Jennings, R (1960) 'The Mental Health Act 1959', *The Modern Law Review*, 23 (4) 410–424.
Wills, A (2005) 'Delinquency, Masculinity and Citizenship in England 1950–1970', *Past and Present*, 187 (1) 157–185.
Wilson, D S (2006) 'A New Look at the Affluent Worker: The Good Working Mother in Post-War Britain', *Twentieth Century British History*, 17 (2) 206–229.
Winnicott, D (1944) *Getting to Know Your Baby: Six Broadcast Talks*, London: Heinemann.
Winter, J (2002) 'The Trial of Rose West: Contesting Notions of Victimhood', C Hoyle and R Young (eds) *New Visions of Crime Victims*, Oxford: Oxford University Press.
Winter, J (2004) 'The Role of Gender in Judicial Decision Making: Similar Fact Evidence, the Rose West Trial and Beyond', *International Journal of Evidence and Proof*, 8 (1) 31–46.
Wolcott, V W (2001) *Remaking Respectability: African-American Women in Interwar Detroit*, Chapel Hill, NC: University of North Carolina Press.
Wolff, L (1995) *Child Abuse in Freud's Vienna: Postcards from the End of the World*, New York: New York University Press.
Wootton, B (1959) *Social Science and Social Pathology*, London: Allen and Unwin.
Wootton, B (1978) *Crime and Penal Policy: Reflections on Fifty Years' Experience*, London: Allen and Unwin.
Worrall, A (1990) *Offending Women: Female Lawbreakers and the Criminal Justice System*, London: Routledge.
Wray, M and Newitz, A (1997) 'Introduction', M Wray and A Newitz (eds) *White Trash: Race and Class in America*, London: Routledge.
Wray, M (2006) *Not Quite White: White Trash and the Boundaries of Whiteness*, Durham, NC: Duke University Press.
Wykes, M (1998) 'A Family Affair: The British Press, Sex and the Wests', C Carter, G Branston and S Allan (eds) *News, Gender, and Power*, London: Routledge.
Yorkshire Post, 27 April 1957.
Young, L (1954) *Out of Wedlock*, New York: McGraw Hill.

Young, M and Willmott, P ([1957] 1962) *Family and Kinship in East London*, London: Penguin.
Yuval-Davis, N (1997) *Gender and Nation*, London: Sage.
Yuval-Davis, N (2006) 'Intersectionality and Feminist Politics', *European Journal of Women's Studies*, 13 (3) 193–209.

Index

abjection, 14, 18–19, 58
Adames, Hilde, 100, 174
affluent society, 89–90
Ahluwalia, Kiranjit, 6
Allen, Wanda Jean, 35–8, 72, 85
Allitt, Beverley, 60–2
anxiety, *see* cultural anxieties

backlash (against feminism), 34
Bain, Marilyn, 114–15, 116–17, 150
Baird, Doreen, 137–41
Barbie and Ken murders, *see* Homolka, Karla
Barrow, Clyde, *see* Parker, Bonnie
Beale, Caroline, 16
Beck, Martha, 46–8, 85
  and Fernandez, Raymond, 46–7
Bell, Mary, 57–9, 84
Bentley, Derek, 96
Bernardo, Paul, *see* Homolka, Karla
Borden, Lizzie, 66–8
boundaries
  cultural, 10–11, 16, 45–6, 65, 70, 80, 86, 142, 173
  of feminism, 3
  gender, 1, 6, 7, 8, 12, 38, 92
Brady, Ian, *see* Hindley, Myra
Britishness, 95, 125, 128, 172–3
Butler, Rab, 161

Caillaux, Henriette, 11
A Calendar of Murder, 100
Campbell, Shirley, 130–3, 140–1
capital punishment, *see* death penalty
Chubb, Edith, 144–9, 153
citizenship (in mid–twentieth-century Britain), 95, 173
Collins, Veronica, 119–24
companionate marriage, 93, 142
consumerism, 92, 122, 142

cultural anxieties, 7, 9, 10, 11, 30, 38, 40–1, 45, 47–8, 59, 68, 75, 83–6, 90, 118, 128, 153, 170–3
cultural criminology, 10
cultural meaning, 9–10, 83–6, 102, 169–73

dangerousness, 54–7, 58, 61, 62, 133, 136
death penalty
  in England and Wales, 96–7
  and women, 6, 8, 31–2, 33, 37, 72, 97
declinism, 90
de Melker, Daisy, 78–80, 84
discourse, 4, 23, 101
  discourse analysis, 23, 103–5
  shadow discourse, 104
dominant woman, 40, 46, 125–7, 162
Doudet, Celestine, 68–71
duty, 165

Ellis, Ruth, 96–7
Evans, Timothy, 96
Everson, Norma, 111–14, 116–17, 150
evil, 54–5, 62, 63
execution, *see* death penalty

family, 31, 36, 165–6
female homosexuality, *see* sexuality
female masculinity, 24–38, 106–17, 150
  and criminology, 24–7
  and sexology, 27–9
femininity
  appropriate, 6, 18, 19, 103, 164–9
  norms of, *see* gender norms
  regulation of, 6, 7, 8, 83–6, 164–9
  stereotypes of, 2, 3, 5, 7, 26, 34, 73–4, 143
  symbolic, 11, 16–18, 65, 73, 83–6, 95, 143, 169

203

femme fatale, 46, 122, 123
Fernandez, Raymond, *see* Beck, Martha
filicide, *see* women who kill; their own children
Fletcher, Alice, 124–8

gender construction, 12–14, 91
gender norms, 1, 3, 6, 12, 13, 15, 39, 92
genre, 4–5
 film noir, 47
 gothic, 4–5, 159
 melodrama, 5, 146
 road, 49
 romance, 47, 120–1
Gunness, Belle, 75–8

Hargreaves, Renee, 149–54
Harvey, Sarah, 155–60, 163
haunting, 104
Hindley, Myra, 19, 84
 and Brady, Ian, 1, 41–2, 44–5, 99
Homicide Act 1957, 89, 96–7, 160,
Homolka, Karla, 85
 and Bernardo, Paul, 42–6

immigration, 9, 125, 142
intersectionality, 14–15, 34, 36, 37, 67, 85, 113–14, 131, 140, 167
iteration, 104

Jennion, Yvonne, 107–11, 116–17, 150
Jones, Genene, 59–60, 62

liminality, 5, 19, 40, 50–1, 58, 71, 75, 85, 118, 141
Lonely Hearts Killers, *see* Beck, Martha
Lyons, Alice, 100, 174–5

Macmillan, Harold, 89
meaning, *see* cultural meaning
Mental Health Act 1959, 53, 56, 129
microhistory, 9, 169
Mitchell, Alice, 27–8
modernity, 90, 128, 153, 170–2
 anti-modern, 128, 140, 142, 153, 171–2
 modernisation, 89–90, 92, 140

Moors Murders, *see* Hindley, Myra
motherhood, 2, 3, 94, 143, 145, 148, 153
 unmarried, 155, 157–8

narratives, 4–5, 15, 120
nodal point, 103

paid work (and women), 91–2
Parker, Bonnie, 50
 and Barrow, Clyde, 48–9
pathology
 psychological, 47, 50, 131–3, 134–6, 139, 141
 sexual, 26, 29, 36, 41, 47, 69, 79, 93, 110, 113, 151, 165
 social, 36
performativity, 13, 114, 116, 140, 153
problem families, 129, 142
prosecution (for murder), 98–9
prostitution, 118–19, 125
psychopathy, 50 – 57, 58, 60, 62, 131, 133, 134–6, 137–8, 140
 moral insanity, 51
 personality disorders, 53–7, 60–3
 and sexuality, 28, 110
Puente, Dorothea, 80–3

recuperation, 65, 68, 71–3, 148
respectability, 63–6, 68, 69, 70–1, 92, 94–5, 142–4
 lack of, 154–5, 162–3
risk society, 62

serial killing, 31, 32, 34
sexuality, 165
 heterosexuality, 3–4, 31, 39, 40, 44, 48, 92–3, 116
 inversion (sexual), 27, 29, 36, 108–9
 lesbian, 27–9, 31, 33, 35, 36, 106–17, 150
Shah, Zoora, 13–14
social change, 10, 11, 30, 31, 40–1, 59, 80, 83–6, 102, 117, 170
spinsterhood, 67–8, 143–4, 146, 150, 154
Sterry, Helen, 133–7, 140–1
stock stories, 4

Thornton, Sara, 6
trangression, 18–19, 166
Tucker, Karla Faye, 71–3, 86

underworld (urban), 116, 118, 122–3

West, Rose, 40
 and West, Fred, 30–1
Wigginton, Tracey, 19
Wilson, Mary, 160–3
witches, 73–83, 154–5, 157, 161–2

Wolfenden Report (Report of the Committee on Homosexual Offences and Prostitution), 89–90, 118
women who kill
 abusive male partners, 1–4
 children (their own), 1–4
 feminist research on, 2–4, 7, 165
 typologies of, 5, 19
 unusual cases of, 1, 2, 3–4, 11
Wuornos, Aileen, 1, 32–5, 72, 85

Printed in Great Britain
by Amazon